A HISTORY OF THE UNITED STATES

/ of the United States

Philip Jenkins

St. Martin's Press
New York

A HISTORY OF THE UNITED STATES
Copyright © 1997 by Philip Jenkins
All rights reserved. No part of this book may be used or reproduced
in any manner whatsoever without written permission except in the
case of brief quotations embodied in critical articles or reviews.
For information, address:

St. Martin's Press, Scholarly and Reference Division,
175 Fifth Avenue, New York, N.Y. 10010

First published in the United States of America in 1997

This book is printed on paper suitable for recycling and
made from fully managed and sustained forest sources.

Printed in Hong Kong

ISBN 0–312–16361–4 cloth
ISBN 0–312–16362–2 paperback

Library of Congress Cataloging-in-Publication Data
Jenkins, Philip, 1952–
A history of the United States / Philip Jenkins.
p.   cm.
Includes bibliographical references (p.   ) and index.
ISBN 0–312–16361–4 (cloth). — ISBN 0–312–16362–2 (pbk.)
1. United States—History.   I. Title.
E178.1.J35   1996
973—dc20   96–24515
                                                        CIP

Contents

List of Tables

List of Maps

Preface

The present history is not a lengthy book, and it would be easy to imagine a book of this size seeking only to offer either an introductory sketch of the political history of the United States, or of economic history, or cultural, or demographic, or religious. Attempting to integrate all these elements into one volume might well appear an ambitious and even a foolhardy undertaking, and presumably I have omitted topics that some readers would have thought essential. While admitting that the choice of emphasis must tend towards the subjective, I think the book justifies itself in terms of its overall goal, which is to present a short and readable overview of the major themes and patterns of American history, and thus to provide a framework for more detailed reading or research.

I might also explain what may appear to be an overemphasis on groups easily categorized as the outsiders of American history: racial minorities most obviously, but also political and religious dissenters. While writing history 'from the bottom up' is a fashion that has rather fallen out of favour, it is still justified in the American context because of the peculiar nature of that nation's traditions. Briefly, to describe someone as 'marginal' assumes a norm or mainstream, and for much of American history it is rarely clear exactly who or what can be termed either mainstream or marginal. In religious terms especially, much thought and behaviour that would appear quite bizarre in other nations has been perfectly 'normal' in America, and has to be treated thus. I would request the reader's tolerance of the degree to which the book does indeed stray towards the 'margins' – wherever these are actually located.

Introduction

Historians have often argued over the issue of 'American exceptionalism', the idea that the United States is somehow subject to rules and trends distinct from those prevailing in other advanced countries. At its worst, this tendency can lead scholars to a rosy consensus theory, which argues that Americans are somehow immune from the passions or problems that affect other comparable societies, so that symptoms of grave political or social tension are ignored. However the enormous size of the nation and the difficulties of internal communication genuinely did create circumstances quite different from those in Europe, and ensured that American history would indeed develop in some fundamentally different ways. These structural differences provide many of the themes that shaped American history from the earliest years of settlement to the present.

The terrain that eventually became the continental United States covers some three million square miles, or almost eight million square kilometers. Excluding Hawaii and Alaska, the greatest distance from north to south is about 1600 miles (2572 km); from east to west, 2800 miles (4517 km). Alaska and Hawaii added another 600 000 square miles (1545 square km). To put this in perspective, modern-day France has a surface area of about 220 000 square miles; Great Britain and Ireland combined cover 120 000 square miles; the reunited Germany covers almost 140 000 square miles. In other words, continental United States alone, excluding Canada, is about the same size as the whole of Europe: one nation covers an area as large as the forty or so jurisdictions that make up greater Europe. Throughout American history the remarkable size of the New World created both problems and opportunities to which Europeans were generally quite unaccustomed and unprepared.

The sheer scale of America posed unique problems for governments, and the interior of the country is marked by natural features that could easily have become political frontiers, especially the Appalachians and the Rocky Mountains. This situation offered rare opportunities for those who feared official control. Throughout its history there have been groups who have escaped an impossible political situation by internal emigration, usually to the fringes of settled land. This was the course taken for instance by dissident Puritans in the 1630s, by North Carolina vigilantes in the 1770s, by Mormons in the 1840s. Others have created utopian colonies in the wilderness, where governments have had neither the power nor, usually, the will to reach them. What is remarkable is not that corners of the country have occasionally contemplated secession, but that any core remained for them to secede from.

Threats of separatism or schism had to be counteracted by political flexibility and technological innovation. It can be argued that American history has been shaped at least as much by its modes of transportation as by its political parties, and the successive worlds created by the sailing ship, the Conestoga wagon, the steamboat, the train and the automobile differed from each other quite as much as the eras so often described by merely political labels. This is especially true of urban development. As Thoreau wrote in the 1850s, 'Boston, New York, Philadelphia, Charleston, New Orleans and the rest are the names of wharves projecting into the sea (surrounded by the shops and dwellings of the merchants), good places to take in and to discharge a cargo'.[1] Forty years later another observer might well have described the cities of that era as chiefly rail depots. Transportation has also shaped American politics. In the late nineteenth century, political control or even regulation of the railroads was one of the key issues dividing radicals from conservatives. More recently, racial conflicts have often pitted the predominantly white suburbs against the mainly minority populations of the inner cities: a geographical schism initially made possible by commuter railroads, and later by cars and superhighways.

The tendency of populations to race ahead of the structures of government explains in large part the frequent resort to violence and vigilantism in frontier communities, though the American history of violence requires a far more substantial explanation than just the influence of the frontier. As we will see, in the nineteenth century both eastern cities and the southern countryside were at least as subject to the rule of the gun as the cattletowns and mining camps of the far west.

The fact that the United States became and remained a nation means that we tend to speak of 'regions' and regionalism, when those component units were often larger than the most substantial nations elsewhere in the world. Today the one state of California possesses an economy that would make it the sixth power in the world, were it to gain political independence. American federalism necessarily differed widely from any European parallel, if only because the individual states were generally larger than, say, the small kingdoms that eventually made up Germany or Italy. There was also the assumption that the union of the states need not be an eternal bond, at least until the relationship with the national government was transformed by the circumstances of the Civil-War. Extreme diversity between and within regions has always been one of the major features of American life.

Related questions of scale and regionalism have often had political implications. From at least the mid-eighteenth century, some visionary Americans recognized that their destiny lay in expanding across the whole country, though few ever realized just how swiftly this goal would be achieved, and how rapidly the nation's demographic centre of gravity would wing towards the Mississippi. Political plans had therefore to be conceived with this expansion in mind for decades to come, a consideration that seldom troubled European leaders. In the early nineteenth century the course of the crucial debate over slavery was entirely based on the potential of westwards expansion, and the political implications for this in terms of the balance of slave and free states.

The larger the country became, the greater the danger that distinct regions might perceive their fate in very different terms. In foreign policy, New England and the north-east often had a European orientation that seemed bizarre or even disloyal to westerners, who saw little reason to intervene in Europe's political entanglements, while viewing Great Britain more as a bitter rival than a fond parent. In different forms, this division affected American attitudes to the War of 1812 no less than the First and the Second World Wars. In the 1990s it continues to shape American views of the nation's commercial and industrial future, with the powerful attractions of the Pacific Rim steadily counterbalancing the European orientation of the east coast.

The other perennial regional division was that between north and south, an inevitable distinction based on the radically different climates and economies of the two sections. In fact, from colonial times onwards the two societies looked so different and perhaps so irreconcilable that we should scarcely wonder at the near breakdown of national unity in the 1860s. The question should perhaps not be why civil war came in 1861, but how unity was achieved in the first place, and maintained unbroken for decades afterwards?

Different regions produced their own distinct cultures, the exact nature of which has given rise to much debate. The question of 'Southern-ness' has been a popular topic for such works, though the very term betrays the prejudice that it is the south that is untypical from an American or even world norm. In fact one could equally well argue that it was rather the north of the early nineteenth century that produced a set of cultural and intellectual assumptions that were bizarre by the standards of the contemporary Western world, while the aristocratic, rural and deferential south was a much more 'normal' entity than its egalitarian, urban and evangelical neighbours. For anyone acquainted with the astonishing social turbulence of the northern cities before the Civil War, it is a curious conceit to speak of a uniquely southern tendency to violence.

However it is certain that the cultures of north and south diverged from the end of the seventeenth century over the question of African slavery: not (initially) its legality, but over the degree to which that institution would be fundamental to the American economic order. From 1700 to the 1950s the south was characterized by a simple racial division, in which whites possessed vastly greater status and economic privilege than blacks. Though similar distinctions prevailed at times in the north, not until the 1920s did enough blacks live in this region to pose the 'American dilemma', the 'Negro problem', in an acute form. Regionalism was thus integrally connected with the race conflict that has been so intractable a part of American life, and has shaped cultural and social history, no less than political.

The fact that black Americans have so often been consigned to the role of an inferior labouring caste means that American history has frequently diverged from that of Europe in terms of class formation and class attitudes. While America does have a thriving tradition of working-class organization and solidarity, this has often been sabotaged by racial hostilities and the implementation of 'divide and rule' strategies, that have successfully set blacks and whites against each other. The presence of a substantial racial minority thus means that the fundamental concepts of race and class have been confounded in the United States in a way that appeared utterly alien to European observers – at least until they began to encounter the same problem with the diversification of their own ethnic populations from the 1950s onwards. It was in the 1970s that the leaders of Britain, France, Germany and other nations began to realize, however ruefully, that the racial experiences of the United States provided valuable lessons that might be taken to heart in their own societies. In Europe too, racial agendas now pervade debates on topics such as social welfare and criminal justice, in ways that have been familiar in the United States since the time of slavery.

Racial polarization in the south was parallelled by the growing ethnic complexity of the north and later of the remaining regions of the country. While the south could rely for decades on a profitable plantation agriculture, it was inevitable that the north would move towards industrial expansion, and probably the associated urbanization. The availability of jobs and free land made the United States an immensely tempting destination for migrants, initially from northern European groups whose links with the American continent dated to colonial times, but eventually to other groups, whose voyages were made possible by advances in ocean transportation. While the ethnic division in the south was literally written in black and white, the rest of the United States became steadily more polyglot, and diverse in both ethnic and religious terms. And though other countries have experienced vast population movements, no nation has known such prolonged, near-continuous immigration as the United States, with all that implies in terms of economic growth, social mobility and intercommunal relations.

The size and diversity of the United States mean that American national unity has had to be preserved by political means quite distinct from those of Europe, and the creation of national ideologies sufficiently flexible to be adapted to a rapidly changing population. The symbolism of England and its monarchy sufficed for much of colonial history, and did not need to be transformed too massively to accommodate the needs of a new nation, with the elevation of a hero president to near-kingly status. This was equally true in religious matters, where an established church was succeeded by a number of independent but none the less militantly Protestant denominations. The coming of new ethnic and religious groups complicated this matter. As a consequence the United States has tended to emphasize notions of over-arching patriotism and national destiny that appear excessive to European eyes, most strikingly devotion to the flag as a much displayed national symbol. All ethnic newcomers have to some extent accepted a constructed national mythology, the features of which include the 'Pilgrim Fathers' and their first Thanksgiving, hero figures such as George Washington and Abraham Lincoln, and mythical readings of the Civil War and the Old West. In turn they are allowed and even encouraged to add their own particular bricks to the wall, so that Columbus Day became the festival of Italian-American pride, while several nations find cultural heroes in the multi-national friends and advisers of George Washington. In recent years African-Americans have added their own figure to the national pantheon: Martin Luther King Jr, the only hero to be commemorated with a holiday of equal weight to those of Washington and Lincoln.

Remarkably, perhaps, for a country that emerged with a militantly anti-aristocratic ethos, American patriotism has often been expressed in military and even militaristic terms. No less than seven presidents owed their election chiefly to their military careers, even when, as in the case of William Henry Harrison and Theodore Roosevelt, the engagements in question were far from impressive; and countless other candidates at both federal and state level have made a great deal of their war records (the seven obvious cases are Washington, Jackson, Harrison, Taylor, Grant, Theodore Roosevelt and Eisenhower; Kennedy and Bush might perhaps be added to the list). In domestic politics, military veterans' groups have often played a major political role, usually on the most conservative and 'patriotic' side of affairs.

National unity and patriotism gain strength from military values, but are other qualities sacrificed? As the defence functions of government grew in the middle of the twentieth century, the militarization of American society raised critical questions about the possibility of reconciling republican and democratic goals with a national security state and an imperial presidency. What, for example, becomes of values like the openness of government, above all in an area such as foreign policy? These questions have been at the heart of

American political debate since before the Second World War, and became acute during crises such as the Vietnam War, Watergate and the Iran–Contra crisis. 'National Security' has also had the effect of increasing the size and intrusiveness of government to levels that may ultimately prove incompatible with the democratic forms outlined in the US constitution.

Americans often exaggerate the uniqueness of their ethnic complexity, this in itself reflecting the basic national myth of the 'melting pot'. In reality most European nations have to some extent drawn on multiple ethnic groups, most obviously in the case of entities such as the Austro-Hungarian state. Even the British Empire was formed and ruled by the several nations of the British Isles, in addition to Huguenots, Jews and others. On the other hand, migration to America from 1820 onwards made it a far more complicated ethnic quilt than any other advanced state, while diversity existed in a democratic framework: from the 1830s, in fact, in a world of radical mass democracy. In contrast to the Habsburg or Romanov Empires, therefore, the complex interests of America's constituent groups had to be resolved through interest-group politics and coalition building. The consequences of this will often be discussed in the following pages, but certain themes can readily be identified.

One is the American tradition of stigmatizing 'dangerous outsiders', conspiratorial plotters whose clandestine deeds threaten both the security of the republic and the American way of life. Identifying such groups serves to unite the main-stream or 'normal' national community, while excluding some other groups, usually of a religious or ethnic character, though this agenda is often left unspoken. The democratic nature of American politics and the open press leaves public discourse vulnerable to such manifestations of hysterical denunciation, what Richard Hofstadter called the 'Paranoid Style' of American politics.[2] American history can be written in terms of the successive 'outsider' groups who have allegedly challenged the national polity, from Illuminati and

Masons to Catholics and Jews, Communists and Satanists. Linked to the paranoid style is the theme of symbolic politics, the tactic of attacking a rival group not directly but through some characteristic of that group, which might be condemned or even prohibited. The history of American moral purity campaigns and drug prohibitions is in large measure a story of ethnic self-assertion against outsiders, defined in terms of race or religion. Though all too easily dismissed as mere 'moral panics' or 'witch-hunts', irritating digressions from the central issues of party debate or class conflict, these moral struggles are in fact at the heart of American social evolution.

Ethnic diversity contributes to understanding the religiosity that has always been such a notable feature of American life. In colonial days the amazing novelty was the coexistence of numerous religious bodies without state establishment; today it is the continuing force of radical and evangelical religion in an age of advanced technology and social organization. Moreover new ideas and social trends in the United States tend to express themselves in religious forms rather than political, in the formation of new churches rather than political parties. This can be partly explained in terms of the the role of the churches in providing a portable ethnic identity and solidarity for different groups, whose abandonment of religious forms is thus associated with the betrayal of a whole culture. The link is all the stronger because American churches are not generally identified either with the state or with a ruling caste. Moreover, social and geographical mobility have always added to the attractions of churches as ready means of providing social networks and assistance in otherwise unfamiliar new territories. Though true of most communities, these points are amply illustrated by the triumph of the black churches in maintaining a preeminence in African-American life over the last two centuries. Whatever the reasons, the continued strength of religious ideas has constantly shaped American political discourse, both in utopian and apocalyptic directions.

In 1842 Charles Dickens visited the United States, and he subsequently published accounts of his visit in the books *American Notes* and *Martin Chuzzlewit*. Both works were understood by Americans as deeply hostile in their ruthless denunciation of slavery, of the pervasive violence and hypocrisy of American life, and of the shallow and sensational media, among much else. To understand Dickens' critique, it is important to recognize him as merely one of countless European observers who travelled to America expecting to find a larger and improved version of Great Britain, and was shocked to find instead a radically different society with its own characteristic flaws and virtues. It is exactly that mix of familiarity and alien strangeness that Europeans have so often found confusing, and occasionally horrifying, but the flaws lay as much in their expectations as in the reality they have encountered.

For various reasons – size, ethnic and racial diversity, religiosity – the United States has from its earliest days evolved a culture radically different from that of its European roots, and any attempt to fit American society into a European mold ultimately results in distortion. Though not immune to wider economic and political trends, the history of the United States has to be viewed in the context of a separate continent no less than merely another nation.

Notes

1. Henry David Thoreau, *Cape Cod* (New York: Apollo, 1966) pp. 312–13.
2. Richard Hofstadter, *The Paranoid Style in American Politics* (New York: Knopf, 1965).

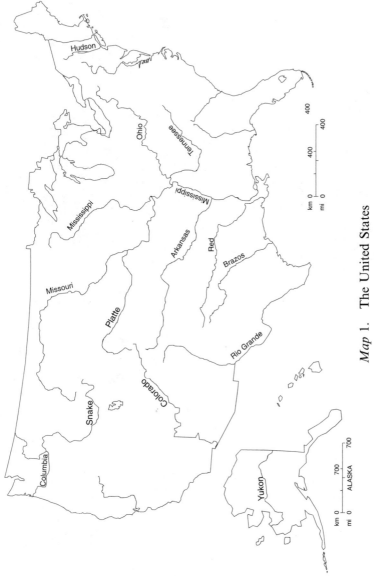

Map 1. The United States

I

. . . .

Unnamed Lands: The European Settlement, 1492–1765

In the 1490s European sailors began reporting their encounters with new lands in the western hemisphere. Though the 'discovery' is often associated with Christopher Columbus, he had many equally inquisitive contemporaries and writers of the day gave priority to the claims of a fellow-Italian named Amerigo Vespucci, from whom 'America' takes its name. The first explorers touched chiefly on lands in the Caribbean, but it soon became apparent that the New World represented an almost unimaginably vast continental land mass, the exact dimensions of which would not be appreciated for another century.

Beginning with Columbus' Spanish employers, several European nations sought to create in the New World great empires modelled on the motherland. New Spain was followed by New France, New Netherland, New England and even New Sweden, in each case implying that the social and political patterns of the home country could successfully be transported across the Atlantic and flourish in this very different soil. These aspirations would prove futile, as settlers adapted to the distinctive conditions of the new land and took advantage of its unique opportunities, to the chagrin of imperial authorities. For the British especially, whose colonizing ventures would ultimately prove by far the most successful, the movement towards religious and social diversity became irresistible, placing a grave strain on any chance of political solidarity.

In 1492 these considerations were in the distant future. As the Europeans discovered a land wholly new to them, their immediate attention focused on the possibly limitless wealth that might be found here, and assessing the alien populations they now encountered.

THE NATIVE POPULATION

Having discovered the 'Indies', Columbus naturally termed the inhabitants Indians, an enduring error that modern writers are anxious to correct by using the term 'Native Americans'; though 'American' itself merely commemorates the name of another European explorer, and one far shiftier than Columbus. Who were these natives? For centuries white observers concocted countless explanations, usually with the goal of fitting them into a recognizable historical scheme. Were they perhaps the descendants of a lost wave of earlier settlers, perhaps Egyptian, Hebrew, even Welsh? The need for such hypothetical roots was all the greater when nineteenth-century explorers found the remains of medieval mound structures in southern Ohio and along the Mississippi valley, evidence of lost cultures far too sophisticated to be associated with the ignorant 'savages' they saw around them.

The existence of native peoples on the American continent can actually be traced back to Palaeolithic times. For many years the peopling of North America was dated by means of the stone tools that appeared so widely some twelve or fifteen thousand years ago, the so-called Clovis points, which were associated with the hunting of now-extinct mammals. Presumably these were used by hunters who had crossed the land bridge that once joined Alaska to Siberia. More recently it has been argued that although a human presence in the landscape is hard to detect before the invention of stone artifacts, people might have been living in America for many years before the Clovis epoch. A growing body of evidence suggests much earlier human activity, certainly about 25 000 years ago, and more controversial claims give dates of forty or fifty thousand years. Nor need the first settlers have been confined to entering via the land bridge, as they may have navigated their way along the coasts in small vessels. One oddity is that some of the oldest confirmed occupation sites are to be found in South America, suggesting that the families migrating from Siberia must have expanded rapidly over their huge new domain, presumably following herds of game. By the time that civilizations were beginning to emerge in the Old World, Native American communities were often living in settled groups, at least for parts of the year, and there were far-flung trading routes.

The exact size of the pre-Columbian population is difficult to determine, not least because the question is politically contentious. Those who take an essentially benevolent view of the European settlement minimize the Indian presence, so that North America is seen to have been a *terra nullius*, land belonging to nobody and thus open to claim and use. Recently the opposite view has become fashionable, with extremely high estimates of the extent of the native population, the suggestion being that white invaders were responsible for the genocide of flourishing, pre-existing communities. There is often an added implication here that the destroyed cultures represented a kind of ecological harmony that was obliterated by selfish capitalist and Christian Europeans. While a demographic catastrophe certainly did occur in Central and South America, the situation to the north was different, as the numbers were much smaller and the pace of conquest far slower. The most plausible suggestion is that around 1500 AD at least two million people lived north of what is now the Mexican border.

Within what is now the United States, geography conditioned several main environmental and cultural regions, Alaska falling into the distinct Arctic/sub-Arctic zone. The eastern half of the country can be termed the woodlands, an area of dazzling dietary wealth in game and fish, supplemented by cultivated squash, gourds and, above all, corn. Coastal populations made heavy use of the resources of the sea – fish and shellfish. By the twelfth or thirteenth centuries, easterners were living in a series of complex and prosperous societies. The abundant forests provided wood for impressive long-houses, and some settlements grew into major fortified towns with imposing temples. These people left their mark on the landscape in the form of tombs with elaborate grave goods, and public ritual structures that would have been quite familiar to the ancient Europeans who built Stonehenge and megalithic monuments. The most impressive are the extensive mound sites, which can be seen as humbler versions of the pyramid temples of Central America, and some great earthwork complexes and geometric enclosures. The Moundsville Complex of West Virginia and the Serpent Mound of Ohio are among the finest surviving remnants of this cultural flowering.

The Hopewell culture flourished in the first few centuries of the Christian era, and mound building was revived in the Mississippian Age (ca. 800–1500 AD). By the twelfth century the largest mound settlements probably had several thousand residents at any given time, quite comparable to the middling towns of contemporary Europe. There is some debate about the exact correspondence between the archaeological perceptions of the mound builders and the historical tribes encountered by the early white settlers. However some of the tribal groups constituted powerful and long-enduring political realities, especially the Iroquois league of the Five Nations (later Six) based in the area of New York state. Formed in the sixteenth century, this federation remained a formidable military presence until the early years of the United States. In the south-east were complex tribes such as the Creeks and the Cherokees.

Centralized settlements and even urban development were also found in the desert of the south-west. This was a very difficult environment, critically dependent on climatic cycles and rainfall, and placing a high premium on the collection and saving of water. From about 1000 AD, large village communities developed there and made resourceful use of natural features to create well-defended settlements or pueblos, at the centre of which were *kivas*, round, partly underground chambers used for religious rituals. The pueblo communities, which often lasted for several centuries, maintained links with the more celebrated cultures of Mexico. Today this area contains by far the largest and most heavily populated reservations in the United States. The Navajo community in New Mexico and Utah today numbers almost 150 000, more than the next twenty biggest reservations combined.

Conventional European stereotypes of 'Indians' usually concern the horse-riding and buffalo-hunting cultures of the Great Plains region, tribes such as the Lakota (Sioux) and Cheyenne, although in reality this societal structure was relatively late to appear. The plains were sparsely populated until historically recent times, when eastern communities began to settle, armed with the newly discovered bow and arrow. And though horses had existed in North America in prehistoric times, they had been extinct for millennia and were only reintroduced by Spanish settlers in the eighteenth century. Once returned, the horse provided the basis of the powerful and militarily dangerous culture encountered by nineteenth-century Americans. Plains society was based on the apparently inexhaustible buffalo herds: there may have been 60–70 million buffalo in any given year before the 1840s.

Further west were still more varied ecologies, including the Great Basin, centered on Utah and Nevada and inhabited by tribes such as the Utes and Paiutes; and the plateau region of modern Idaho. In much of what later became southern California, the harsh desert conditions prevented the existence of all but small, impoverished groups dependent on foraging. In the Pacific north-west, in contrast, large village settlements flourished, based on the rich fishing and the harvesting of sea mammals. Social structures were complex, and awareness of social distinctions was finely tuned. These sophisticated groups also developed magnificent visual arts, most evident in the awe-inspiring totem poles so avidly collected by nineteenth-century Europeans. Native population densities were probably at their highest on the Pacific coast.

European explorers and settlers found much in North America that was priceless, even though it would be centuries before they discovered the precious metals they sought. They found crops such as Indian corn, tobacco and sweet potatoes, all of which were integrated into their own agricultural systems. In exchange, even the best-intentioned left a disastrous legacy in the form of European diseases that decimated native populations long before there was any systematic policy of 'Indian removal'. This process was accelerated by famine resulting from the destruction of familiar environments and (from the eighteenth century) the spread of liquor. The effects of disease, war and environmental collapse were harrowing. In California the Indian population was probably around 300 000 in 1750, but less than 50 000 by the 1860s. Sometimes destruction by biological means was quite deliberate, as in the 1760s when the British ransacked smallpox hospitals for contaminated bedding to offer as gifts to the Ottawa peoples. For all the savagery of the centuries-long wars, North American Indians suffered far less from bullets or cannon shells than what has been termed the 'biological unification of mankind'.

THE CONQUISTADORES

As in South America, the first European presence in the north was Spanish, when Juan Ponce de Leon sighted Florida in 1513. After the fall of Mexico in 1519–20 the Spanish conquistadores travelled north and south to seek new empires, often drawn by tales of wealthy cities beyond the next range of mountains or over the desert. Sometimes the stories were true, and by 1533 the great Inca civilization had been discovered and crushed. North America offered much poorer pickings. In 1528 Alvar Nuñez Cabeza de Vaca took part in an expedition to Florida, the first major venture into what would become the territory of the United States. He spent several years with Indian tribes before returning to Mexico City, where the stories he disseminated of wealthy northern cities caused much excitement, and two new expeditions were launched as a result.

In 1540 Francisco Vázquez de Coronado travelled in quest of the fabled wealth of the mythical 'Seven Cities of Cibola'. Though he found nothing to rival the splendours of Mexico or Peru, his search represented the first European exploration of what are now the south-western states of the United States, and Spaniards discovered the Grand Canyon in northern Arizona. His followers journeyed far enough into the plains country to be astonished by the vast herds of roaming buffalo. At just that time Hernando De Soto was engaged in a three-year exploration of the towns and temples of the south-east, penetrating into Georgia and as far as the southern Appalachians. He travelled over sections of at least ten of the later American states. Both Coronado and DeSoto reached the Mississippi River.

By 1565 the Spanish settlement at St Augustine, Florida, had become the first permanent European settlement in North America, and there were sporadic ventures further north and west: by 1603, the Spanish had even reached the shores of Alaska. Santa Fe in New Mexico was founded in 1610. In the seventeenth and eighteenth centuries the Spanish authorities in Mexico sought to consolidate their power in the northern territories that constitute the present states of Texas, California and New Mexico, but they met determined resistance from some of the better-organized tribes, for example the Navajo. In 1680 a massive pueblo revolt caused a severe setback to Spanish settlement and evangelization in New Mexico, and a Yaqui rising in 1740 resulted in the death of a thousand Spaniards.

Despite this the missionary endeavour continued. By the end of the eighteenth century there was a network of some thirty mission stations in Texas alone. San Antonio was the main political centre, with its own fort or *presidio* (1718), and the mission station that later gained legendary status as the Alamo. From the end of the seventeenth century, missions spread north from Baja California along the Pacific coast, and celebrated evangelists such as Juniper Serra sought not only to convert the natives, but also to integrate them into the imperial economy as farm labourers and herders. Here too there was a structure of *presidios*, centred on Monterey, and by the 1760s the northwards expansion was sustained by the fear of possible military and imperial rivalry with Britain and Russia. From 1762 to 1801 Spain ruled the once-French territory of Louisiana, giving it theoretical sovereignty over a major portion of the continent.

By the time the United States came into being, therefore, Spanish explorers and missionaries had ranged widely over the western half of the country and Spanish settlements would later become the nuclei of such large cities as Albuquerque (New Mexico), Tucson (Arizona), San Antonio and El Paso (Texas). Los Angeles originated as a village, founded in 1781 to promote colonization. The geographical breadth of Spanish exploration is illustrated by the names still used for the land of the mountains (Montana), the snowy region (Nevada) and the area of richly coloured rivers (Colorado). Across the south-west the Spanish evolved an economy and a culture that would later earn worldwide fame as that of the 'American' west, with its *vaqueros* or cowboys and their skill with horse and rope. Many of the familiar words of this world are in fact Spanish, including ranch, corral, lasso, lariat, chaps and bronco. Both the word and the concept of the rodeo are Spanish in origin.

In the sixteenth century North America was included in that part of the New World the Pope had designated for Spanish domination. This dispensation was soon challenged by a host of newcomers, the most powerful of whom were the French. In 1535 Jacques Cartier explored the St Lawrence river and began a series of colonizing attempts that ultimately bore fruit in the founding of the 'city' of Québec (really a trading post) in 1608. By the 1630s colonization was extending along the St Lawrence, and in 1663 New France became a crown colony under Louis XIV. In the early seventeenth century the French authorities sponsored Jesuit expeditions with the aim of creating a spiritual and political empire among Christianized Indian tribes such as the Algonquins and Hurons, chiefly in the modern Canadian province of Ontario. The missions were devastated in the middle of the century and many missionaries martyred, but French authority continued to expand. In 1675 the Catholic see of Québec had ecclesiastical jurisdiction over the whole of French North America. In 1713 Britain received territorial concessions in Canada, but the awe-inspiring French presence was symbolized by the new fortifications of Louisbourg (1717).

In 1673 the governor of New France despatched an expedition, led by Louis Joliet and Jacques Marquette, to establish whether the great Mississippi flowed south or west, towards Florida or California. The discovery that it entered the Gulf of Mexico was crucial for later French settlement, and the Mississippi now became the central artery of a New World empire that appeared set to dominate the continent as Spanish power steadily declined. Canadian colonists voyaging along the Mississippi to the Gulf of Mexico gave the name of the current French monarch to the new province of Louisiana. In 1680 Father Hennepin explored what later became Minnesota. French settlements appeared at Biloxi in Mississippi, Cahokia in Illinois (1699), Detroit in Michigan (1701) and Mobile in Alabama (1702). The city of New Orleans dates from 1718. In 1749 a new expedition mapped

After decades of neglect, English interest in the New World revived with the country's geopolitical contest with Spain: by 1579 Sir Francis Drake was even making an implausible claim for lands he had discovered in northern California. In 1584 geographer Richard Hakluyt wrote that English colonization 'may stay the Spanish king from flowing all over the face' of North America, and serious attempts at colonization followed shortly thereafter. Between 1585 and 1590, colonizing ventures focused on Roanoke in North Carolina, where a short-lived settlement sprang up. Though this venture had little long-term significance, perhaps the major symbolic outcome was the birth of a baby named Virginia Dare, the first English child born in the New World (1587).

Colonization efforts revived after 1603, under James I, directed at several points from Maine southwards. In 1606 Parliament created the London and Plymouth Virginia Companies to promote settlement, and the following year the London Company set up an enduring colony at Jamestown in what is now southern Virginia, near the site of a deserted Spanish mission. The early days of the venture were perilous as the colony was located in a particularly unhealthy region. Of the 104 colonists present in June 1607, only 38 were still alive the following January, most of the remainder having succumbed to typhoid and dysentery, aggravated by hunger – 1609 was 'the starving time'. Sickness continued to claim many colonists until 1624, when the demise of the Virginia Company and the creation of a royal colony permitted reform and a general reorientation. Skirmishes with the Indian population also caused heavy losses, above all the bloody war of 1622, which claimed the life of perhaps 350 colonists; but here too the gravest dangers had been removed by the middle of the decade. By 1634 Virginia's population was approaching five thousand; forty thousand by the 1670s.

Nor, at first, was the economic situation much more sound. The initial prospectus announced plans for a subtropical plantation to grow 'sugar cane, oranges, lemons, almonds and aniseed'. None of these proved successful, and conditions only changed for the better in 1612 with the introduction of tobacco. Smoking became an enormously popular fad in England and western Europe, and the fortunes of Virginia boomed. So did those of the other Chesapeake Bay colony: Maryland, founded in 1632 as a proprietorship for Cecilius Calvert (Lord Baltimore) with the goal of creating a refuge for persecuted English Catholics. The two hundred settlers who arrived in the new land in 1634 were equally divided between Protestant and Catholic. Maryland offered an atmosphere of religious tolerance that was attractive to many besides Catholics, but in 1655 relations became violent and Puritan settlers defeated a Catholic force. Matters remained tense until 1689, when the Calvert supremacy was overturned, and the favourable position of Catholicism destroyed.

The Marylanders entered the tobacco trade with the same enthusiasm as the Virginians. By the 1650s the two colonies together were annually exporting some five million pounds of tobacco, and their future was assured. By 1700 Chesapeake tobacco made up four fifths of the value of the exports from British North America. Within the cash-poor colonies, tobacco remained the normal means of exchange well into the eighteenth century, so that even the salaries of colonial clergy were specified in terms of so many pounds of tobacco, Truly, this was an economy built upon smoke.

Many immigrants travelled under the terms of indentured servitude, a contractual relationship by which an immigrant agreed to work for a master for several years in order to pay off the cost of passage. Though the prospect of eventual liberty made this a different issue from that of slavery, the conditions of transportation and work were often little better than those of slaves. Servants were similarly subject to virtual sale upon arrival, in conditions that would later become notorious in the slave markets auctioning newly arrived Africans, and were likewise subject to physical and sexual abuse by unscrupulous masters. In the seventeenth century the end of a term of servitude promised the opportunity to establish of a good livelihood by farming, but in later decades former servants were more likely to retain their menial status. Servitude of this sort became progressively less attractive to Europeans, while the previously soaring population of western Europe stabilized after the mid-seventeenth century. The consequent lack of white labour encouraged planters and farmers to seek new sources, and in 1717 the British government made transportation to the New World a legal punishment for crimes that would earlier have brought the death penalty. Even this could not solve the problem, and the new cash crops being developed in the southern colonies imposed working conditions that in themselves constituted a virtual death sentence for white settlers.

A solution was found in the use of African slaves. The first known slave importation in the British colonies occurred in 1619, though the Spanish and Portuguese had had long experience in this practice, having already transported perhaps a million Africans. Slavery did not represent a major force in British lands until after the 1680s. In 1670 Sir William Berkeley estimated that among th 40 000 Virginians, there were only 2 000 black slaves and 6 000 white servants. By 1700 there were 10–20 000 slaves in British America out of a total population of 275 000, perhaps five per cent of the whole. Virginia, Maryland and North Carolina all doubled their slave populations between 1698 and 1710. On average about three thousand Africans were imported each year between 1700 and 1790. The tempo accelerated during the 1760s, when over 7 000 slaves entered North America each year. Probably 300 000 were imported during the course of the eighteenth century. After an apparent ending of the slave trade in the 1780s, a brief revival at the opening of the new century brought in a further 40 000 Africans. Throughout the second half of the century the African proportion of the population never fell below one fifth, and in some regions was far higher than that. By 1775 Virginia had about 500 000 people and Maryland 250 000, and perhaps a third of this combined population had their origins in Africa.

NEW ENGLAND

For many years, popular perceptions of the early history of
America were dominated by the experiences of settlers in
New England, and especially the colonies based around Plymouth and Massachusetts Bay. As a consequence generations
of American schoolchildren were imbued with a highly coloured account of the religious and sectarian motives behind
their country's origins. 'Puritan' became synonymous with
settler or colonist, and the first Thanksgiving provided a
richly religious symbol for the beginnings of the white presence in the New World. Apart from ignoring the vast history
of earlier French and Spanish settlement, this was misleading
in downplaying the importance of the mid-American colonies, which became economically viable far earlier than their
northern counterparts. The northern, 'Pilgrim' emphasis is
only explicable in terms of the rhetorical battles over the
nature of American society in the early nineteenth century,
and New England's need to present itself as the authentic
America, rather than the slaveholding, aristocratic and secessionist south.

The Puritan settlement of New England was a result of the
dissatisfaction of some clergy and laity with the adequacy of
the reform of the Church of England under Queen Elizabeth I, and by the survival of what they perceived as popish
practices. English Puritans had initially engaged in a political
struggle to control the national church with a view towards
enforcing their own opinions, but by the end of the sixteenth
century it had become apparent that this would not be
possible, and that further agitation would meet severe repression. From about 1615 Protestant militants were also
alarmed at the growth of Arminian thinking within the established church, that is, ideas that moderated or softened the
stringent Calvinist theology. In response, small groups
formed that despaired of the national church and envisioned
a purified church composed of companies of visible saints, a
spiritual elect free from the unregenerate masses. These sec-

taries stemmed mainly from London and the trading towns of south-east England, and they generally followed leaders trained in the Cambridge colleges. The first 'gathered churches' took refuge in the Netherlands, where they were hospitably received but were unlikely to maintain their English language and identity in the coming years. The separatists or independents now focused their efforts on the 'New England' over the seas, in 'the northern parts of Virginia.'

Sailing on the *Mayflower*, a hundred Pilgrims reached Cape Cod in November 1620. Finding themselves beyond the authority of Virginia, the colonists devised for themselves a 'Compact' of self-government, and thus began the colony that settled at Plymouth shortly afterwards. The group established friendly relations with the Wampanoag Indians, who generously taught them about the food of the new land. The miracle of their survival was celebrated in the first Thanksgiving in 1621, but the colony remained small, with barely 300 people by 1630.

Plymouth was soon overshadowed by its neighbour at Massachusetts Bay, which received its charter in 1629. Within a year, there were 2 000 settlers in Massachusetts, mainly living around Boston harbour. The northern colonies were immensely strengthened over the next decade as high church and Arminian opinions gained ground in England. Fifteen to twenty thousand colonists had arrived by 1640, including 65 ministers, and settlements proliferated. This 'New England' expanded into new regions. By 1636 Thomas Hooker had led a hundred people to Hartford, which became the basis of Connecticut and was soon recognized as a colony in its own right (in 1662 it was augmented by the previously separate colony of New Haven). By the middle of the century Massachusetts Bay had some 15 000 European settlers, with another 2 500 in Connecticut, about 1 000 in Plymouth and perhaps 2 000 all told in the fringe colonies of Rhode Island, New Hampshire and Maine. Boston had emerged as the obvious capital of the region, with 3 000 residents by 1660. When war threatened in 1643, Massachusetts Bay was the core of an entity called the 'United Colonies of New England'.

The religious justification of the new colonies was expressed in the missionary outreach to the native communities. The key figure here was John Eliot, pastor of Roxbury, who by the 1650s had translated the catechism and some of the Scriptures into Indian languages. His missionary venture also involved the formation of Christian communities, 'praying towns' on the model pioneered by the Catholics in South America and elsewhere. By the 1670s several thousand natives had been converted to Christianity. Such relatively benevolent relations have to be set against the often extreme brutality of military encounters with native peoples. In 1636 the war against the Pequots involved the massacre of entire villages, in which several hundred Indians may have perished in single incidents.

ORTHODOXY AND HERESY

Later accounts of the Puritan colony regularly describe early Massachusetts as an extreme theocracy, and there is no question that the settlers did indeed view their world as a new Israel, to which the Old Testament injunctions applied with special force. Theirs was a city upon a hill, and Boston was a new Jerusalem, in which moral and religious conformity were severely enforced for fear that an angry God would punish his errant people. Fundamental to the ideology of the new colony was the Old Testament notion of the covenant between God and his people, a contract that required scrupulous observation. However, few of these ideas were necessarily remarkable from the point of view of contemporary Protestant Europe, or indeed from mainstream religious opinion in Stuart England, which similarly enforced church attendance and penalized a huge range of moral misbehaviour that would today be regarded as entirely a matter for the individual. Obligatory days of fast and thanksgiving were similarly a familiar English practice in an age that viewed the moral and natural universes as intimately linked. And while the first codes of Massachusetts laws appear draconian, they differed little in tone or severity from the statutes of the Cromwellian republic.

The Massachusetts Puritans were strictly orthodox Calvinist Christians, with ideas on matters such as the Trinity and the Virgin Birth that would have been largely accepted by any mainstream Anglican or even Catholic. They were not prepared to accept the slightest deviation or even speculation on basic matters, which was a difficult position when so many individual believers had their own interpretation of the Scriptures. As the political crisis mounted in England in 1640, the collapse of ecclesiastical control inevitably meant the growth of extreme sectarian opinions and their propagation through books, pamphlets and personal visits by missionaries. Between 1630 and 1670 New England was beset with repeated crises involving the heretical speculations associated with sects such as familists, antinomians, anabaptists and, most nightmarish of all, Quakers. Each successive confrontation with the religious intolerance of the Massachusetts colony promoted the expansion of neighbouring settlements.

The first doctrinal crises erupted in the mid 1630s with the liberal views of Roger Williams and Anne Hutchinson. Williams held extreme views on religious toleration and the state's role in enforcing religious conformity: for him, 'forced worship stinks in God's nostrils'. He was accused of wishing to extend tolerance to pagans, Jews and Turks, and assuredly to all Christian believers. For incorrect ideas, he recommended the approach, 'Fight only with words not swords'. His eccentricity extended even to the notion that lands should never be acquired from the Indians without proper payment. By 1635 he had been exiled with his followers, who built a new refuge in the area of Providence in the later Rhode Island colony.

Anne Hutchinson was a recent English immigrant who held religious discussions among a circle of pious Boston women. This separate female activity was suspect in its own right, but her mystical approach also led her to underplay the human role in obtaining salvation through bible reading, church attendance and 'works'. She thus fell into what the orthodox considered the heresy of antinomianism, and in 1637 she and her followers were tried for 'traducing the ministers'. A claim that her actions were inspired by direct revelation sealed her fate, and she was exiled the following year. She naturally found her way to the new colony in Narragansett Bay. Other dissidents followed. Antinomian exiles from Massachusetts were also among the first colonists of New Hampshire, though the settlement there was far more diverse in motive.

From about 1640 Rhode Island represented a liberal phenomenon unique in the Christian world and possibly on the planet, all the more remarkable for its establishment at a time of such violent strife between and among the various Christian denominations: this was after all the height of the Thirty Year War in Europe and the worst period of the German witch-craze. In 1647 Rhode Island abolished witch trials. The colony's 1663 charter contains the astonishing affirmation that 'every person may at all times freely and fully enjoy his own judgment and conscience in matters of religious concernments'. For the next century Rhode Island enjoyed an evil reputation among orthodox New Englanders as a spiritual Sodom, the baneful influence of which was reflected in the mystical and occult speculations that are recorded in villages along the southern coasts of Massachusetts and Connecticut. The Puritan Cotton Mather called the area 'the sewer of New England'. About 1640 Rhode Island became the home of the American Baptist movement, and it later gave rise to sectarian Baptists such as those who accepted the Jewish Sabbath – the 'Seventh Day Baptists'. Apart from its cranky Christian movements, Newport had a core of Jewish families from 1677, and in 1763 became home to America's first public synagogue. Scorned by their narrow-minded neighbours, Providence and Newport consoled themselves by becoming the leading trading ports of the region in the following century.

The most extreme of the sectarians were the Quakers, whose activities caused some of the darkest chapters in early colonial history. Originating in England in the 1650s, the group challenged virtually all the most fundamental beliefs and values of the day by claiming that Christ was found in the Inner Light that guided each believer. As radical democrats, Quakers rejected symbols of social hierarchy and submission such as the doffing of the hat to superiors, and insisted on the use of the intimate 'thou' and 'thee'. They challenged the power of clergy by vocally disrupting the formal services of the 'steeple houses', and their rejection of oaths threatened to destabilize the basis of civil government. Worse, some of the most active and articulate preachers were women. From 1656 Massachusetts repeatedly persecuted the Quaker missionaries, ordering severe beatings and exile, threatening worse if they dared return; as of course they did. Between 1659 and 1661 four Quakers were hanged on Boston Common. One was a woman, Mary Dyer, who had been Anne Hutchinson's closest friend. By 1676 Quaker settlers were seeking toleration in new American lands and a settlement was founded in West New Jersey.

In England, too, Quakers represented the ultimate test for any proposed toleration law, and persecution reached a new height under the Tories in the early 1680s. However, Quaker leader William Penn was viewed kindly by King Charles II and his brother the Duke of York, and in 1681 Penn received a proprietorial charter for the land that would become Pennsylvania, 'Penn's Woods'. The Quaker settlement extended into parts of what later became Delaware and New Jersey. The settlement was an immediate success: by July 1683, 50 vessels had arrived to raise the population to 3 000, an influx parallelled only by the early immigration to Massachusetts Bay.

In 1682 Penn's 'Great Law' for the new colony offered tolerance to 'all persons who confess and acknowledge the one almighty and eternal God to be the creator, upholder and ruler of the world', with the proviso of orderly behaviour. In its first decades the colony sought to institutionalize Quaker principles in a law code that minimized the death penalty and made creative use of jails and workhouses, but the period of experimentation ended with the adoption of the English criminal code in 1718. This was part of a compromise whereby Quakers were relieved of the necessity to take oaths in order to hold office, being granted instead the right to affirm loyalty.

Such sweeping tolerance was tempting to the religious minorities of Western Europe, including German sectarians whose position was deteriorating in the confessional states of the day. German-Americans date their history from the day in 1683 when the first group of settlers set up a colony at Germantown, now in suburban Philadelphia. There were also the inevitable Baptists – English, Welsh and Irish – whose congregations in the Philadelphia area founded the first American Baptist association in 1707. By the turn of the century the orthodox regarded Pennsylvania as a sectarian zoo, much as they had earlier viewed Rhode Island, and like that older colony Pennsylvania's tolerant atmosphere encouraged a boom in trade and agriculture. By the middle of the eighteenth century Philadelphia had surpassed Boston as the leading city of British America; by 1770 Philadelphia vied with Dublin for the position of the Empire's second city.

While the search for religious refuge motivated many British colonists, other territories were settled as a result of economic or imperial self-interest. In 1664 the English took possession of the Dutch colonies headquartered in New Amsterdam, which was then renamed New York. England now had control of the former Dutch and Swedish territories in the New World, and this also served to remove a potential threat to the security of the New England and the Chesapeake colonies. Also in these years, British settlement was spreading to the lands south of Virginia into the Carolinas. Settlement there had been proposed as early as 1629, and the area received its name from King Charles I, then in power,

Table 1.1   The formation of British America

British colonies	Approximate date of first European settlement
New England	
Connecticut	1634
Massachusetts	1620
New Hampshire	1623
Rhode Island	1636
Vermont	1724
Maine	1624
Middle Atlantic	
New Jersey	1664
New York	1614
Pennsylvania	1682
South Atlantic	
Delaware	1638
Georgia	1733
Maryland	1634
North Carolina	1660
South Carolina	1670
Virginia	1607

rather than his son, under whom the scheme was actually accomplished decades later. The northern part of Carolina was settled in the 1650s, the south from about 1670 (Table 1.1). Older settlements also achieved colonial status in their own right: Rhode Island in 1647, New Hampshire in 1679.

By about 1675 the English settlers had staked their claim to the eastern seaboard, with at least a nuclei of settlements stretching from the borders of Spanish Florida in the south to the present states of Maine and Vermont. Inland the colonists had pressed as far as the Fall Line, where further river navigation was prevented by rapids. In the next generation they would begin to move into the foothills of the Appalachians and the mountain valleys that stretched from the Carolinas and Virginia into New York.

CRISIS, 1675–92

By the late 1670s, that part of God's Israel that was New England was prospering in many ways, but serious difficulties were becoming apparent. In 1675 a devastating war broke out between the colonists and the local Wampanoag Indians led by Metacom, 'King Philip'. The war dragged on for a year and resulted in the death of six hundred colonists and perhaps three thousand natives. In 1676 the prospect of a general Indian confrontation led to widespread demands for improved military preparations and the devolution of more power from the colonial capitals to the frontier communities themselves.

In Virginia the detonator for unrest was the governor's embargo on further penetration into Indian lands without his permission, and the erection of forts to enforce this. Discontent culminated in an open rebellion led by Nathaniel Bacon, who united frontiersmen and servants in a populist campaign based on anti-elite and anti-aristocratic politics, as well as a rejection of unjust taxation. The rebels even drew slave support, ensuring that it would be regarded by later radical historians as a pioneering example of lower-class militancy and interracial collaboration: even if the dissidents had as one of their chief goals the suppression of the Indian menace. The capital of Jamestown was burned, and the English government was forced to send a thousand soldiers to hold the colony.

Tensions grew during the next decade. After the triumph of the king's party in England in 1683, the court party sought a general revision of the charters of the English boroughs, which had caused so many constitutional perils during the previous 50 years. In a related move, a new imperial policy was signalled by the revocation of existing colonial charters, including that of Massachusetts in 1684. By 1686 *Quo Warranto* proceedings had been instituted against all the charters of colonial America, and there were plans for new regional structures, perhaps a 'Dominion of New England' under a governor directly responsible to the king. This trend raised all kinds of concerns – constitutional, religious and personal: the new king was the Catholic James II, who was believed to harbour absolutist intentions. Without the charters, all the property arrangements in the colonies would be thrown into doubt, and at the least the colonists potentially faced huge rises in quitrents. At worst the colonists might find themselves as oppressed as the Irish, and as open to some kind of recolonization. At the end of 1686 Sir Edmund Andros was installed as governor of the Dominion of New England, and by 1688 the dominion extended from the Delaware River to the St Lawrence, including New York. In addition to being authoritarian, the governor and his circle also made conspicuous use of the Anglican service book, which for New England Puritans was barely removed from popery, and protests became widespread.

In November 1688 the Dutch stadholder William of Orange landed in England to confront King James, who by the end of the year had been driven from power. When the news arrived in America some months later it caused a general revolution. Boston was put under the rule of a Council of Safety until the restoration of traditional government in May. In New York a German adventurer named Jacob Leisler led a social revolution based on his command of the militia, and as the prospect of a French invasion became daily more real, Leisler emerged as a dictator. He retained his position until 1691, when he refused to acknowledge the authority of the new governor and was executed. The revolution of 1689 in Maryland resulted in the triumph of a Protestant Association formed in opposition to the proprietor, Lord Baltimore, whose family lost their position in the colony until they converted to the established church. The capital was also moved from Catholic Saint Mary's City to Protestant Annapolis ('Anne Arundel Town'). A warrant was issued for the arrest of another proprietor, William Penn, calling for his capture for treason, and his proprietorship was suspended. Throughout 1689 all the colonies experienced a greater or lesser degree of upheaval until all eventually proclaimed the new royal family.

Even when government had been more or less restored, other questions lingered. The old charters had been forfeited and new documents were often not obtained for years: not until 1691 in the case of Massachusetts. Moreover the new charters were often quite different from the old, and in New England it changed the criterion for political participation from the traditional notion of church membership to the more English property qualification. It was also at this point that the Plymouth plantation was absorbed into the colony of Massachusetts. Also, the bold Stuart vision of a united British America could scarcely be forgotten. Though Andros's rule as governor was intolerable, a weighty precedent had been set for future joint efforts in a common imperial interest.

The dream of a godly New England was in deep difficulty and the problem was exacerbated by the war situation. In 1690 New England had allied with New York in a combined campaign against New France, a disastrous failure that had contributed to the economic ruin of British America. The depth of the fear and disillusionment in those years is illustrated by the Salem witch panic which erupted in February 1692 following the discovery that some teenage girls were dabbling in folk magic and divination. The resulting spiral of hysteria and accusation resulted in dozens of people being charged with witchcraft by the middle of the year, and twenty being executed. Though again this affair has become part of the common folklore of Puritan America, the incident was wildly untypical and would have been unimaginable in circumstances less desperate or unsettled than those of the early 1690s.

THE BRITISH COLONIES IN THE EIGHTEENTH CENTURY

By about 1640 the British presence in North America was an established fact. The British domain had about 27 000 residents in 1640, and thereafter the population expansion was prodigious, passing the 100 000 mark in the mid-1660s and reaching a quarter of a million around 1700. Thereafter, the number more or less doubled every 24 years or so, suggesting a steady annual growth rate of 3 per cent, a rate that continued until almost the end of the nineteenth century. There were about 470 000 people in 1720, a million in the early 1740s and two million by the mid 1760s. In 1790 the first federal census found that the new United States had just under four million inhabitants. This number doubled to about eight million by about 1814, to sixteen million by the late 1830s, 32 million by 1861, and 64 million by about 1890. To put this demographic achievement into context, if this extraordinary rate had been maintained until the present, then the United States would have a population of around a billion, rivalling that of China.

As the colonial population grew, it also became more evenly distributed among the colonies (Table 1.2). In 1700 by far the heaviest population concentrations were in the three colonies of Massachusetts, Maryland and Virginia, which between them accounted for over 60 per cent of the people of British North America. By 1770 the share of population of these three areas had reduced to about 40 per cent, a relative decline that reflected growth in the new colonies of Pennsylvania and North Carolina. Even tiny Rhode Island grew from 7 000 inhabitants in 1700 to 50 000 by 1765.

Formal divisions between the colonies mask the more fundamental regional distinctions, which for example meant that the natural Chesapeake region straddled the official frontier between Virginia and Maryland. In the mid-eighteenth century there were essentially six major regions,

Table 1.2   Population growth, 1700–70

	Population (thousands)		
	1700	*1740*	*1770*
New England			
Connecticut	24	70	175
Massachusetts	70	158	299
New Hampshire	6	22	60
Rhode Island	6	24	55
Total	106	274	589
Middle Atlantic			
New Jersey	14	52	110
New York	19	63	185
Pennsylvania	20	100	275
Total	53	215	570
South Atlantic			
Georgia	–	–	26
Maryland	31	105	200
North Carolina	5	50	230
South Carolina	8	45	140
Virginia	72	200	450
Total	116	400	1 046

broadly three each in the north and the south, and each producing significant urban growth.

The northern parts of New England had poor agricultural soil but superb timberlands. There were also rich opportunities for fishing, whaling and commercial shipping, based on the city of Boston and smaller centres such as Gloucester and Salem. By 1730 Boston's population was approaching 16 000, a level that remained steady until the revolution. In the first half of the century British settlers expanded rapidly into the northern regions that would become Maine and New Hampshire: there were some 6 000 white settlers there in 1690, 60 000 by 1760.

Southern New England merged into the New York colony, which was characterized by better soils and substantial trade along the Hudson River to Long Island Sound. This commerce was already laying the foundations for the later prosperity of New York City, which had 25 000 people in 1760. Other thriving ports included Newport in Rhode Island, the fifth largest city in British America, with 11 000 people in the 1760s. The significance of coastal towns and regional ports was equally apparent in the wealthy Delaware River region, dominated by Philadelphia, a city of some 25 000 people in 1760, 45 000 by the 1780s. Elsewhere urban development was slow, and centres such as Williamsburg, Richmond and Annapolis were quite paltry in comparison with true cities such as Boston and Philadelphia.

Further south the Chesapeake region retained its tobacco economy, but river trade also gave access to the agricultural produce of the hinterlands and permitted the development of large-scale commercial production of wheat and corn in the rich Piedmont region of Maryland, Virginia and North Carolina. This produce found its outlet in the port of Baltimore.

At the southern extreme of the British lands were the Carolinas, which in 1712 were formally divided between north and south. North Carolina, together with Southern Virginia, was the core of a new tobacco region, but the colony diversified its economy through timber and naval stores. The southern third of this territory was not settled until 1733, when it became the colony of Georgia. By the middle of the century the rice and indigo plantations of South Carolina and Georgia supported a rich trade, reflected in the urban development of Charleston (then, correctly, 'Charles Town') and Savannah. Charleston in the 1760s had 12 000 people, making it the largest urban centre south of Philadelphia. This extreme southern section made the most intensive use of slaves, even more so than the Chesapeake.

The cities served as centres for the diffusion of new standards of 'improvement' and culture, usually emanating from

London or Paris. In 1704, publication of the *Boston News-Letter* began the continuous history of the American press, and by the 1770s every colony but Delaware and New Jersey had at least one newspaper: Boston, Philadelphia and New York had 15 between them. In 1732 Benjamin Franklin began publication of his popular *Poor Richard's Almanac*. Franklin was a prominent scientist who worked tirelessly to make Philadelphia a model for civic improvement. In 1743 he founded the American Philosophical Society. By the middle of the century most major towns had a network of clubs, societies and discussion groups. From 1710 the colonies were brought closer together by a postal system. The growth of public institutions and signs of 'civilization' were marked in Philadelphia, which acquired a medical school in 1765 and the colonies' first permanent theatre the following year.

As the colonies grew, they naturally evolved their own distinctive cultural and social patterns, and formulated ways of life that would come to be recognized as 'American'. In terms of government and law, however, America in this era was far more British than it had been before the 1690s, when the weak British state had had little capacity to keep its wayward children in line. Eighteenth-century British governments were more anxious to enforce some kind of imperial conformity, however minimal. The growth of royal government is reflected by the constitutional status of the colonies. By 1775 no less than eight of the thirteen colonies were under royal charter; Pennsylvania, Maryland and Delaware remained proprietary colonies, while Connecticut and Rhode Island were corporate colonies, under charters obtained by the colonists themselves on American soil. The days were long gone when government revolved around the church and the franchise was conditional on membership of a religious body. In royal colonies, in fact, the right to vote had depended on membership of the established church. All colonies now had a governor appointed either by the king or the proprietor, and a legislature complete with two houses on the Westminster model. And as in England, laws passed by such a body required the signature of the monarch. The process of 'normalization' is suggested by the imposition of English criminal law with all its capital sentences on Quaker Pennsylvania, hitherto one of the more radically distinct states.

The colonies were integrated into the Atlantic trade routes of the wider empire. American ships carried colonial produce to the British Isles, other European centres and the West Indies, major items including tobacco, naval stores and timber. In turn they imported English manufactured goods. Colonial shipping was also involved in the notorious 'triangular trade' with Africa and the Caribbean: rum was sent to Africa to help with the purchase of slaves, who were shipped to the West Indies; which in turn supplied molasses to North America. By 1710 this trade was supporting 60 ships operating out of Newport alone; by 1750 perhaps half the town's 340 ships were engaged in slaving. The ports also supported a lively amount of privateering during the prolonged Anglo-French wars. This activity often shaded into virtual piracy, but was carried out under the justification of empire.

The colonies had never been egalitarian, either in theory or in practice, and there had always been a wealthy and powerful elite. The eighteenth century was, however, marked by a significant polarization of wealth, and the emergence of powerful new elites. In the middle colonies these tended to be planters and landowners with vast estates, like the fifty or so Virginian families who held office as magistrates and served on the governor's council. Examples included the Byrds, the Lees, the Randolphs, and the Carters, the splendour of whose life-style is illustrated by surviving mansions such as Westover and Carter's Grove.

In Maryland Richard Tilghman, who had immigrated in 1657, and his son and namesake succeeded in accumulating some 15 000 acres on the eastern shore. Richard junior first served in the colonial legislature in 1697, and over the next 90 years no less than 10 of his sons and grandsons followed him into that body. Their dominance over two counties, reflected in numerous offices such as justice of the peace and vestryman, was cemented by wide marriage alliances with other local magnate families. However even the Tilghmans were dwarfed in wealth and power by the Carrolls of Carrollton. Charles Carroll (1737–1832) left an estate with a total value of some $1.4 million, and landholdings of 57 000 acres. Landed magnates like these formed the self-confident core of the patriot resistance during the 1770s, and Carroll would be one of the signatories of the Declaration of Independence.

Nor were the American gentry a uniquely southern phenomenon. New York was one of the most feudal of the colonies, with vast landed estates that had been founded by the Dutch along the Hudson river. Around 1700 just four families (Philips, Van Cortlandt, Livingston and Van Rensselaer) owned 1.6 million acres of this colony. The cities also developed a patrician elite of traders and financiers, equally tied to the political leaders of provincial society. Philadelphia was dominated by great Quaker families such as the Cadwalladers, Lloyds and Biddles. In 1770 the top 5 per cent of Boston taxpayers controlled half the city's taxable assets, while since 1690 the proportion of Bostonians lacking taxable property had grown from 14 per cent to 29 per cent.

Colonial politics were shaped by the tension between the provincial elites and the mass of colonists, both frontier settlers and the growing populations of the towns. Clashes between 'ins' and 'outs' were compounded by religious and ethnic rivalry. In Pennsylvania the pacifism of the Quaker elite was anathema to Presbyterian (and Scottish–Irish) residents in the border lands, who demanded consistent policies of military preparedness. Before the 1740s legislatures in Philadelphia were reluctant to vote for military supplies to combat pirates or Indian incursions. Rivalry between the metropolis and the hinterlands exploded in 1764 when a group of back country vigilantes known as the 'Paxton Boys' massacred some peaceful Indians and threatened to march on Philadelphia.

In the Carolinas, frontier opposition to the colonial government was institutionalized in the Regulator movement of

1766–71 which was a cross between a populist anti tax movement and a vigilante organization. Regulator rhetoric attacked the corrupt and self-satisfied elites who grew rich from places and sinecures paid for by the people's taxes, while failing to deliver the services and protection required of any government. In 1771, 2 000 regulators 'pursuing the Indian mode of fighting' were defeated in a major battle with the governor's forces at Alamance. Their anger with the colony's eastern elite led many frontiersmen to migrate further west, and even to support the loyalist side in the revolution.

THE RELIGIOUS DIMENSION

The evolution of colonial society can be illustrated by the history of its churches and religious denominations, and the extreme diversity of American religion has its foundations in the colonial period. Throughout its history, both colonial and national, America has been characterized by religious standards and practices that were unusual by the standards of the rest of the Christian world. Particularly astonishing to most other Christian societies in the seventeenth and eighteenth centuries was the notion of a host of competing denominations, which were also independent of state control or sponsorship. Although estimates of members or attenders would be speculative, Table 1.3 presents a rough idea of the changing numbers of churches and meeting houses claimed by the various denominations in the colonial era.

In the mid-seventeenth century worship was clearly dominated by the Congregationalists, chiefly in New England, and the Episcopalians, mainly around the Chesapeake. A century later the situation had become considerably more complex. By 1780 the Congregationalists had about 30 per cent of churches, while the Presbyterians, Baptists and Episcopalians had a total of 55 per cent between them. In other words, the

Table 1.3   The religious affiliations of the British colonies, 1660–1780 (thousands)

	1660	1740	1780
Congregationalists	75	423	749
Episcopalians	41	246	406
Dutch Reformed	13	78	127
German Reformed	–	51	201
Catholics	12	20–40?	56
Presbyterian	5	160	495
Lutherans	4	95	–
Baptists	4	96	457
Quakers	–	–	200
Jews (synagogues)	1	–	6
Total (approximate)	150	1200	2500

four main denominations claimed about 85 per cent of the total number of places of worship. German groups (Lutheran and Reformed) were already making a strong showing in the second rank of religious denominations. The list at this point is somewhat misleading because it fails to include the meeting houses of the Methodists, who were soon to constitute a powerful denomination in their own right.

These figures illustrate the considerable progress made by the English established church, reflecting the general drift of the colonies towards 'normal' English practices and laws. The Anglican Church was a powerful presence from the earliest days in colonies such as Virginia, Maryland and South Carolina, where it took on the character of a real establishment. Virginia recognized little separation between church and state, with the elected parish vestry as the key institution of civil government, with jurisdiction over an immense range of civil and moral regulations. The minister in effect held office at the pleasure of the local landowners and merchants. By 1760 there were about 60 Anglican clergy in the colony.

Technically, the Anglican Church in the Western hemisphere was under the jurisdiction of the Bishops of London, but from 1689 this notional authority was supplemented by the presence of active commissaries, who sponsored considerable expansion. They in turn were supplemented by the distinctly high-church missionaries of the Society for the Propagation of the Gospel, who found remarkable opportunities in Congregationalist New England, where from the early eighteenth century intellectual debate in the universities led many to become dissatisfied with traditional positions. In 1722 seven members of the Yale faculty signed a statement expressing doubts about the validity of non-episcopal ordination, and several of the group subsequently sailed to England for reordination. This manifestation of high-church sentiment caused horror in traditionally minded Puritan circles, giving concrete evidence of their fear of creeping popery. Episcopal advances were also evident in tolerant Pennsylvania, where Christ Church in Philadelphia proved an influential centre. By the 1720s the Anglican Church was enjoying a general vogue.

Nonetheless, the growing strength of the Anglican Church did not conceal the heterogeneous nature of American religious life, and the radically different nature of the cultural landscape from anything prevailing elsewhere in the Christian world. Anglicans and Congregationalists coexisted and competed with other Protestant groups, especially Presbyterians, who poured in from Ulster in the middle of the century, and Baptists and Quakers, who found in America a tolerant haven they so conspicuously lacked in most of Europe. Most not only had numerous individual congregations, but also widespread federal groupings, whether regional synods or associations.

Dominant religious groups faced neighbours who not only employed a different rhetoric and theology, but even used a different language. For example the acquisition of New York brought the British government a population adhering to the Calvinist Dutch Reformed Church, which in the eighteenth century was granted official support wherever the majority of settlers so wished. A German presence flowered with mass migration from about 1720. The German Reformed and Lutheran churches both represented respectable communities with a tradition of state establishment in their respective homelands, but there were also numerous sects, including different forms of anabaptism and still more bizarre groups deeply imbued with occult, mystical, utopian, pacifist and communitarian ideas. The latter developed a strong affinity for Pennsylvania, where groups such as the Brethren and 'Dunkers' flourished, together with their countless offshoots. This was exemplified by the Protestant monastery of Ephrata, where celibate perfectionists lived communally. More towards the religious mainstream, Pennsylvania also possessed a strongly organized Lutheran network with its own Ministerium.

The religious commitment of the early settlers was manifested in their promotion of learning, both to create a literate laity able to read the Scriptures and to build up a learned ministry. The Congregational settlers of New England gave high priority to the development of religiously oriented colleges: Harvard was founded in 1636, Yale in 1707. Other denominations were active in promoting their own colleges, mainly founded in the mid-eighteenth century, which together would constitute the elite institutions of American higher education. Anglican endeavours produced the College of William and Mary in Virginia (1693), Kings College in New York (1754, later to become Columbia University) and the Philadelphia school that would become the University of Pennsylvania, (1755). The Baptists sponsored Brown University in Rhode Island (1764), while New Jersey's Princeton (1746) had Presbyterian roots. Also in New Jersey, Rutgers University (1766) was associated with the Dutch Reformed church.

THE GREAT AWAKENING

The various denominations were all affected to a greater or lesser degree by a religious revolution that swept the colonies from the late 1730s: the 'Great Awakening'. This was by no means a purely American event, but distinctly American circumstances did create the necessary preconditions, specifically the ambiguous state in which the descendants of the New England Puritans found themselves.

Originally the 'gathered saints' had found it relatively easy to identify likely members, who were then subjected to intense questioning in order to prove the authenticity of their conversion. But what about their children and grandchildren, who had grown up in the group and had no necessity of a dramatic spiritual rebirth? Were they to be admitted or excluded? In 1662 the New England churches proposed a 'halfway covenant', a new class of membership for the sons and daughters of saints. In sociological language, the Congregationalists were making a classic transition from the status of a sect (voluntary and committed) to that of a church, in which membership becomes hereditary, and thus more formal in character and more at ease with the surrounding culture.

By the 1730s there was growing tension between the rhetoric of evangelical theology and the reality of life within a relatively comfortable state-sponsored and tax-financed church. As in contemporary Germany, some Protestant clerics denounced the comfortable illusions of the saints in Zion, and urged that neither prodigious academic learning nor simple conformity to social rules was any form of true Christianity. They urged instead that Christianity demanded a heart-conversion, a shattering psychological event in which the individual recognized his or her absolute sinfulness and total reliance for salvation on the merits of Jesus Christ. This was to be followed by a fundamental reorientation of one's life towards God and away from the vain pleasures of this life.

The American Awakening is customarily linked to the work of Jonathan Edwards, minister of Northampton, Massachusetts, whose sermons urged his congregation to consider themselves as 'sinners in the hands of an angry God', sinners who could only be saved from everlasting fire by an immediate and decisive act. His words met an enthusiastic response, and soon it was remarked that everyone appeared to be asking, 'what must I do to be saved?' By the end of the decade spiritual concerns were aggravated by increasing threats to everyday existence, including the outbreak of 'King George's War' with Spain and a general economic and commercial crisis. In 1741 there was a supposed slave conspiracy in New York, in which blacks were said to be conspiring with both foreign enemies and Catholic agents.

By 1740 the revival was in full flood with the emergence of a series of itinerant preachers who engaged in striking oratorical feats, and whose fluency and passion gave them superstar status. George Whitefield's preaching tours in 1739–40 were a phenomenal success, and the wild zeal inflamed by the revivalists was exemplified by James Davenport, who engaged in twenty-four-hour harangues that whipped his audiences into hysteria. Conservatives depicted him as a grim warning of the lunacy and social disruption to which 'enthusiasm' would lead. On the other side, evangelicals denounced educated ministers who lacked the conversion experience required as a basic qualification for spreading the word of God. In 1740 Presbyterian Gilbert Tennent preached his famous sermon on 'The Dangers of An Unconverted Ministry', urging the superiority of godly zeal over worldly learning. As the established clergy were 'dead men', how could they beget living children? Tennent withdrew somewhat after disturbing encounters with men such as Davenport and Count Zintzendorf, a German mystic who was venturing deep into unorthodox speculation.

These debates enjoyed a long afterlife in American religious history, and most denominations were affected to some extent. Should preference be given to ministers who were godly and zealous, or to the properly trained and ordained? The class implications were obvious, and some evangelicals were willing to ask whether God had specifically prohibited the prophetic spirit from descending on African slaves? The Baptists, typically, were split between Old Light Regulars, who were suspicious of enthusiasm, and New Light Separates, who wanted a reborn membership. Similar tensions affected the Presbyterians, as well as German groupings such as the Lutherans, members of the Reformed Church and Mennonites.

In some cases actual schisms occurred, and the Methodists separated themselves from their Episcopalian origins towards the end of the century. By 1768 New York had a distinct Methodist chapel. The movement seemed doomed when John Wesley forthrightly condemned the revolutionary cause, but by the 1780s Methodism emerged as an American church, with a huge potential for growth. By 1790 the Methodist Episcopal Church had claimed 40 000 adherents in the new United States. The German churches spawned evangelical sects such as the United Brethren and Evangelical Association, which grew dramatically at the end of the century. Revivals and awakenings proved a lively incentive to new settlement, as families and groups set out to form new villages where they could live in godliness and unity: from New England especially, 'New Light' settlers spread west into Ohio.

The 'Great Revival' reached its height in the early 1740s, but it is difficult to pinpoint its end. Though other events throughout the century are usually listed as separate and distinct phenomena, these were in fact continuations or outgrowths of the original explosion. In German America the height of enthusiasm occurred in the 1750s and 1760s. In Virginia, activity by Methodist and New Light Baptist preachers caused social turmoil sporadically from the 1740s through to the 1770s, and prepared the way for the democratic challenges to political authority during the revolutionary years.

As in England in the 1650s, the gentry-dominated country-side of Virginia was appalled by the impudence of the itinerant Baptist preachers, who refused to honour traditional symbols of social status and were accordingly subjected to violence and abuse by squires and mobs. Between 1768 and 1776 some 50 preachers were jailed for varying terms. For 20 years there were recurrent feuds over official refusal to license preachers and meeting houses, and tension reached new heights when the Baptists made mass conversions among the slaves. The first black Baptist congregations emerged in Georgia and Virginia in the mid-1770s. Though not explicitly democratic or egalitarian, the enthusiasts emphasized dangerous ideas, above all the search for merit in personal spiritual experience rather than wealth, social status and intellect.

By the 1760s the spread of evangelical religion was encroaching on the political sphere, demanding the vast expansion of rights and freedoms not far removed from the designs of the political militants. These issues included freedom to preach, freedom from paying taxes to support the establishment, freedom from civil discrimination on basis of faith, and the extension of these rights to all denominations. Religious and political establishments came to stand or fall together in colonial America.

THE ANGLO–FRENCH WARS

Though the British colonies were developing a thriving cultural and economic life of their own, their prosperity depended on the tense international relationship with France. From the early eighteenth century, France was a leading military and commercial force on the North American continent and the Anglo-French wars usually had repercussions in America, so that military preparedness was a constant factor in the political life of the colonies. From 1689 to 1763 the wars caused regular revisions of the boundaries between the various colonial possessions – though captured fortresses and colonies were often returned at the end of hostilities – while devastating population losses occasionally resulted from raids and invasions. The scale of destruction was exacerbated by the Indian allies employed by both sides, forces that rarely observed even the primitive niceties of European warfare. Throughout the period the British maintained a firm alliance with the Iroquois, and the French with the Algonquins and Hurons, so that European conflicts were extended into proxy wars between these surrogates.

In line with European events, Anglo–French colonial warfare erupted between 1744 and 1748, when the British took the key fortress of Louisbourg. The peace settlement made little progress in defining the boundaries between the disputed border territories in Acadia and the Great Lakes, and a further round of combat was inevitable. In 1753 the French built a chain of forts in the Mississippi–Ohio River area, which the British viewed as their possession, and specifically along the Allegheny River in western Pennsylvania. The British troops sent to evict them were defeated the following year at Fort Duquesne (later Pittsburgh) in a campaign that incidentally marked the military debut of a Virginian officer, George Washington. With war under way, colonial representatives took a step with implications that can be seen as far-reaching in retrospect: the calling of a congress at Albany in New York to discuss united action and even a form of political union – perhaps a United Colonies of America. The need for urgent measures intensified with every new French success over the next two years. Most harmful for British prestige was the defeat of an expedition led by General Braddock against Fort Duquesne, in which ambushed British regulars retreated in disorder. For Benjamin Franklin and others, the sight of this humiliation left long memories and an influential impression of the fragility of British power. Worse, Braddock's disaster was a direct consequence of failing to heed the warnings of colonial officers such as Washington. Perhaps Americans knew best how to manage their own affairs.

Map 2   North America in 1713

Map 3   North America in 1763

From 1756 the war in America merged into the larger European struggle, usually known as the Seven Years War, and new political and military leadership gave a remarkable impetus to the British forces. Between 1758 and 1760 British forces took most of the key French fortresses, including Louisbourg, Ticonderoga and Niagara in what later became New York state, and Fort Necessity in Pennsylvania. The capture of Fort Duquesne (Pittsburgh) ensured British control of the crucial forks of the Ohio River. British victory at Québec in September 1759 not only crippled the whole French military effort, but virtually ended the war. Under the Treaty of Paris in 1763 the French empire in North America was destroyed, with the exception of some islands and fishing rights. Canada and New France became British possessions, while France rewarded its enfeebled Spanish ally with the territory of Louisiana. Spain, meanwhile, lost its Florida lands to the British.

The British Empire now dominated the whole of North America east of the Mississippi. Though the term 'New England' had come to have a strictly regional significance, it was the British model of the new world that now triumphed over 'New France' and other competitors. That ultimate achievement would prove to be doomed by the very fact of victory, as imperial success created the essential preconditions for the independent American nation.

2

Revolution and Nation Building, 1765–1825

TOWARDS SEPARATION

In the decade after 1763 the colonies developed a ferocious self-assertiveness that would lead to a full-scale war of independence and separation from British rule. The presence of aggressive French and Indian neighbours had placed a severe limit on any likely colonial dissatisfaction with British authority, as royal forces might at any time be needed to combat invasion. Removing the French factor gave the colonists more liberty to consider their long-term goals and aspirations. The British in turn had to consider the complex needs of a more diverse population. Apart from the British colonists, imperial subjects in North America now included the Catholic, French-speaking residents of Canada and the Indian allies who had played so critical a role in earlier victories. The Indians were a source of special concern as a series of worrying frontier wars erupted in 1763: though associated with the name of the chieftain Pontiac, these probably reflected a lingering French influence.

From the British imperial point of view, it made excellent sense to limit the westward expansion of the colonists into Indian lands, while granting toleration and some self-government to the French Canadians. There were also economic considerations in limiting expansion, including the interests of fur traders and land speculators. In 1763 the Crown declared the Appalachians the limit of the British colonies, and marked everything west of this as Indian territory, an injunction that was already beginning to fall apart by the end of the decade. The Québec Act of 1774 extended the limits of that province into the region north of the Ohio river. Still worse, British policy in Québec involved toleration of and even collaboration with the Catholic church. Neither policy was acceptable to the British Americans, for whom imperial considerations were a distant reality.

The end of New France also persuaded the British to restructure their rule in their transatlantic colonies, to seek a self-financing governmental structure that would pay for an American garrison from American resources. While the issue of taxation became the central grievance in colonial politics, it was intertwined with many other issues, above all colonial trade. For over a century the British had regulated trade and manufacturing in their overseas possessions through the Navigation Acts, which required that goods exported from the colonies must be shipped in a British vessel in order to foster the native merchant fleet. The 1760s saw old-established practices becoming bitter grievances, partly through new British laws, but also because of altered colonial sensibilities.

In 1764 the Sugar Act resulted in tax being levied on molasses brought to the colonies from the possessions of other countries, with the familiar aim of persuading customers to buy their supplies from British colonies. It also gave tax officials extensive rights of search and seizure to ensure enforcement. The Act was desperately unpopular, and in 1766 the tax was reduced significantly, setting the precedent that bad laws could be challenged successfully. The same fate befell the Stamp Act of 1765, which required tax stamps to be placed on newspapers, legal papers and other items of commerce. It was this law that evoked the slogan 'taxation without representation is tyranny', raising the threatening issue of the political status of the colonists within the empire. That autumn, delegates from nine colonies met in New York to formulate a protest against the Stamp Act. In 1767 the

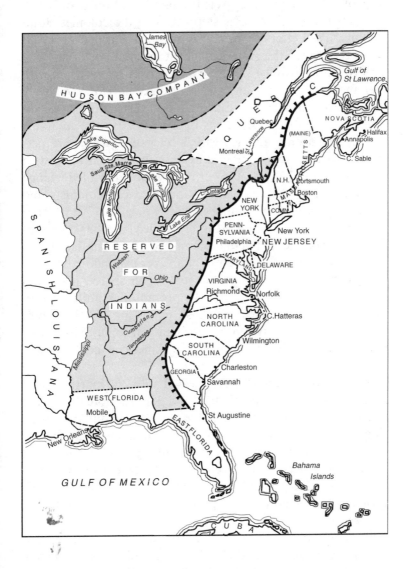

Map 4   British colonies on the eve of revolution

controversial Townshend Acts brought about the taxation of tea, paper and other items shipped in to the colonies. John Dickinson's 'Letters from a Pennsylvania Farmer' (1767–8) elegantly argued the American constitutional position.

Between 1766 and 1775 these battles over tax recurred with ever increasing force, and the protesters developed a lively network of propaganda and organized resistance, based on clandestine clubs of the 'Sons of Liberty'. Boston militants formed a working alliance with local gangs, who were persuaded to turn their energies against the British instead of each other. In 1765 and 1767 crowds in Boston rioted against the Stamp Act. Meanwhile relations between colonists and British troops were becoming steadily worse. In 1770 violence between soldiers and a Boston crowd led to a 'massacre' of five colonists, the first actual bloodshed of the conflict. From 1772 Boston became the centre of an ever-expanding network of Committees of Correspondence, which shared news and planned common actions, thereby promoting a united American identity in the face of British repression. At that point the Townshend tax system was bringing in some £300 a year, while the military presence in the American colonies was costing £170 000.

The political atmosphere injected into the partisan and religious struggles an ideological and populist note that might otherwise have been absent, but which now acquired a strong tinge of anti-elite, anti-aristocratic feeling. This was true of Virginia's conflicts over religious liberty and the itinerant Baptist preachers; of the Regulator Movement in the Carolinas; and of New York's agrarian rebellion in 1766, in which farmers and tenants were pitted against the great feudal estates.

By 1773 the colonies were becoming ungovernable, and dissidents in Boston and elsewhere were obviously engaging in military preparations. In 1773 Boston militants destroyed a cargo of East India tea in Boston harbour, the renowned 'Boston Tea Party', a flagrant violation of British law and authority. In response the Coercive (or 'Intolerable') Acts introduced an iron-fist policy. Boston harbour was closed and British authority over Massachusetts was sternly reasserted. At that point open revolt was inevitable, and trouble spread well outside the limits of Boston. When Rhode Island protesters burned the stranded British sloop *Gaspée* in 1772, the British responded with a Commission of Inquiry to identify the malefactors and sent them to England for trial, an act that in effect suspended the criminal jurisdiction of the colony. The affair was seen as a 'flagrant attack upon American liberty in general', and provided further ammunition for the Committees of Correspondence. In September 1774, a Continental Congress met in Philadelphia to discuss American grievances, and to order a boycott of British and Irish manufactures.

In April 1775, British determination to crush potential rebellions had reached the point of ordering the arrest of rebel ringleaders, forcibly breaking up massed protests and seizing of arms. A weapons raid on 19 April led to the first real battles of the war, when troops led by General Gage met forewarned colonists at Lexington and Concord in Massachusetts. Though casualties were few, the battles stirred up militancy among the colonists, and soon British soldiers were encountering armed units of 'minute-men', so-called because they pledged to be ready at a minute's notice. In June, fighting between patriots and regulars in Boston culminated in an American defeat at the 'Battle of Bunker Hill'. By that time, the Continental Congress had emerged as a *de facto* rebel government of the colonies in arms, with George Washington as supreme commander of American forces. In August the British officially declared that the colonies were in a state of rebellion.

WAR AND INDEPENDENCE

While well-trained, the British army was far too small to hope to suppress a full rebellion across the vast territory of the

American colonies. Even with the aid of loyal militias and German (Hessian) mercenaries, British forces in America probably never exceeded 50 000 at any given point. On the other hand they had the great advantage of nearby bases, at Halifax, Nova Scotia, and in the West Indies. Moreover, the British were not fighting a completely united foe, in that many colonists (perhaps a quarter of the whole) were hostile to the rebellion to the point of taking up arms, and these 'Tories' were so strong in some areas that the 'War of Independence' became a savage civil war marked by massacres and the brutal ill-treatment of captives. John Adams suggested that if they had not been kept in line by radical neighbours to both north and south, both New York and Pennsylvania would have joined the British. The whole continental army had a strength of some 20 000, inferior in training and discipline to the British.

The British strategy in the early stages of the war focused on the destruction of the major centres of patriot militancy. The Americans' goal was to survive as a political and military force long enough to encourage some of England's foreign foes to intervene on their behalf, in other words to show that this was an authentic national revolution rather than an overgrown riot by farmers and apprentices. Though they achieved their goal, victory was obtained slowly and at great cost, and was not absolutely assured until 1781, the seventh year of war. At least until late 1777 there were many moments when the American venture seemed foolhardy and doomed to failure.

During 1776 the major victories for the rebels came in the south, where Tory/Loyalist forces were beaten in Virginia and North Carolina. In March the arrival of American artillery on the heights above Boston persuaded the British commander, General Howe, to evacuate the city, but this triumph was followed by months of near fatal setbacks for the American cause. Patriot armies were driven from Long Island, Howe's soldiers captured New York city, and American armies were forced to lift their siege of the British fortress of Québec. The military climate was therefore distinctly bleak that summer when the Continental Congress gathered in Philadelphia to discuss the changing political context of the war. Hitherto patriot rhetoric had concentrated on asserting the rights of British subjects within the empire and under the crown. With the growing violence and the British blockade, the emphasis now shifted to political independence, a radical departure that required proper justification to the international community.

In January the cause for independence had been stated forcefully in Thomas Paine's pamphlet 'Common Sense'. This was one of the most influential writings of the age and sold 150 000 copies. The issue was debated throughout June, with John Adams the main advocate of independence. Apart from the central issue of sovereignty there were also tensions between individual colonies, as well as disagreement between north and south over the slave question. Thomas Jefferson drew up the document that eventually became the Declaration of Independence, adopted by the Congress on 4 July, 1776 (see Appendix).

Relying on Enlightenment ideas of nature and contract theory, in the document Jefferson pronounced the 'self-evident truth' that 'all men are created equal, that they are endowed by their Creator with certain unalienable rights, that among these are life, liberty and the pursuit of happiness. That to secure these rights, governments are instituted among men, deriving their just powers from the consent of the governed. That whenever any form of government becomes destructive to these ends, it is the right of the people to alter or to abolish it, and to institute new government . . .' The British monarchy had violated the original contract by countless 'repeated injuries and usurpations, all having in direct object the establishment of an absolute tyranny over these states'. These crimes were listed at length, leading to the ringing conclusion that the 'the representatives of the United States of America, in General Congress, assembled . . . do solemnly publish and declare, that these united colonies are, and of right ought to be free and independent states; that they are absolved from all allegiance to the British Crown, and that all political connection between them and the state of Great Britain, is and ought to be totally dissolved'.

The rhetoric was magnificent, but it could not in itself improve the military situation, which by the end of 1776 had reached a desperate pass. The loss of New York shifted the scene of battle to New Jersey, where in the last days of the year Washington plotted a brilliant counterstroke. On 26 December, his forces crossed the Delaware River to launch a surprise attack at Trenton, and this was followed by a victory at Princeton in early 1777. This at least stabilized the American position in the middle colonies. Meanwhile the King of France had been secretly subsidizing the rebel regime.

A change of fortune came about in 1777, thanks less to Washington's generalship than to confusion within the British command. The main British offensive of that year involved a coordinated attack by General Burgoyne's forces, moving south from Canada, while Howe campaigned in Pennsylvania. Howe was relatively successful and captured Philadelphia in September. This secured a potentially valuable position for the new campaigning season, while Washington's army was forced to endure the coming winter in dire circumstances at nearby Valley Forge. Poorly supplied with food and shelter, these 'winter soldiers' suffered hardships that have earned them a place in the patriotic mythos. But the northern arm of the British endeavour had gone badly awry, and Burgoyne's 8 000 troops found themselves cut off in upper New York state. Their surrender in October 1777 was a military and diplomatic disaster that encouraged the French to enter the war as an American ally in early 1778. This meant trained troops and, more critically, a French fleet that could successfully challenge British naval superiority. By 1780 Spain and the Netherlands had also joined the international coalition against Britain.

The war now entered a new phase, in which American troops were successful on most fronts. In June 1778 Washington himself fought the last major engagement in the middle region, an indecisive encounter at Monmouth Court House in New Jersey. Vital for later westward expansion were the victories achieved in Kentucky and along the Ohio valley, leading to the decisive victory at Vincennes in 1779 (see below). All along the border territories American forces now gained the upper hand over the Indian and Tory raiders who had been devastating border settlements, and this back-country struggle involved some of the worst atrocities of the entire war.

Even at that late stage, the British had some cause for optimism, including the near-successful betrayal by the American commander Benedict Arnold of the fortress at West Point. Meanwhile discontent among Washington's forces at Morristown drew dangerously close to open mutiny. In the south, the British captured Charleston in May 1780, and shortly afterwards virtually destroyed an entire American army in a major victory at Camden. The surrender of 5 000 American soldiers in this campaign represented the greatest single debacle for the patriot cause in the whole war. The British general, Cornwallis, followed his triumph with a campaign into North Carolina and Virginia, where he chose Yorktown as his headquarters. He was assisted by a new commander on the British side, none other than Benedict Arnold. Successes continued into June 1781, when a British raid on Charlottesville came close to seizing much of the Virginia legislature, including Jefferson and most of that state's patriot leadership.

That summer Yorktown became the target for a major combined operation of French and patriot forces, supported by a powerful French fleet that forced the British Navy to withdraw support. In October Cornwallis was forced to surrender his 8 000 men, and the land war was virtually over. British naval victories over the next two years meant that the ensuing peace settlement was nothing like as ruinous as it might have been. Under the Treaty of Paris (1783) the new United States emerged with boundaries stretching from the Atlantic to the Mississippi, though Britain retained its Canadian and West Indian possessions. The establishment of the Mississippi boundary – almost as an afterthought – was in reality an amazing diplomatic success for the new United States.

THE AGE OF CONFEDERATION

In 1783 the United States of America became a free and united nation, but its future seemed far from certain. The war was accompanied by much violence against Tories and loyalists, many of whom fled to Canada and Nova Scotia. Perhaps 50 000 exiles chose this route, and in 1784 the British created the province of New Brunswick specifically for the exiles. By 1791 the remaining British possessions were partitioned between upper and lower Canada, the former being the new territories of the exiled loyalists. The number of slaves who escaped during the fighting is hard to ascertain, but there were certainly tens of thousands.

Within the United States, the prolonged war had obviously caused great social and economic disruption. The American government had financed the war with 'Continental' paper money that had rapidly become worthless, and there was a burdensome public debt. In 1780 Congress proposed to redeem the paper currency at the ungenerous rate of forty to one. Inflation ran out of control. By 1783 the payment of soldiers was badly in arrears, which was all the more dangerous as the victorious army had the power to enforce its wishes if it so chose. That March there were rumblings of sedition at the army headquarters in Newburgh, New York, and a conspiracy of uncertain dimensions to demand the money due to the soldiers: otherwise Congress should know that 'in any political event, the army has the alternative'. On this occasion, discontent was suppressed by an emotional appeal from Washington himself.

This was not a happy inheritance for the new government, which faced real uncertainty about its proper scope and activities. While the state governments were familiar entities with well-defined responsibilities, there was less assurance about the national government, which was established under the Articles of Confederation agreed by Congress in 1777 and ratified in 1781. Indeed, the confederation was closer to an international alliance than a real federal system as each state was designated as a sovereign entity. Each also commanded a single vote in the legislature, to the disgust of the larger and more populous states which found themselves thwarted by the whims of smaller neighbours. While signatory states agreed to do certain things, such as pay taxes to the national confederation, there were no real enforcement mechanisms to make them do this. While there was a nominal president of the Congress, the office had little in common with the powerful executive of later decades.

Foreign policy became all but impossible under confederation, as each state tended to look after its perceived self-interest, and foreign powers recognized this fact as a painful reality. The British knew well that effective treaties would have to be made with the states on an individual basis. This was dangerous enough in normal times, but in the 1780s there were serious threats from the remaining colonial neighbours, the British in the Great Lakes region, the Spanish in Florida and the Louisiana Territory, and the Indian tribes in alliance with either or both of these. Some states believed it was in their interests to confront these neighbours, others favoured appeasement and the maintenance of trade. A 1786 proposal to concede the Mississippi navigation to Spain made wonderful sense to New Englanders, who had little to lose from the thwarting of western expansion, but it seemed an act of near-treason to southerners. Who was to say which regional self-interest would prevail? In what sense, if any, did a Boston merchant share a common interest with a Georgia planter, still less a Kentucky frontiersman? North and south were each natural and well-defined regions, but what did they have in common with each other?

Lacking the protection of a central government, it was tempting for Americans to seek the protection of the Spanish or English in order to trade and settle in their lands; and while initially only groups of individuals were prepared to abandon their American loyalty, there were rumblings that whole territories or states might soon find it convenient to secede. A similar lack of concerted action ruined efforts to coordinate trading policy. Some states attempted to negotiate treaties with other powers, to the exclusion of their American neighbours, and different jurisdictions levied taxes and tariffs on trade between the former colonies. States with active ports taxed goods entering en route to inland neighbours, and different states used different financial mechanisms, even minting their own money.

Interstate rivalries were accentuated by uncertainty over contested land claims. Connecticut, for example, claimed extensive lands to the west that were currently in the possession of Pennsylvania, and rival settlers established forts and engaged in lethal battles. For thirty years after independence, most states exhibited a real hostility to the formal mechanisms of English law, and many courts ostentatiously rejected the whole careful framework of common law and precedent on the basis that this was a mere hangover of colonial oppression. Without a legal framework, the likelihood was that disputed lands would simply fall to the best-armed and most aggressive party.

Contempt for strict legality and the enormous disparity in state policies excited the fears of the propertied that political republicanism might soon involve an attack on social hierarchy. In most states the great majority of farmers were burdened by heavy debts, made all the more severe by the extreme shortage of the cash money that was required to pay debts and taxes. Merchants and creditors secured the passage of laws demanding that debts be paid in gold or silver rather than worthless 'Continental' paper. Worse, under the surviving English practice, unpaid debts could well lead to indefinite imprisonment until accounts were satisfied. If debtor groups organized politically under the new and extended political franchises, what was to prevent them from passing laws that postponed or even abolished existing debts, in effect causing a massive transfer of wealth between the classes? Similarly, classical education had made enough political leaders familiar with the Roman precedent of an agrarian law, a seizure of great estates to be redistributed among the poor and propertyless. If a given state decided on such a radical course, there were no national or federal institutions to prevent it.

The American population had powerful recent memories of taking direct action to cure social grievances caused by perceived exploitation and excessive taxation. From 1784 debtors' movements mobbed courthouses and sheriffs' auctions to sabotage the collection system. Fears for property and social order reached a height in 1786 with the outbreak of Shays' debtors' rebellion in western Massachusetts, significantly led by a revolutionary war soldier who had fought at Bunker Hill. Though the back of the rising was broken in December, guerrilla fighting lingered on into the following spring. While not a particularly bloody movement by the standard of contemporary Europe, the rising served as the crucial incentive to begin the process of constitutional reform and revision.

Schemes for change were already under discussion. In 1785 representatives from Maryland and Virginia had met at Alexandria to discuss matters such as tolls and fishing rights, and Congress had been urged to take over the regulation of American commerce. Under the far-sighted influence of Virginian leader James Madison, the plan for a new constitutional convention was further developed at a meeting at Annapolis, Maryland in 1786. The convention itself began its deliberations in Philadelphia in May 1787, with 55 members representing every state except Rhode Island.

MAKING THE CONSTITUTION

The ensuing debate on the proposed national constitution proceeded with a remarkably high degree of rhetorical sophistication, in which many of the delegates emerged as figures of intellectual distinction. James Madison represented an advanced strand of Enlightenment political thought with roots in the late seventeenth-century English world of the philosopher John Locke and the scientist Isaac Newton. Madison, like most of his colleagues, accepted a form of contract theory in which government was instituted by the people, who therefore had the right to change it as they wished, as long as they respected basic and inalienable rights, including property. While government was necessary, it was prone to expand beyond its proper boundaries, and a system of mutual checks and balances was required. Conventionally there were three main functions of government – legislative, executive and judicial – and a successful system would preserve the greatest possible separation between them. In Newtonian terms, they might be conceived as natural forces to be kept in a stable relationship akin to that of heavenly bodies. Madison therefore favoured a strong national government, but one constantly limited by internal checks and balances.

Madison's was assuredly not the only scheme, and his role as a radical innovator should not be exaggerated. In fact it now appears that the influence of Charles Pinckney of South Carolina on the final plan was greatly underestimated by generations of historians. And there were other ideas: Alexander Hamilton favoured a model closer to that of the British monarchy and aristocracy, as a way of checking the mob passions he so dreaded. However the idea of balancing and separating powers was widely accepted. In the model ultimately adopted there would be three branches of government, with a legislature (Congress), an executive headed by the president, and a federal judiciary with its apex in the Supreme Court. In addition to mutual scrutiny between the branches of government, there would also be a healthy tension within the branches, especially within the legislature.

In order to prevent the government from being subjected to radical alteration on the strength of a passing whim of the electorate (say, in the matter of debt abolition), the constitution provided different terms for the various elements of elected authority in the hope that at least part of the government would remain secure in office until a particular panic or enthusiasm had passed. All members of the lower house, the House of Representatives, were to be liable for popular election every two years, and would thus be the most closely attuned to public opinion. Senators would not be subject to popular election (this was later reversed by the seventeenth constitutional amendment, ratified in 1913) and would generally be chosen by state legislatures. Senators would serve six years, with one third of the whole body subject to change every two years on a rotating basis. The president would serve for four years. In the judicial branch, federal justices would be appointed rather than elected, serving until they died, retired or were removed by impeachment. Throughout American history this staggering of terms and conditions of office has been criticized for thwarting an overwhelming popular will, most dramatically in the New Deal era of the 1930s; but equally the less responsive nature of the Senate and Supreme Court has also prevented presidents and Congress from enacting swift and ill-considered legislation. For good or ill, this was certainly what the framers of the constitution intended.

Deciding on the virtues of a closer union was easy compared with the question of how the constituent states should resolve disputes, especially when one state or region felt its interests were being threatened. The states varied enormously in size, wealth and population. According to the 1790 census, Virginia was by far the largest state, with 748 000 people, while at the opposite extreme were Rhode Island with 69 000 and Delaware with 59 000.

Table 2.1   The population of the states in 1790 (in thousands)

	Total	Non-white	Slave*	
Massachusetts	378	5.0	0	
Connecticut	237	6.0	3	(1.3)
Rhode Island	69	4.0	1	(1.4)
New Hampshire	142	0.6	0	
Vermont	86	0.3	0	
New York	340	26.0	21	(6.2)
Pennsylvania	434	11.0	4	(1)
Delaware	59	13.0	9	(15.3)
Maryland	320	111.0	103	(32)
Virginia	748	306.0	293	(39.2)
Kentucky	74	12.1	12	(16.2)
Tennessee	36	–	–	
North Carolina	394	106.0	101	(25.6)
South Carolina	249	109.0	107	(43)
Georgia	83	29.4	29	(35)

*Percentages in brackets

Should each state be represented in proportion to its population, in which case three or four large states would hold indefinite hegemony? This was the basis of Madison's Virginia Plan, which had its greatest appeal among the delegations from the three largest states – Virginia, Massachusetts and Pennsylvania. It was supported by other southern states who rightly believed that current demographic trends would benefit their region most, making them all large and populous within a decade or two. Alternatively, each state might hold one vote in a national council as under the confederation, so that Virginia or Pennsylvania might find itself consistently thwarted by Rhode Island and Delaware. This was part of the New Jersey Plan favoured by smaller states. Each course in its pure form was unacceptable to one or other bloc, and the convention almost came to grief in its opening days as Delaware threatened immediate withdrawal over the threat of proportional representation.

The solution was found in adopting different standards for different parts of the government on the lines of the 'Connecticut Compromise' (Connecticut often played a key role in the debates, as a regular intermediary between the south and the New England states). Within the legislature the principle of popular representation would hold for the House of Representatives, which was to be most closely attuned to the popular will, and states would be granted one Representative for every 30 000 persons. (The current figure is far larger, an apparent violation of the constitution that continues because no one has felt inclined to challenge it.) In the Senate each state, however strong or weak, had two senators. The necessity for laws to pass through both houses thus gave satisfaction to both factions – the large states and the small. This compromise owed something to the practice of the Iroquois Confederation, in which each tribe held one vote regardless of size. The main precedent was the English parliament, in which seats were divided between counties and boroughs. The Senate thus corresponds to the more prestigious county seats, roughly two per county, while the House of Representatives parallels the borough seats, which fluctuate in number in theoretical correspondence to changing social and political circumstances.

So part of the legislature could be elected according to population. But what population? The founders agreed that a federal census would be necessary, and this could give a reasonably accurate idea of the number of human beings in the new nation. Some, however, were not legally free. In 1790, 790 000 Americans were of African descent, almost one fifth of the whole and a far larger proportion than in any subsequent era; and over 90 per cent of these were slaves. The proportions were far larger in some regions, so that perhaps a third of the residents of Maryland and Virginia were not free, over 40 per cent in South Carolina. In parti-

cular counties the proportion of slaves was over 70 per cent
of the whole. Did these slaves count towards the population
that gave a particular state its electoral strength? Initially the
south said that they should, and the north equally naturally
that they should not. The eventual compromise followed the
principle of confederation years, stating that the slave population would count, but at a discount to free white people.
The actual language is interesting. States would be allotted
representatives based on the number of 'free persons . . . and
excluding Indians not taxed, three fifths of all other persons'.
The word that is not present, of course, is 'slave', an omission
found throughout the document.

As in 1776, the founding fathers in 1787 were painfully
aware of international public opinion and its potential influence in any likely conflict with countries such as Britain. It
was vital to maintain the American persona as a haven of
republican virtue and liberty, which would be so compromised by the frank discussion or acknowledgment of the slave
dilemma. This concern was also evident from the steps taken
to ensure that a new federal government would not abolish
the slave trade. Such a measure was probable in the long
term, but a twenty-year delay was provided. Quite intentionally, the actual clause of the constitution dealing with the
mater is so arcane that it would perhaps elude any unsuspecting reader, referring as it does to Congress having no power
to prohibit 'the migration or importation of such persons as
any of the states now existing shall think proper to admit'
before the year 1808. Though 'migration' is mentioned first,
the substance of the clause concerns the subjects of 'importation', who were slaves.

Closely related to the slave question was the issue of the
western lands, the territories between the Alleghenies and the
Mississippi that would become an enormous source of wealth
and future expansion. Several states had claims on these
areas, ranging from the plausible to the outrageous: many
seventeenth-century charters specified western boundaries on
the Pacific coast, and Virginia for one still sporadically

claimed such an empire. These notional claims would have to give way to the reality of new states to be carved out in the west, but the question then arose of how the partition should be achieved, and under what conditions? Would slavery be permitted, along with all other forms of private property? Apart from the north–south divide, states with a vested interest in western lands obviously viewed the issue differently from those such as Delaware that had no outstanding claims. In addition the vast fortunes of land speculators (many of whom were also legislators) depended on the legal settlement of the west. Meanwhile there was the obvious danger that legal and governmental feuds could cause such discontent that those in the newly settled areas might rebel and secede.

The critical test for US policy was the treatment of the north-west territories, that huge region that eventually became the five states surrounding the Great Lakes. Virginia ceded its claims in this region to the national government in 1784, and in 1787 the Northwest Ordinance outlined the future governance of the region. This devised an orderly and gradual procedure for the admission of new states, a model that would ultimately be followed until the continent was united from ocean to ocean. The new areas would enjoy the status of territories under appointed governors until the population had grown to 60 000, a level sufficient to support a state government. Even in the 'probationary' stage the settlers would not be separated from the American polity, while the new states would enjoy complete equality with their better-established counterparts. The ordinance also offered a comprehensive plan that prohibited slavery, while granting the right of slave owners to hunt down escaped fugitives. The scheme not only lubricated the constitutional debates, it also influenced American national policy on slavery up to the civil wars.

From the start of the convention, revising the terms of union met fierce opposition, and the actual process of debate involved almost daily trade-offs, bargains and shifts of factional allegiance. This is perhaps less remarkable than the fact that a document emerged at all, to be submitted for ratification by the various states. The ratification process was bitterly contentious, with federalists and anti-federalists often refighting the battles of Philadelphia, while sometimes moving to newer issues that had not been so central there.

Delaware, Pennsylvania and New Jersey ratified the constitution in 1787, eight other states followed suit in 1788. The accession of New Hampshire in June 1788 was critical as this provided the ninth vote required for the constitution to come into effect. But the matter was still not settled as vital states such as New York and Virginia were still debating the issue. The necessity of winning the battle was called forth in the *Federalist*, the most important literary monument of this era. This was a collection of papers answering objections to the new frame of government, authored by Alexander Hamilton, James Madison and John Jay. On the other side, the anti federalists could draw on figures of impeccable patriotic credentials such as Patrick Henry. In Virginia especially, it took a hard battle before the federalists eventually triumphed.

Important in this phase was the issue of a bill of rights, a document modelled on the English declaration of 1689, which specified the rights of the subject of a just monarchy. Virginia had issued a sweeping statement of rights in 1776, under the primary authorship of George Mason, and there was pressure to have such a document incorporated directly into the constitution. Eventually, a bill of this sort was appended to become the first ten amendments to the constitution in 1791. It serves as a catalogue of the traditional grievances of the Protestant Whig tradition, a document that can only be understood in the context of decades-long struggles against oppressive governments from the time of Charles II to the days of George III and John Wilkes. The document thus specifies limits to the power of the government to establish a state church, to curtail free speech or quarter soldiers on its population in times of war; to disarm the loyal citizenry, or to trample their rights in criminal courts or abolish juries; to inflict cruel and barbarous punishments. Though these rights originally applied solely to the federal power, successive court decisions have extended them to the realm of the states, and in the twentieth century these amendments have had an incalculable effect on the workings of government and law enforcement.

By the end of 1788 the United States was in place as a federal nation. North Carolina joined in 1789 and Rhode Island in 1790 (Table 2.2). In 1791 the union also admitted Vermont, which had seceded from the jurisdiction of New York in 1777. Like Rhode Island, Vermont joined the union with great reluctance and in response to scarcely veiled threats.

A NEW NATION

The new nation went on to evolve distinctive institutions. George Washington was elected president in 1789 (Table 2.3), and was careful to balance a high regard for the prestige and prerogatives of his office with avoidance of monarchical temptations. His personal prestige lent power to the office, while making the presidency a focus of patriotism and national unity. In 1794 Washington dealt ably with the first domestic crisis of the new system, when thousands of Pennsylvania farmers refused to pay a tax on whisky, requiring the president to send in 13 000 troops against the 'rebellion': numbers on each side were larger than in most battles of the revolutionary war. His action was vital as it probably prevented the movement from spreading throughout the western regions. Washington's decision not to seek a third term in 1796 proved a weighty precedent that was subsequently taken to have something like the force of law, and was not challenged until Franklin D. Roosevelt sought re-election as president in the perilous circumstances of 1940.

Table 2.2   The states, 1787–1820

	Year of admission to union	Modern capital
Delaware	1787	Dover
Pennsylvania	1787	Harrisburg
New Jersey	1787	Trenton
Georgia	1788	Atlanta
Connecticut	1788	Hartford
Massachusetts	1788	Boston
Maryland	1788	Annapolis
South Carolina	1788	Columbia
New Hampshire	1788	Concord
Virginia	1788	Richmond
New York	1788	Albany
North Carolina	1789	Raleigh
Rhode Island	1790	Providence
Vermont	1791	Montpelier
Kentucky	1792	Frankfort
Tennessee	1796	Nashville
Ohio	1803	Columbus
Louisiana	1812	Baton Rouge
Indiana	1816	Indianapolis
Mississippi	1817	Jackson
Illinois	1818	Springfield
Alabama	1819	Montgomery
Maine	1820	Augusta
Missouri	1820	Jefferson City

The national government now created a capital city, which was essential if the federal administration was to avoid the jealousy that would arise from the selection of any existing centre. Philadelphia would have been the most likely choice, and indeed served as interim capital from 1790 to 1800. The site selected for the new capital was virgin territory on the border between Maryland and Virginia, and thus equally

Table 2.3   Presidential election results 1789–1820

	Winning candidate	Electoral votes*	Losing candidate	Electoral votes
1789	George Washington	69	None	–
1792	George Washington	132	None	–
1796	John Adams (F)	71	Thomas Jefferson (DR)	68
1800	Thomas Jefferson (DR)	73	Aaron Burr (DR)	73
1804	Thomas Jefferson (DR)	162	Charles Pinckney (F)	14
1808	James Madison (DR)	122	Charles Pinckney (F)	47
1812	James Madison (DR)	128	DeWitt Clinton (F)	89
1816	James Monroe (DR)	183	Rufus King (F)	34
1820	James Monroe (DR)	231	John Q. Adams (DR)	1

*Figures for the popular vote are not available before the 1820s.
F = Federalist; DR = Democratic-Republican.

accessible from both north and south. It was also conveniently close to the thriving ports of Alexandria and George-
town, as well as to the seat of the nation's leading statesman,
Washington's estate at Mount Vernon. In 1800 Washington
DC was declared the national capital. Despite an ambitious
initial design by Pierre L'Enfant, it would be decades before
the seat of government developed a real life as a major city in
its own right. Even in 1850 the city's population was barely
50 000.

One remarkable development of the new system occurred
in the judicial branch, where the Supreme Court of the United States swiftly acquired an importance far beyond that
envisaged by the framers of the constitution. The first chief
justice was John Jay, who saw the office as essentially a part-
time function. From 1801 to 1835, however, the office was
held by John Marshall, who made the role of the court a

pivot of the federal government and an extraordinarily effective check upon the other branches. His decision in the 1803 case of Marbury v. Madison established the principle that the Court had the right and duty to overrule laws passed by Congress when those laws violated the constitution. Leaning to the federalist side of the contemporary political spectrum, Marshall favoured a strong government that upheld and defended property rights against the possible intrusion of radicalism. Over the next three decades this led to a series of decisions defining the power of state and federal governments to award or revoke privileges, monopolies and property grants. His approach is illustrated by the 1810 case of Fletcher v. Peck, which concerned vast land grants by the legislature of Georgia in circumstances of extensive bribery. Marshall decided that despite the surrounding corruption, a state could not simply rescind rights that had achieved the status of a contract, the implication being that legislatures should not have the dangerous authority to trample over property rights.

In 1819 Marshall decided another critical case concerning an attempt by the state of Maryland to tax the federal Bank of the United States. As so often, Marshall went far beyond the strict issues involved in the case to announce a far-reaching doctrine of implied powers. Although the constitution might not have declared every specific power that the US government was to have, the government indeed had implicit powers that enabled in to carry out the overarching goals required in nation building, and that in areas of conflict, state jurisdiction was overruled by federal. Thus, 'Let the end be legitimate, let it be within the scope of the constitution, and all means which are appropriate . . . are constitutional'. This was a charter for national development and governmental expansion with implications that would not become fully apparent for many years to come. Marshall's decisions also ensured that American political debates would often revolve around questions of constitutional law, and thus end up in the judicial arena.

REPUBLICANS AND FEDERALISTS

As president, George Washington ostentatiously stood above factions and parties at a time when the very word 'party' had unpleasant and even conspiratorial connotations. Nonetheless the 1790s witnessed the birth of an American party system, and the conflict between the two sides often approached real violence. Though foreign policy issues predominated, these generally served as vehicles for domestic concerns. Broadly, two groups emerged: the Federalists, led by John Adams and Alexander Hamilton, and the Republicans, who looked to Thomas Jefferson (despite the name, the Republicans of this era are regarded as the direct ancestors of the modern Democratic Party, and Jefferson's adherents are known by the label 'Democratic-Republican'). In domestic terms, Federalists favoured a stronger central government and were in sympathy with the commercial and financial interests that were strongest in New England. Republicans emphasized agrarian interests and states' rights, and found their strongholds in the southern states, especially Virginia.

The division between the two was apparent from the earliest days of the union, in disputes over the creation of a national financial system along lines proposed by Hamilton. In the first years of the republic the Treasury Department, which Hamilton headed, was by far the best organized of the offices of state, and was far larger than its rivals in the Departments of State and War. This gave Hamilton an institutional foundation from which he could promote his views on such delicate and potentially critical matters as the crippling scale of the public debt. Despite objections that the creditors of the new nation were greedy exploiters who deserved little consideration, Hamilton's *Report on Public Credit* insisted on the United States paying its obligations in full, in order to establish national credit on foundations as rock-solid as those of contemporary England. This scheme caused sharp controversy in 1790, echoed the following year when

Hamilton proposed a national Bank of the United States to maintain fiscal stability. Further, he advocated a strong governmental role in supporting and expanding manufactures and the means of communications upon which they depended. Together these ideas posited a national government of a scope far more expansive than that described by the constitution, but Hamilton justified his views on the theory that once a republic was established, its continued health required firm national institutions: in other words, a pioneering version of 'implied powers'. The bank proposal was supported by Washington, but savagely criticized by Jefferson, Edmund Randolph and others, who saw it as a gross violation of constitutional principles, and moreover a dangerous and monopolistic concentration of power. For the critics, Hamilton was seeking to turn the United States into a facsimile of that very England from which the Americans had only recently gained independence.

Overseas issues intruded into the conflict with the outbreak of war between England and France in 1793. Both sides had naval and commercial interests that impinged upon American sovereignty, and the British offended national sentiment by searching American ships for contraband and press-ganging American sailors. The British also maintained a military presence in the forts of the north-west, in violation of the Treaty of Paris. The many real and potential grievances were exploited by the Republicans, who saw Britain as a traditional enemy and the upholder of alien principles of aristocracy and monarchy. Republican anger was especially aroused by the Jay Treaty of 1794, which oriented American trade and policy decisively in the direction of Britain while removing the contentious British garrisons.

Conversely the Federalists viewed revolutionary France as the epitome of the worst in human society, the result of what happened when a nation abandoned traditional standards of respect and social hierarchy. And while Britain had violated American sovereignty, this was barely significant when set against the continuing French aggression at sea, and the clear attempts to subvert American politics through bribery and revolutionary propaganda. In 1797 diplomatic endeavours to remove the French naval danger were complicated by crude attempts to bribe the US representatives. As the mysterious French agents were referred to by code letters, the incident became known as the 'XYZ Affair', and it nearly led to open war between the two nations. By 1798, the warships of the new US Navy were regularly engaging the French in combat, and the situation was not calmed until after Napoleon gained power in France the following year.

Partisan conflict reached dangerous proportions in 1798 with an outbreak of panic over the machinations of supposed revolutionary conspirators, organized by the German Illuminati sect and operating through Masonic lodges. In the conservative view, these extremists were not only seeking to establish a political dictatorship, but were also planning to eliminate religion, the family and sexual morality, and the radicals found their leader in Thomas Jefferson. In response to the perceived threat, the federal government passed the draconian Alien and Sedition Acts, which imposed stringent penalties on free speech, criminalized criticism of the government and proposed the deportation of unruly foreigners. The measure looked like a prelude to forcible suppression of the Republicans, and there was talk of civil war and a breakdown of the hard-won constitutional union. Jefferson and Madison wrote the 'Resolutions', subsequently passed by the legislatures of Virginia and Kentucky, in which they drew strict limits on the powers of the federal government, which was presented as a dissoluble compact between the states.

Tensions remained high into the election year of 1800, when Jefferson defeated Adams in a campaign marked by hysterical propaganda on both sides. Following 'the revolution of 1800', his enemies saw the new president as a revolutionary dictator potentially quite as extreme as the new French Emperor Napoleon, with whom he was felt to have many points of resemblance. Despite the impeachment of some Federalist judges, Jefferson proved far more moderate than feared, and indeed operated the presidency according to the Federalist concept of a strong national government.

It was this advocate of limited government and states' rights who undertook the high-handed act of purchasing the Louisiana territory from France in 1803, a deed that had no discernible warrant in the constitution. The measure was justified only by its outcome: the Purchase lands covered some 830 000 square miles, almost doubling the national territory of the United States. Potentially, of course, it threatened to call into being a gaggle of new states that together would swamp the influence of Federalist New England, but it removed the nightmare prospect of a Napoleonic presence in New Orleans. The following year Jefferson sponsored an expedition by Meriwether Lewis and William Clark to explore the new lands, in a two-year venture that brought American land claims to the shores of the Pacific. It was also Jefferson's administration that proposed a national system of canals and roads. This included a national road that would unite east and west, an early example of the federal government using its powers to promote the development of the new lands. The project was begun in 1811 and ultimately stretched from Maryland to Illinois.

The real concern about extremism focused not on Jefferson but on his volatile vice president, Aaron Burr, who may indeed have had dictatorial ambitions. In 1804 there was a Federalist scheme to get him elected as governor of New York, as the precursor to the secession of New York and New England. This was prevented by Burr's killing of the Federalist leader, Alexander Hamilton, in a duel in New Jersey. In 1805–6 Burr was active in a mysterious scheme that involved gathering thousands of followers, possibly with a view to invading and occupying Spanish territory in Florida, or perhaps organizing some form of western secession from the United States. Conceivably his followers may have believed he was acting with the approval of the president on a private and semi legal scheme like that which had led to the acquisition of Louisiana. Burr was charged with treason but acquitted. The 'Spanish Conspiracy' was inevitably employed as a partisan weapon against the Republicans.

THE WAR OF 1812

The Federalist–Republican schism remained central to American politics throughout the presidency of Jefferson and his successor, James Madison, and culminated in the divided reaction to the war of 1812. This followed long dissatisfaction with British and French naval policies of blockade and impressment. Sometimes the provocations were quite unashamed, as in the 1807 incident in which a British frigate attacked the US warship *Chesapeake* in Chesapeake Bay. The United States reacted to such outrages with a series of its own embargoes between 1807 and 1809, which had the disastrous effect of virtually shutting down American commerce with Europe. In 1809 the French agreed to respect the American flag at sea, but Britain did not and pressure for war mounted.

Once again the political split assumed regional forms, with the 'war hawks' concentrated in the south and west and pitted against dovish New England. While the frontier leaders had less to fear from British retaliation, they also stood to gain by possible advances into Canada and Florida and the removal of the British-allied Indians blocking new settlement. The eventual declaration of war was a narrow decision, supported by a 79 to 49 vote in the House of Representatives and a Senate majority of only 19 to 13. Over the next two years the states of Massachusetts, Connecticut and Rhode Island demonstrated such hostility to 'Mr Madison's War' that their leaders often sailed close to treason. The Rhode Island legislature voted against permitting the state militia to be called into national service, and the governor threatened to disobey any federal orders that appeared contrary to the constitution. The governor of Massachusetts called a public fast to bemoan a war 'against the nation from which we are descended'.

The ensuing war was a complex matter lacking any one major front. Most of the land fighting involved American attempts to secure control of Canada. An American invasion failed disastrously in 1812, and US forces repeatedly suffered heavy casualties. Frontier skirmishes forced the Americans to abandon Fort Dearborn, at the heart of the later city of Chicago, while Detroit was briefly in British hånds. The following year the Americans won a critical naval victory on Lake Erie, which led to land victories over the British and Indians at the Battle of the Thames, and also to the American recapture of Detroit and much of Michigan. Border fighting ultimately proved indecisive, and the United States realized that Canada was not likely to fall within its power in the foreseeable future. If not exactly a 'Canadian War of Independence', these events ensured that US history would be confined to the southern half of the continent.

British dominance at sea was rarely challenged effectively, though American privateers damaged British commerce. For a while, it seemed that the United States would leave the war with considerably less than it began, and even with its newly won independence badly compromised. British hopes reached new heights in the Summer of 1814, with the prospect of a successful invasion of New York state by thousands of army regulars made available by the suspension of war with France. A British expeditionary force also burned the public buildings of Washington DC, causing a severe financial panic. British negotiators now presented an extraordinary package of demands as the price of peace, including the creation of a huge Indian buffer state that would incorporate most of the later states of Wisconsin, Illinois, Indiana, Ohio, and Michigan. The new entity would be supported militarily by British fleets on the Great Lakes, from which US warships would be excluded. The British also reasserted their traditional legal right to navigate the Mississippi, which would be a blow to American ambitions in the west. Such claims seemed less fantastic with President Madison in flight from his capital, and the British pressing hard in both the Chesapeake Bay and along Lake Champlain.

But the American forces held their own. Baltimore stood firm, despite a naval bombardment that eventually became the subject of the American national anthem, 'The Star Spangled Banner'; while another British advance was crippled by a naval defeat on Lake Champlain. The last major battle of the war occurred in January 1815, when General Andrew Jackson defeated British forces attempting to take the city of New Orleans. The battle occurred a month after the signing of a peace treaty at Ghent, and had no direct impact on the course of the war; though victory here may in the long term have saved Louisiana for the United States. The final peace settlement essentially called for restoration of the territorial *status quo* and ignored the issue of embargoes, which had been made obsolete by the end of the Anglo-French wars. The peace agreement also failed to secure the protections which the British had earlier demanded for their Indian allies.

The United States concluded the war with its national independence reasserted, and with a new sense of patriotism and confidence. National unity was enhanced by the disastrous decision of the New England leaders to convene a meeting in Hartford at the end of 1814. Despite some Federalist extremism and talk of secession, the convention was generally moderate in tone, and it proposed amending the constitution rather than outright secession. But deliberations came to public attention just as the nation was celebrating victory at New Orleans, tainting the Federalist Party with treason. The opposition was crippled, leaving James Monroe to win overwhelmingly in the 1816 election, and again in 1820. For a decade the United States was virtually a one-party state. Just three men occupied the presidency between 1801 and 1825 (Table 2.4), a record to be proud of in a new nation emerging from a bloody revolution, especially when the first decade of nationhood had been so marked by factional conflict and threats of civil disorder.

Table 2.4   Presidents of the United States, 1789–1829

	Time in office	*Party*
George Washington	1789–97	None
John Adams	1797–1801	Federalist
Thomas Jefferson	1801–9	Democratic-Republican
James Madison	1809–17	Democratic-Republican
James Monroe	1817–25	Democratic-Republican
John Quincy Adams	1825–9	Democratic-Republican

Monroe's standing at home gave greater weight to American international pronouncements. In 1823 he proclaimed the famous 'Monroe Doctrine', called forth by the war of liberation waged by the Latin American nations against their Spanish colonial masters. Following suggestions that Spain might be assisted militarily by the autocratic nations of Europe, united in a 'Holy Alliance', Monroe declared that the United States would tolerate no European political interference in the western hemisphere. While this seemed an amazingly ambitious prohibition, the scheme fitted well with British concerns about discouraging any future Russian role in the Americas, and thus met no serious objection from London. The full importance of the doctrine would not become apparent until the second half of the century, when the United States would have the power to enforce its will against foreign intruders.

EXPANSION

At the start of the century the United States was in the midst of a long period of both internal development and external expansion at a pace barely parallelled in human history. During the revolutionary crisis of the 1770s the colonists were already breaking through the boundaries that had kept them tied to the seaboard. There were several well-recognized routes to the west, including the Mohawk Trail through upstate New York; the Cumberland road, which ran from Maryland into the present area of West Virginia; and the legendary Cumberland Gap, which led from the Carolinas into Kentucky. Further south, settlers from Georgia could skirt the southern limits of the mountains and open up Alabama and Mississippi. Once across the Appalachians, the critical transportation routes were the great rivers flowing to the Mississippi, especially the Ohio and the Tennessee. Pittsburgh's central position in the river networks allowed it to serve as the jumping-off point into West Virginia and Ohio.

Though the migration was a vast and autonomous popular movement, there were some key leaders. In 1775 the pioneer Daniel Boone opened the Wilderness Road into Kentucky on behalf of the significantly named 'Transylvania' company, seeking to push American frontiers 'beyond the woods' into Bluegrass country. Settlements initially clustered around Lexington, and statehood was achieved in 1792. The area's population approached 100 000 by 1792 and 220 000 by 1800. In 1778 George Rogers Clark determined to defend Kentucky from British and Indian attacks by carrying the war into enemy territory, and thus led the forces of Virginia in an ambitious campaign against the later territories of Illinois and Indiana. His victory at Vincennes in 1779 established future American land claims in the 'old north-west' and the Great Lakes region.

The new lands often fell into a shadowy legal realm, where borders were ill-defined. The first settlers of eastern Tennessee were under the clear rule of no one colony or state, facing rival claims from Virginia and North Carolina, and had to compose a separate constitution for self-government, the Watauga Association. The situation was not resolved until the Northwest Ordinance of 1787, which provided a legal and political framework for western settlers. Thereafter progress was rapid: Kentucky gained admission to the union in 1792,

Tennessee in 1796 and Ohio in 1803. By 1815 Pittsburgh and Lexington were substantial settlements with perhaps 8 000 inhabitants each, with Cincinnati, Louisville and St Louis already at 2–3 000. In 1808 St Louis became home to the *Missouri Gazette*, the first newspaper west of the Mississippi.

The United States now eliminated Spain as a potential rival for western lands. In 1795 the Pinckney Treaty opened the navigation of the Mississippi to American trade, while in 1818 future president Andrew Jackson's campaign against the Seminole peoples led to a virtual US invasion of Florida. (Jackson also executed two British subjects in the course of his provocative action.) The following year Spain recognized the *fait accompli* by agreeing to sell its formal title to the territory. Spanish control of Central and South America was broken in the nationalist revolutions of the 1820s, and henceforward the main US rival to the south would be the relatively weak nation of Mexico.

By 1830 American expansion west was already so far advanced as to have created a state in Missouri and heavy white settlement in Arkansas and Michigan, while settlers would flood into Iowa following the removal of Indians there in the next few years. The non-Indian population of what later became the mid-west stood at only 51 000 by 1800, but there were 1.6 million people by 1830, over nine million by 1860, and by the latter year the area housed 29 per cent of the national population (Table 2.5). The mountainmen and trappers already ranging through the plains and rockies by the 1820s were the first portents of the next great migration wave of the mid century.

Table 2.5   US population 1790–1820 (in millions)

Census year	National population
1790	3.93
1800	5.3
1810	7.2
1820	9.6

INDIAN CONFRONTATION

The settlers were not moving into unpopulated territory, and conflict erupted with the native inhabitants. A major problem was the different concepts of legality held by the respective sides: while whites believed they had bought a given area quite fairly, Indians often argued that the sellers had no right to trade in tribal property, and even that land as such could not be sold. The north-west territories were the scene of repeated battles in the mid 1790s and again in 1808–9, and some of these engagements were decisive, for example the Battle of Fallen Timbers, which in 1794 resulted in the destruction of Indian power in Ohio.

In 1811 the Americans faced one of their most serious challenges to date when the Shawnee leader, Tecumseh, sought a vast confederation that could challenge the United States along the entire length of its borders, from Canada to Mexico, while simultaneously allying with British military strength. Tecumseh was one of the great diplomats on the continent at that time, and his military experience dated back to the 1780s. He was supported by his brother, a visionary known as the Prophet, who might well have supplied the spiritual dimension required to power a major crusade. If the interpreters are to be believed, Tecumseh was an inspiring orator with a historical vision. Opposing collaboration with whites, he is said to have asked, 'Where today are the Pequot? Where the Narragansett, the Mohican, the Pokanoket? . . . They have vanished before the avarice and oppression of the white man, as snow before a summer sun'. Even with such strong leadership, Indian resistance continued to be futile. In 1811 the Prophet was defeated by Governor William Henry Harrison of Indiana at the battle of Tippecanoe. Tecumseh was killed in the battle of the Thames in 1813, and the following year General Andrew Jackson defeated the Creeks of Georgia at the Battle of Horseshoe Bend.

In 1814 the British demanded peace terms with the Americans that would have created a permanent Indian territory in

the north-west, but military events during the following
months made that unrealistic, and after 1814 the Indians
were left without foreign allies. In 1819 the Treaty of Saginaw
recognized US hegemony in the north-west. The Indians
signed away six million acres, or about one sixth of the area
that became the state of Michigan. In 1832 a failed campaign
by the Sac chief, Black Hawk, allowed the United States to
consolidate its position throughout Illinois and to penetrate
into Iowa.

The obvious growth of white American power gave the
Indian peoples few options. They could attempt to unite
along the lines advocated by Tecumseh, but a concerted
and sustained effort of this sort would be virtually impossible. Other than westward migration, the only remaining
choice was to seek to become American, to evolve a new
civilization that whites might respect and treat in terms of
reasonable equality. This was the course pursued in the south
by the peoples who became known as the 'Five Civilized
Tribes': Cherokee, Choctaw, Chickasaw, Creek and Seminole. These groups had a long tradition of village settlement
and agriculture, and it was relatively easy for them to adapt
their styles of clothing and political organization to European
models. The transition was welcomed by missionaries, who
saw Europeanization as a critical accompaniment to evangelization. It also seemed to fulfill Jefferson's dream that the
tribes should be led 'to agriculture, to manufactures, and
civilization'. The Tribes even came to own slaves, the ultimate sign of civilization. Europeanization was symbolized by
the brilliant Sequoyah, who devised a written version of the
Cherokee language. In 1828 there appeared the first issue of
the newspaper *The Cherokee Phoenix*.

For all their efforts, circumstances were badly weighted
against the native peoples. By 1830, perhaps 60 000 Indians
occupied the 25 million acres of land in the old south-west,
land that was desperately sought after by settlers, planters
and speculators. Throughout the 1820s pressure for their
removal mounted, and the inauguration of President Andrew

Jackson in 1829 provided the ideal opportunity for the advocates of white settlement: as Jackson asked, 'what good man would prefer a country covered with forest and ranged by a few thousand savages to our extensive republic, studded with cities, towns and prosperous farms?' Still worse for the Indians, in 1829 gold was discovered on Indian lands in Georgia. The tribes were pressed to accept relocation in a new 'Indian Territory' west of the Mississippi, and at least some elements of the leadership did consent. In 1830 Jackson signed the Indian Removal Act. These actions were probably illegal as well as high-handed, and Jackson ignored the condemnation of the US Supreme Court. Over the next decade the civilized tribes were uprooted, often at the points of US army bayonets. The resulting forced migration of the Cherokees was called the Trail of Tears, and it claimed the lives of thousands of Indians. The incident also ignited yet another gruelling war in the south-east, as the Florida Seminoles chose to resist rather than perish. Between 1820 and 1845, the number of Indians living east of the Mississippi probably fell from around 120 000 to under 30 000.

ECONOMIC GROWTH

In addition to expansion on land, the new United States swiftly became a sea power of the first rank, a development that caused real concern to British observers long before American industrial preeminence was even considered a remote possibility. In the first half of the nineteenth century American shipping benefited from international circumstances, as European nations relied on American sources for meat, grain and cotton during the Anglo-French wars. American improvements in technology and business organization were reflected in the new clipper ships and packet boats, as well as innovative techniques in navigation. New England ports such as Nantucket, New Bedford and Provincetown dominated the international whaling industry, which reached its height around 1840. In 1820 a Connecticut sealer made a pioneering voyage that established US claims in Antarctica. In addition the speedy American ships continued to engage in illegal slaving long after 1808, the official date of abolition. By 1861 the American merchant navy possessed a tonnage of 2.5 million, a figure far higher than in any subsequent part of the century.

American owners and captains had to be inventive in seeking new routes, as the British initially discouraged US trade with familiar destinations such as the West Indies. The Americans began trading with the Baltic, and from 1784 they were active in the China trade, giving the United States the opportunity to undersell the products of the British East India Company. Over the next four decades the ships of New England ranged freely over the Indian Ocean and the China Seas. It was an American warship·that opened Japan to the West in 1853, and American Protestants came to regard the evangelization of China and East Asia as a task peculiarly assigned to them by the deity. Though America did not exactly rule the waves, it made an impressive effort, above all in the Pacific.

Mercantile capital accumulated from these shipping ventures became the primary source of American industrial development, which began in earnest from about 1810. Industry also ultimately benefited from the embargoes and wars, which forced consumers to rely on domestic manufactures. The maritime linkage contributed to the location of early enterprises in New England, near the key ports, but development here was also assisted by the ready availability of water power. The model site of the new era was the textile town of Lowell in Massachusetts, where the first mill was founded by the patrician Francis Cabot Lowell in 1812, together with a partner whose money stemmed from the East India trade. The town of Lowell became the 'Manchester of America', but was admired less for its productivity than the extreme paternalism exercised over its workforce. As an industrial proletariat was unsuitable for the American republic, the mill-girls of Lowell were expected to work only long enough to acquire enough money to establish themselves when they returned to their proper role as rural housewives. Lowell stood on the Merrimack River, which also provided the power for the textile complexes at Manchester and Nashua in New Hampshire and Lawrence in Massachusetts.

Rhode Island offers another case study. As early as the 1780s Moses Brown began a cotton-spinning enterprise there, complete with plagiarized versions of the latest British technology, and power looms had appeared in the state by 1815. The state already had a hundred cotton-spinning mills, employing 7 000 workers. An industrial boom developed after the war of 1812. By 1832 investment in the Rhode Island textile industry was triple the sum invested in maritime trade, which began a relative decline. The growth of steam power and railroads permitted a still greater expansion of textile manufacturing after 1830, while other firms ventured into metal casting and the construction of steam engines. By 1860 about half the state's population was engaged in manufacturing. In Maryland, similarly, a cotton textile industry that began in 1808 was by 1860 producing goods worth two million dollars. The American iron industry also developed apace in the late eighteenth century, based on the timber supplies of regions such as Pennsylvania. Though charcoal-fuelled smelting was obsolete by English standards, the clearing of forests to supply the furnaces served a double purpose in opening new lands for agriculture. Pittsburgh was already a sizable manufacturing town by 1815.

Throughout the first half of the century, government played a decisive if controversial role in American economic growth, and Henry Clay epitomized those national-minded thinkers who saw future development as dependent on political action, on governmental promotion of canals and turnpike roads, railroads and manufactures. This also required the defence of emerging native industry. In 1816 and 1824 Congress approved high tariffs of the sort required for Clay's 'American System', but throughout these years industrial interests had to fight hard against the different concerns of southern plantation owners and farmers. In 1819 the upsurge in American industrial and urban growth was halted by a disastrous financial panic, which caused grave doubts about the wisdom of economic nationalism, and indeed of the whole industrial future to which the nation had so recently seemed irrevocably committed. By 1820 Clay was lamenting the failure to break economically with England: Americans were still 'politically free, commercially slaves'.

FREEDOM IS A HABIT

By contemporary standards the society that emerged from the revolution was radically democratic, in the sense of granting political franchise to a large majority of white men, and even in some cases to black men. (Of course women and most blacks would have to wait many years for their due share in the political process.) While property qualifications remained in some places, inflation greatly reduced their effect on the size of the electorate. Several states gave the franchise to resident taxpayers rather than property holders. In addition to granting the vote, the new states made it much easier to exercise that right, by holding frequent elections and expanding the number of polling places. This was essential in a society of such diffuse settlement.

State governments from the mid 1770s onwards made bold advances in matters of declaring individual rights and ordering legal reforms, on the basis that social abuses were an English inheritance that should be abolished together with the power of the monarchy. Eight states had issued bills of rights as separate documents by 1784, and four others incorporated such documents into their constitutions. The pioneering Virginia Bill of Rights, adopted in June 1776, was an aggressive statement of natural rights theory, with the consequent assertion of all the basic rights that would eventually find their way into the US constitution: rights against double jeopardy and self-incrimination, high bail and excessive punishments; assertion of jury trial; and freedom of the press. Religious issues were especially important here, and the Virginia document announced that 'all men are equally entitled to the free exercise of religion according to the dictates of conscience'. In Pennsylvania the radical constitution of 1776 was equally humane, democratic and secular.

Between 1775 and 1820 many aspects of American life were transformed by the breakdown of traditional orthodoxies and controls, and the application of democratic doctrine far outside the sphere of government and party politics. The implications of democratic ideals for military affairs were painfully evident in the War of 1812, when US campaigns regularly came to grief due to the nature of the popular militia. Well suited to resist invasion, the state forces were hopelessly inadequate for any more complex struggle, with their insistence on electing officers regardless of abilities. They also carried out mass debate on controversial orders, and rejected those they disliked. This meant, for example, that forces returned home when they had fulfilled the strict terms of their engagement, no matter how inconvenient for the war effort, and they were extremely reluctant to venture outside American territory. Certainly republican government was in no danger from such forces, but nor could the United States hope to achieve the status of a significant military power.

In the law, meanwhile, the break with England permitted state legislatures and courts to experiment with easier divorce procedures and expanded property rights for married women: impressive for the time, though tentative by the standards of the twentieth century. In 1790 Pennsylvania became the first jurisdiction anywhere to restrict the death penalty essentially to homicide, a trend that soon spread across the United States, and in the 1840s Michigan undertook the radical step of abolishing capital punishment altogether. The United States in the early nineteenth century was the first society in human history where commission of a serious crime generally led the perpetrator to prison rather than the gallows or block. Most states rapidly curbed and then abolished the process of imprisonment for debt, which had been the largest single cause for incarceration in colonial times, and remained so in England for over a century afterwards.

Legal liberalization was accompanied by a general distrust of English precedent, and indeed of formal legal mechanisms, and some states actually prohibited trained lawyers from serving on their supreme courts. This taste for innovation was all the greater in the 'legal periphery' of the new border states, from which daring experiments originated and spread to the major jurisdictions. Not until the conservative writings of jurist James Kent in the 1820s did American law acquire a well-defined body of precedent and case law that in effect stabilized the future course of legal development.

RELIGION AND CULTURE

Legal developments raised the question of exactly how far colonial social assumptions should properly be abandoned as part of the trappings of aristocracy and tyranny. This social transformation was equally marked in matters of religion. Early national America had been dominated by relatively sober denominations such as Presbyterian, Congregationalist and Episcopalian, which enjoyed a status close to establishment in particular states and regions. In the first half of the nineteenth century there was a dramatic shift towards newer groupings that placed far less emphasis on a trained and learned ministry, and preached a universal salvation more in keeping with the political democracy of the age. Hierarchy and centralized structures similarly gave way to the loose federalism of the Baptists and Methodists. Between 1800 and 1840 Baptist membership nationwide grew from 170 000 to 560 000, while the Methodist ranks swelled from 70 000 to 820 000, with a further increase to perhaps 1.6 million on the eve of the Civil War. The rising sects were ideally suited to frontier conditions, where trained ministers were a scarce commodity and the ideal evangelist was an itinerant armed with little more than a Bible. Ministers rode circuits, establishing 'cells' of true believers wherever they could gain a hearing and preaching an individualistic doctrine of free grace, individual responsibility, conversion and regeneration.

American religion was repeatedly shaped by the successive enthusiastic revivals that would be such characteristic elements of the American cultural landscape for the next two centuries, and which were modelled on memories of the 'Great Awakening' of the 1730s. The late 1790s brought a 'Second Awakening', which originated in New England with the students at Yale and other colleges. The timing was significant, coming at the time of a attack on the Republicans for their supposed atheism and 'infidelity', which showed the need for the nation to reassert its orthodox heritage.

Expectations were renewed by the upsurge of popular spirituality that erupted in the south and west, where a great assembly at Cane Ridge, Kentucky, in 1801 became the legendary standard by which all later revivals were judged, a 'second Pentecost'. Such mass gatherings were marked by amazing emotional and ecstatic outbursts, dancing and laughter, 'barking' and 'the jerks'. Observers remarked on 'the impassioned exhortations; the earnest prayers; the sobs, the shrieks or shouts, bursting from persons under intense agitation of mind; the sudden spasms which seized upon scores, and unexpectedly dashed them to the ground'. There would be repeated local revivals in addition to the national events of 1798 and 1857, and the 'popular' denominations benefited accordingly.

THE GROWTH OF SLAVERY

The spread of democratic principles had an obvious impact on the position of the wholly unfree, whose status posed such grave questions about the ideals of the new society. Anti-slavery sentiment grew at the end of the century, and most northern states abolished the institution, starting with Vermont in 1777 and ending with New Jersey in 1804. Even so there were still 30 000 slaves in the northern states at the turn of the century, about half in New York alone. The slave trade officially perished in 1808. The free black communities of the north developed a remarkable solidarity and self-confidence, and an institutional network based on their distinctive churches, mutual aid groups and fraternal lodges. Separate black churches date from the 1770s, chiefly among Baptist and Methodist groups, but in 1816 the African Methodist Episcopal Church became the first such congregation to emancipate itself fully from white legal and financial control.

The expected withering away of southern slavery never occurred, due to the invention of the cotton gin by Eli Whitney in 1793. By separating seeds from cotton fifty times faster than hand sorting, this device created a massive new demand for raw cotton, and promised to supply a vast output to keep pace with the surging demand of the British textile mills. The problem, of course, was exactly how to grow and pick the necessary cotton when production was so intensive in both labour and land. The solution was found in a greater commercial use of plantation slavery, the harshest and least reputable form of an already tainted enterprise. The need for plantation land drove southern settlers into several new states whose climates perfectly fitted them for the spreading economy: Alabama, Mississippi, Louisiana, and parts of Tennessee and even east Texas. The law of supply and demand now had an impact, as the end of the legal slave trade made existing slave stocks much more valuable and reduced the temptation to free any slaves other than those who had wholly outlived their usefulness.

Cotton exports soared from 3 000 bales in 1790 to 178 000 in 1810 and 4.5 million bales in 1860. By 1820 the United States had become the world's largest cotton producer, and perhaps ten states and territories were largely dependent upon the plantation system. Slavery grew alongside cotton production. In 1810 there were a million slaves, by 1830 there were two million. In 1860 the 4.5 million African-Americans constituted almost a seventh of the total US population, and four million of these remained slaves.

The nature of slavery also deteriorated owing to fears of slave insurrection, and the perceived need for vigilance and tighter control. Slave rebellions were nothing new in America, as New York had experienced a troubling rebellion as early as 1712. In 1741 over thirty slaves had been executed for a rumoured insurrection in New York city, and there had been many lesser-known outbreaks. Matters changed radically with the new expectations stirred by the rhetoric of liberty stemming from the American revolution, and from the Haitian rising of the 1790s, which created the first black republic in the hemisphere. Haitian connections with the French territory of Louisiana may have contributed to potential violence in this region, where in 1811 there was a bloody revolt. Rebellions in the United States now became better publicized, and at least in rumour threatened to assume terrifying proportions of regional or national conspiracy.

A series of potent slave leaders emerged: Gabriel Prosser in Richmond, Virginia, in 1800, Denmark Vesey in Charleston, South Carolina, in 1822, Nat Turner in Virginia in 1831. Vesey's plan would have involved the seizure and destruction of Charleston, the nation's sixth largest city at that time, and popular fears are suggested by the ensuing execution of 36 alleged plotters. Turner's rising led to the death of some sixty whites, and for southerners confirmed the imminent peril of 'Haitian' conditions if the slave system ever faltered. These fears were especially directed at free blacks, who could so easily become a source of agitation, and from 1816 slaveholders were prominent in endeavours to repatriate freed slaves to Africa. Southern states now passed laws restricting or prohibiting the manumission of slaves.

From about 1815 the westward population expansion made it apparent that the union would soon have to admit several new states, and this raised the question of their attitude to slavery. The south obviously favoured the admission of states that both practised and permitted slavery, not only because these were likely to share common interests, but also because they would not support any attempt to achieve abolition through an amendment of the federal constitution. As new states were admitted, it became desirable to balance regional interests by maintaining a general parity between slave and free states. The eight states admitted between 1816 and 1837 were admitted in pairs, one with slavery, one without, an informal but effective arrangement. Between 1816 and 1819 the slave states of Mississippi and Alabama joined the union to balance free slavery-free Indiana and Illinois, and by 1819 the 22 states of the union were equally divided between slave and free. However this division was by no means as rigid as it would later become, all the more so since the new free states often had large southern populations. Southern Illinois, for example, attracted thousands from the Carolinas, Virginia and Tennessee, who had migrated along the obvious river routes; and it was far from obvious that the region would opt for free status. Moreover the state maintained a distinctly subordinate legal status for blacks until the 1840s.

The doctrine of parity was consecrated in 1820, when Missouri sought admission as a slave state, meeting ferocious abolitionist sentiment in the north and west. A compromise was achieved whereby Missouri's admission was balanced by that of the northern part of Massachusetts, which became the new (free) state of Maine, but in addition the future westward expansion of slavery was severely circumscribed. American land acquisitions were to be partitioned by a line drawn at the parallel of 36° 30′ north. North of this line, any future states would be admitted as free; south of this, slavery would be permitted. While a workable compromise in the short term, it raised future problems as it constituted the *de facto* partition of the United States into two different societies, defined by the institution of slavery. Nor did it really resolve the concerns of the south, as the 'free' west was vastly larger than the slave region and in a few decades was likely to produce a sizable majority of free states. The results of this conflict would dominate American politics for the next four decades, until finally erupting into massive bloodshed in 1861. Jefferson termed the Missouri compromise debate 'a firebell in the night', possibly even the death knell of the union. For once he spoke as a prophet.

3

Expansion and Crisis, 1825–65

In 1850 Herman Melville's novel *White Jacket* included a vision of American destiny that in retrospect seems intolerably arrogant and hypernationalistic. In his defence, it can only be said that he was expressing views that were far from unusual for Americans of the time, and that this sense of limitless potentiality is explicable in terms of the astonishing progress of his country in the previous three decades. Melville wrote:

> And we Americans are the peculiar, chosen people – the Israel of our time; we bear the ark of the liberties of the world. Seventy years ago we escaped from thrall; and besides our first birth-right – embracing one continent of earth – God has given us for a future inheritance the broad domains of the political pagans, that shall yet come and lie down under the shade of our ark, without bloody hands being lifted. God has predestinated, mankind expects, great things from our race; and great things we feel in our souls. The rest of the nations must soon be in our rear. We are the pioneers of the world; the advance guard, sent on through the wilderness of untried things, to break a new path in the New World that is ours. In our youth is our strength; in our inexperience, our wisdom . . . And let us always remember that with ourselves, almost for the first

time in the history of earth, natural selfishness is unbounded philanthropy; for we cannot do a good to America but we give alms to the world.[1]

To put this into perspective, the population of the United States virtually quadrupled in those years, rising from about eight million in 1815 to some 31 million in 1860 (Table 3.1). This expansion was partly a natural consequence of the free availability of land and economic opportunities that made it relatively easy for the young to set up housekeeping and begin families at an early age. Other factors included the flood of immigrants and the acquisition of new territories in the west. Westward expansion proceeded at a rate scarcely dreamed of in 1800. By 1860 America's key commercial cities included such western upstarts as Chicago, St Louis and Cincinnati. By 1830 one American in five lived in areas that had not been part of the national territory in 1790; by 1850 this had risen to one in three. By the middle of the century New York was the third largest city in the western world, after London and Paris.

It is difficult to recount the history of the United States in those years without constantly resorting to superlatives, to remarkable statistics that showed a degree of development unparallelled in Europe. At the same time this vast expansion was accompanied by growing tensions and injustices, which

Table 3.1   US population, 1820–60 (millions)

Census year	National population
1820	9.6
1830	12.9
1840	17.1
1850	23.2
1860	31.4

arose especially from the movement westward. Americans thus gained a continental empire and became a world industrial power, but in so doing they almost lost their nation.

INDUSTRY AND COMMUNICATIONS

American industrial growth began to accelerate from about 1830, initially in well-established sectors such as textiles and iron. From the 1840s the US economy started to enjoy the benefits of its vast mineral reserves. The importation of British and especially Welsh experts and managers led to the creation of a new iron industry based on coke-fired smelting, which thus employed the magnificent anthracite coal reserves of Pennsylvania. New industrial towns were created to mine the coal and new cities emerged in Pennsylvania, centres such as Scranton, Carbondale and Wilkes-Barre. Pittsburgh now consolidated its role as the 'Birmingham of America', the observers who devised such names still feeling the need to draw English parallels. Between 1840 and 1860 the value of American manufactures rose fourfold.

Industrial and commercial growth were dependent on transportation facilities to a far greater degree than in the relatively small and compact lands of Europe. At the beginning of the nineteenth century Philadelphia owed its position as the preeminent American city to its access to the rich agricultural lands of Pennsylvania, but this supremacy was fundamentally undermined by the building of the Erie Canal in 1825, which provided a convenient water route from the Great Lakes to the east coast via the Hudson River. The canal made the fortunes of New York City, and also of Buffalo, the terminus on Lake Erie. Over the next two decades Philadelphia attempted to compete by utilising a complicated series of water and land routes into the hinterland, but New York ultimately triumphed.

The Erie Canal also made the fortunes of the mid-west, which enjoyed an enviable economic boom as freight rates

plummeted. From the 1840s Michigan and Wisconsin flourished on the strength of the new timber industry and some
amazing mineral finds: copper in the Keweenaw peninsula
and iron deposits around Lake Superior. All these resources
would have been of purely scientific curiosity without appropriate means of transportation. In 1855 the completion of the
Soo Canals 'uncorked' Lake Superior (as Robert Raymond
comments).[2] The expansion of traffic on the Great Lakes
made the fortunes of the rising city of Detroit.

Canal building spread rapidly in the late 1820s, but this
phase was soon superseded by the growth of the rail network.
The Baltimore and Ohio Railroad was chartered in 1827 and
expanded during the 1830s. By the 1850s railways covered
much of the east coast and were reaching towards midwestern
cities such as Cincinnati and St Louis. The 3300 miles of
railway lines in place by 1840 had grown to 17 000 miles by
1854, and 12 000 more were under construction. Rail allowed
the opening of the coal country of Pennsylvania no less than
the cattle ranges of the west. In 1837 Samuel F. B. Morse
demonstrated the first successful telegraph system, and by
1858 messages could be sent across the Atlantic by undersea
cable.

Communications were further improved by the coming of
commercial river steamships, following the model invented
by Robert Fulton in 1807. These did much to open up the
continental heartland even before the expansion of rail, with
all that implied for urban growth. When Charles Dickens
visited the United States in 1842 he recorded his steamship
journeys along the Ohio and the Mississippi to the key river
ports of Pittsburgh, Cincinnati, Louisville and St Louis. All
now recorded booming population growth as metropolises of
the west. St Louis in particular had vast potential as the
junction of the two great rivers, the Mississippi and the
Missouri, and was accessible from the Ohio routes. The
Mississippi trade gave life to other cities too, for example
Natchez, Vicksburg and Memphis, while its distance from the
river routes ensured that once-flourishing Lexington forfeited

its primary role in Kentucky to Louisville – Lexington grew little after about 1820. New Orleans made its fortune as the meeting place between the Mississippi River routes and the seaborne trade of the Gulf of Mexico. By the 1860s the course of the American Civil War would be shaped by the new technologies of rail, telegraph and steamship.

American industrialization proceeded despite a primitive financial system, which made it difficult to obtain reliable credit and offered huge opportunities to confidence men and financial sharks. Financial panics were also a recurrent menace, and caused devastation throughout the economy. The financial disaster of 1819 was followed by comparable horrors in 1837 and 1857. By 1842 even the states of Maryland and Pennsylvania were forced to default on loans, sabotaging American credit and reputation overseas, while the ruinous collapse of the state bank in Alabama illustrated the extreme fragility of the banking system.

CITIES

New industries and modes of transportation transformed the American urban network. Around 1830 the urban hierarchy was dominated by New York, with some 200 000 people, followed by Philadelphia and Baltimore, with around 80 000 each, and Boston at 60 000. By 1860 New York had over 800 000 people, and there were eight more centres with over 100 000. At the heart of industrial Rhode Island the population of Providence rose tenfold between 1820 and 1860, and that was in addition to the network of surrounding factory towns. In Maryland similarly, the city and county of Baltimore grew from 39 000 people in 1790 to 211 000 in 1850, and the proportion of the state's population in the surrounding northern counties swelled from 33 per cent to 59 per cent. This east coast dominance was already being challenged by the upsurge of new cities during the middle of the century, especially in the mid-west, with St Louis, Milwaukee, Detroit, Cincinnati and Cleveland.

Upstart Chicago demonstrated how a city could take spectacular advantage of the new economic opportunities. In 1833 this bustling trading post became the centre of astonishing speculative growth following a rumour that it would serve as the terminal of a proposed Illinois and Michigan Canal. The railway arrived in 1854, and eleven lines soon converged in the city. Chicago emerged as the hub of the mid-west's trade in grain, timber and livestock, surpassing St Louis by the mid 1850s. By 1859 Chicago had a network of vast steam-powered grain elevators, permitting the revolutionary transformation of the region's agricultural commerce: soon the city gave birth to the new industries of commodities trading and futures contracts. By 1865 the Chicago stockyards were in operation, ready to receive the cattle of the western ranches. In 1869 the rail network extended as far west as San Francisco, and the next decade brought the refrigerated railway wagons that allowed the meat packing trade to reach continental and then global markets. Chicago's population grew prodigiously in an age noted for wonders. It recorded less than 5 000 people in 1840, 110 000 in 1860, 300 000 in 1870, and a million before the end of the century.

Urbanization was far less marked further south, where only New Orleans could compare with the northern centres, with 100 000 people by 1840. Cities such as Louisville, Memphis, Charleston, Mobile and Richmond had populations ranging from only 25 000 to 50 000 in the 1850s; while five of the southern states still had no settlement with over 10 000 people. This was partly a consequence of the slower extension of the rail network into the south, but even here the new technology was having an impact. In 1837 a newly created rail junction in Georgia bore the uninspiring name of Terminus; in 1845 it was renamed Atlanta, after the Western and Atlantic Railroad, and the new city grew steadily.

Urban populations were increasingly diverse. The building boom of these years created a vast market for unskilled labour, which was all the more difficult to find given the rival attractions of relatively free lands in the west. The solution was found in massive immigration. Between 1821 and 1840 some 751 000 immigrants entered the United States, a figure that rose dramatically to 4.3 million between 1841 and 1860. The Irish represented a third of the immigrants of the 1830s, and 250 000 more entered between 1840 and 1844. A further 250 000 entered in 1851 alone. The turning point came in the mid 1840s under the impact of the Irish potato famine. Far more people entered the United States in the decade after 1846 than in the nation's history since independence. Two million Irish immigrated between 1840 and 1870, as well as substantial numbers of British and Germans.

In 1850 about a tenth of the American population was foreign born (Table 3.2), and some 70 per cent of the foreign stock population was concentrated in just six states in the north-east and mid-west. In Boston the number of Irish residents swiftly overtook the native-born population during the early 1850s.

Table 3.2   US population, 1850 (millions)

Region	Total population	Foreign born*		Slaves*	
New England	2.73	0.30	(11.0)	–	
Mid Atlantic	5.90	1.00	(17.0)	–	
South Atlantic	4.68	0.10	(2.0)	1.70	(36.3)
East North Central	4.52	0.55	(12.0)	–	
East South Central	3.36	0.05	(1.5)	1.10	(32.7)
West North Central	0.88	0.10	(11.0)	0.09	(10.0)
West South Central	0.94	0.09	(10.0)	0.35	(37.2)
Mountain	0.07	0.004	(5.5)	–	
Pacific	0.10	0.02	(22.0)	–	
Total	23.20	2.25	(9.7)	3.20	(13.8)

* Percentages in brackets

THE NEW POLITICS, 1828-48

In American political life, the years from 1814 to 1825 are generally known as the 'era of good feelings', in which party divisions largely faded into oblivion. Good feelings became scarce in the following decades, as the rising tensions in national life were reflected in factional politics. The old Federalist Party never recovered from the Hartford convention, and the insult 'Hartford Fed' proved a politically valuable tool for years afterwards. Conversely the Democratic-Republican tradition gained new strength from the presidency of Andrew Jackson, and especially the election of 1828. In 1824, Jackson had commanded a larger share of the popular vote than any of his rivals (Table 3.3), but his failure to gain an absolute majority of electoral votes had consigned the decision to the House of Representatives, which supported the candidacy of John Quincy Adams. Enraged by the 'corrupt bargain' between Adams and Clay, the Jacksonians prepared for political war in 1828.

Jackson not only carried that election convincingly, but initiated both a series of policies and a type of rhetoric that ushered in a new age of party conflict. Jackson won by mobilizing social groups and regions that felt themselves to be the victims of surviving privilege in American society: the west against the east, urban labourers against employers, farmers against financiers. Populism was facilitated by the general decline of restrictions on the franchise, so that most free white men had the vote by this time, and all the newer states possessed this system from the time of their admission. In 1840 some 2.5 million votes were cast in the presidential election out of a total population of 17 million. Presidential electors now tended to be chosen by popular vote rather than by state legislatures.

Jacksonian politics were based on a pure spoils system, in which the winning party could expect to assign offices freely to its own followers. Though the idea was not new, it was now linked to a democratic and anti-elitist theory that held

Table 3.3   Presidential election results, 1824–56

Year	Winning candidate	Popular votes (millions)	Losing candidate	Popular votes (millions)
1824	John Q. Adams (DR)	0.10	Andrew Jackson (D)	0.16
			Henry Clay (DR)	0.05
			William H. Crawford (DR)	0.05
1828	Andrew Jackson (D)	0.65	John Q. Adams (NR)	0.50
1832	Andrew Jackson (D)	0.69	Henry Clay (NR)	0.53
1836	Martin Van Buren (D)	0.76	William H. Harrison (Whig)	0.55
1840	William H. Harrison (Whig)	1.30	Martin Van Buren (D)	1.10
1844	James K. Polk (D)	1.30	Henry Clay (Whig)	1.30
1848	Zachary Taylor (Whig)	1.36	Lewis Cass (D)	1.20
			Martin Van Buren (Free Soil)	0.29
1852	Franklin Pierce (D)	1.60	Winfield Scott (Whig)	1.40
1856	James Buchanan (D)	1.90	John C. Fremont (R)	1.40
			Millard Fillmore (Whig)	0.87
1860	Abraham Lincoln (R)	1.87	Stephen A. Douglas (D)	1.38
			John C. Breckinridge (D)	0.85
			John Bell (Const. Union)	0.59
1864	Abraham Lincoln (R)	2.20	George McClellan (D)	1.80

that any man was as technically qualified as another to hold office, and that the decision should properly be based on correctness of political outlook. The use of patronage was facilitated at the local level by the emergence of political machines, of which New York City's Tammany Hall was the best known, which brought out the vote in exchange for the distribution of jobs and favours, services and contracts. Jacksonian democracy took politics into everyday life, for example in the promotion of 'pet' banks and financial concerns that won the favour of the ruling party. In 1837 the Supreme Court followed the new mood when the *Charles River Bridge* case overturned the privileges of an established concern in the interests of opening a market to new business.

This political tendency hastened the conflict with the Bank of the United States, the idea of which had been a basic article of faith for Federalists and economic nationalists since the 1790s. In 1817 the United States created a second national Bank, which from 1823 was headed by the powerful figure of Nicholas Biddle. In 1832 Jackson refused to recharter the second bank, withdrew government moneys and began a campaign in which Nicholas Biddle conveniently served as the perfect propaganda example of eastern big-money privilege.

Jackson's party commanded wide support: it won every presidential election but two between 1828 and 1856 (Table 3.4), and was defeated in 1840 chiefly because the public associated incumbent President Van Buren with the depression following the financial panic of 1837. However an opposition now emerged, which included at least elements of the old Federalist agenda in matters such as the government's role in promoting economic improvements. Supporting industrial and commercial development, these groups thus favoured higher tariffs and viewed Jackson as the fiscally irresponsible demagogue 'King Andrew'. They also protested against the president's withdrawal of the federal role in internal development, suggested by his 1830 veto of the Maysville Road Bill. In 1828 and 1832 the Democrats were opposed by 'National Republican' tickets, and in 1836 the Whig Party came to prominence. The Whigs achieved real success in gaining nationwide support. They put up a respectable showing in every national election from 1836 to 1852, and actually won the presidency in 1840 and 1848.

Though the Whigs were congenial to the eastern financial and industrial factions, it was a measure of how Jackson had transformed American political discourse, and the rhetorical

Table 3.4   US presidents, 1817–65

	Time in office	*Party*
James Monroe	1817–25	Democratic-Republican
John Quincy Adams	1825–29	Democratic-Republican
Andrew Jackson	1829–37	Democrat
Martin Van Buren	1837–41	Democrat
William Henry Harrison	1841	Whig
John Tyler	1841–45	Whig
James K. Polk	1845–49	Democrat
Zachary Taylor	1849–50	Whig
Millard Fillmore	1850–53	Whig
Franklin Pierce	1853–57	Democrat
James Buchanan	1857–61	Democrat
Abraham Lincoln	1861–65	Republican

nature of Americanism that even they had to adopt a 'frontier' ethos. Both at national and state level, the most respectable patricians presented themselves at election time in an improbably rough and backwoods guise, surrounded by symbols such as the log cabin, the coonskin cap and hard cider. In 1840 William Henry Harrison campaigned on the strength of his military victory over the Indians at Tippecanoe in 1811.

THE AGE OF CIVIL DISORDER

The new political world was naturally reshaped by the social changes of the 1830s, by factors such as urbanization, immigration and a new ethnic diversity. The Founding Fathers had written of a future America that was largely an extension of the rural society they knew, a land of farms and plantations, albeit with trading towns and artisans. Nineteenth-century America continued to be predominantly rural, and even in 1850 the urban proportion of the population was only

15 per cent. On the other hand the emergence of the east-coast cities and industrial centres was a traumatic shock to the old order, which lacked the mechanisms to deal with the new conurbations. As a consequence, between about 1830 and 1860 American society was marked by repeated out-breaks of rioting and factional violence, which, had they occurred in contemporary Europe, would have been dis-cussed by historians in the language usually reserved for civil war.

The new cities were marked by intense class conflicts, and working-class organizations now emerged. In 1828 there was a 'Workingmen's Party', while New York city had its radical 'Equal Rights Party', the Locofocos. Working-class politics were most apparent in times of economic setback, such as in 1837, when crowds demanded what they considered fair prices and rents. There was also a current of class politics in emerging industries such as textiles, where strikes became common from the 1830s. In 1860 the shoemakers of Lynn in Massachusetts organized the largest single strike in the ante-bellum United States, a stoppage that spread throughout the towns of New England.

The influence of Jacksonian and radical ideas was reflected in local political battles, in which populist movements struggled against the entrenched privilege of landowners and closed political elites. In New York state, tenants on the great feudal estates organized an 'Anti-Renter' movement in 1839, whose leaders aimed to 'take up the ball of the revolution . . . and roll it to the final consummation of free-dom and independence of the masses'. In Rhode Island, Thomas W. Dorr organized a protest against the electoral structure that gave power only to landowners and ignored the swelling masses of the urban and manufacturing populations in and around Providence. The 'rebellion' became so intense that Dorr's forces claimed to represent a rival government, and Providence approached conditions of civil war. Martial law was declared in 1842, and Dorr was accordingly prose-cuted for treason against the state of Rhode Island.

In addition to the familiar language of class, American politics were profoundly affected by periodic outbreaks of conspiracy theory, which as usual veiled deeper social tensions. One celebrated example concerned freemasonry. In 1826 a renegade Mason named William Morgan disappeared in New York state after threatening to reveal the secrets of the organisation in print. He was certainly kidnapped, and probably murdered. The ensuing outcry resulted in the formation of an anti-Masonic movement pledged to the destruction of secret societies and their sinister influence on American life. This was in part a revival of the Illuminati scare of 1798, which did so much to form later interpretations of social problems. Even today there are theorists who hold that a clandestine Masonic agenda can be read in the symbolism of the US dollar bill, and that the date '1776' listed thereon commemorates the founding of the Illuminati order, rather than American independence.

The movement of the 1820s was a reaction against the perceived power of the closed elites, who obstinately retained control of political and economic life in a democratic republic. Anti-Masonry portrayed a broad conspiracy against morality and religion, orchestrated by clandestine groups that dragooned their followers by means of the bloodiest oaths and threats; and as Morgan's case showed, they did not hesitate to carry these out. In the 1850s ideas of clandestine elites and secret assassination plots were directed against the supposed conspiracy of slave holders, said to dominate the US government. Such conspiracy charges gave rise to political parties and movements dedicated to exposing and uprooting the alleged plotters. An anti-Masonic party was briefly a national electoral presence in 1832, picking up nearly 8 per cent of the popular vote, though members soon drifted into the Whig Party. The anti-Masonic desire to open the political process led it to institute the novel American device of the open nominating convention. The 'slave-power' idea similarly contributed to the rise of the Republican Party after 1856.

Conspiracy fears were especially directed against the Catholic Church. Mass immigration and urbanization both met a sharp reaction from traditionally minded Protestant nativists, who saw the Catholic Church as epitomizing the worst nightmares of autocracy and privilege, magnified by primitive superstition. From the early 1830s antipopery became a staple of American political life and it remained so until the Ku Klux Klan movement a century later. Newspapers and scandal sheets such as the *Protestant Vindicator* proliferated from the early 1830s, as did societies whose whole *raison d'être* was ideological and political confrontation with 'Romanism'. Religious and ethnic divisions influenced party politics, which through much of the late nineteenth century regularly set urban Catholic Democrats against rural and Protestant nativist Republicans. Often the battles between nativists and Catholics were fought out in physical form, by urban street gangs allied to political parties, and to formal organizations such as the fire companies. These battles reached their height in the 1840s and 1850s. There were also symbolic conflicts, such as the decade long battles over temperance and the 'Blue Laws' or the enforcement of the sabbath. While Protestants did not necessarily hope to create utopias by prohibiting liquor and sanctifying the sabbath, the ability to enact such legislation sent a powerful symbolic message about who still controlled the United States. Between 1846 and 1861 thirteen states prohibited the sale of alcohol.

The Catholic issue was perennially explosive, producing large-scale outbreaks in addition to the ongoing gang fights. Sectarian violence was regularly excited by sexually oriented charges against Catholic clergy and nuns. The most notorious was the purported confessions (1836) of a supposed ex-nun named Maria Monk, who told of the murder and secret burial of children born to nuns. The hearing of confession was said to offer the ideal opportunity for priests to seduce nuns, but rectories and convents were believed as a matter of course to be linked by secret tunnels. Catholic churches and convents were believed to serve as storehouses for weapons, in preparation for a possible rising. Infuriated Protestants demanded to raid or search the premises, usually leading to street battles. In Charlestown, Massachusetts, a mob sacked an Ursuline convent in 1834 as part of a vain search for a secret infant graveyard, while 'anticonvent riots' were a fixture of antebellum life. In 1855 an attempt to free a (fictitious) imprisoned nun came close to causing fighting in Providence. Boston had further sectarian rioting in 1837. In Philadelphia in 1844, savage riots between Protestants and Catholics broke out following rumours of arms hoards in a local church: the scale of the confrontation is suggested by the use of cannon on both sides.

Antipopery spawned a number of political sects, fraternities and parties, such as the American Republican Party in 1841, which in 1845 changed its name to the 'Native Americans': hence this political strand in American history is generally termed 'nativist'. The super-patriotic American or 'Know-Nothing' Party opposed alien immigration and Catholic influence, and saw the slavery controversy as a distraction from the cause of true Americanism. The party enjoyed major successes after the 1852 election, which all but obliterated the Whigs and saw Democrat Franklin Pierce returned to the White House with Catholic support. Pierce earned further hostility with his controversial appointment of Catholics and foreigners to official positions, while in 1853 Protestant rage greeted an Italian archbishop whom the pope had sent to investigate the state of the Catholic Church in America. The 1854 elections were a triumph for the Know-Nothings, who gained control of Massachusetts.

The Know-Nothings operated in concert with the fearsome street gangs of the major cities, who used brutal intimidation to deter immigrants and Catholics from voting, but they also exercised a potent influence on mainstream politics. In 1854 the governor of Rhode Island responded to rumours of a Catholic putsch by forming a special armed militia, the membership of which was restricted to native-born white

Protestants. By the middle of the decade the Know-Nothings dominated legislatures throughout New England and elsewhere, and they again won widespread victories in the 1856 elections. In 1855 Know-Nothings fought pitched gun battles with German immigrants in Louisville.

Between 1830 and 1860 American cities were models of misgovernment and civic violence. The exact causes of the latter varied dramatically from year to year, but the overall result was a profound crisis of social order. Matters were aggravated both by the growth of the urban population, and by the enhanced size and partisan commitment of the electorate in the Jacksonian era. Urban elections were often the occasion for factional violence in the streets, as in Philadelphia and New York in 1834, and in several other cities in the worst of the Know-Nothing years. In 1856 Baltimore was the scene of battles orchestrated by 'numbers of the Newmarket Fire Company, and the Rip Raps and other political clubs'.

Crowds sometimes resorted to violence for explicitly economic reasons, as in 1835 when Baltimore erupted following the exposure of a major fraud that had broken the Bank of Maryland. Partly following British traditions, but also in line with American traditions of popular justice, the crowd sought to inflict vengeance on the perpetrators, which gave an element of class warfare to the outbreak. Perhaps twenty were killed on this occasion, a grave but far from unparalleled toll in these conflicts. Violence could erupt over apparently trivial causes. In 1849 New York was the scene of a riot caused by simultaneous performances of *Macbeth*, which symbolically pitted an American actor against the Englishman Macready. The mob took the side of the American, and decided that Macready represented foreign rule, aristocracy, and elite privilege. Thirty died on that occasion.

Such threatening outbreaks persuaded urban governments to consider what had once been dismissed as the irredeemably European solution of policing. The 1844 riots in Philadelphia were on a scale that made middle-class observers ask whether dictatorship might be preferable to such outrageous anarchy.

Over the next decade all the major cities acquired a uniformed force on the model established by Sir Robert Peel's London police. While the new units brought some improvements, religious and partisan struggles for control of the police may actually have caused a deterioration of civil order in the short term. The appointment of Catholic police officers in Boston and other cities was a bitterly contentious issue that paralleled more recent struggles to admit racial minorities to government positions. In New York City, two rival forces struggled for control – a state-sponsored unit backed by Republican nativists, and a city police favoured by Catholic Democrats – and the two literally battled in the streets in 1857. In 1871 New York was torn once more by a battle between Catholic Irish protesters and the militia.

REINVENTING RELIGION

During these years American cultural differences with Europe became more marked, as the American people began to explore the implications of their radically democratic society and the weakness of state or ecclesiastical controls on thought and behaviour. As in politics, the spirit of the time was marked by a sense of limitless opportunity and a thoroughgoing challenge to established or traditional elites, a Biblical casting down of the mighty from their seats. Radicalism was often expressed in religious forms, with the years around 1830 and 1848 being especially productive of new sects and enthusiastic movements

By the middle of the century the older and more staid religious denominations had been supplanted by democratic and enthusiastic groupings. American Christianity was dominated by three huge Protestant denominations: Baptist, Methodist and Presbyterian. The Congregationalist and Episcopalian Churches were firmly relegated to the second rank, where they were already being rivalled by denominations such as Lutheran and Catholic that had had only a limited presence in 1790. Also at this level was the Christian Church/Disciples of Christ, a new evangelical body with entirely American roots that had been forged in the successive fires of revivalism. By the end of the century the national predominance of Baptists and Methodists was still more marked.

While Protestant Christianity was in the ascendant, there were disturbing signs that the shifting ethnic balance might yet undermine this picture. There had only been 30 000 Catholics in the United States in 1790, half of whom were old-stock settlers in Maryland. John Carroll became the first American bishop in 1789, and by 1808 he was an archbishop with four suffragan sees. The Church's position was revolutionized by the mid-century Irish and German influx. By 1870, 7000 priests served seven million Catholics organized in fifty-five dioceses. By 1921 there were twenty thousand priests, twenty million Catholics and over a hundred dioceses.

However horrifying they might have been to the mainstream denominations of colonial days, Baptists and Methodists were both orthodox and acceptable compared with the members of the countless sects that flourished in the United States after the removal of official regulation on spiritual experimentation. The proliferation of heresy and religious innovation proceeded at all levels, intellectual and popular, elite and plebeian. In the more intellectual category was the attack on Trinitarian orthodoxy, and with it many of the once basic Christian doctrines about human sinfulness, the divinity of Christ and his work of atonement. Under the leadership of William Ellery Channing, Unitarianism spread rapidly from about 1820, especially in New England, where its ideas were summarized as involving 'the fatherhood of God, the brotherhood of man, and the neighbourhood of Boston'. Universalism asserted a belief that all would be saved. Both traditions exalted human reason and the potential for social improvement.

By the 1830s the intellectual world of New England was influenced by the new philosophical current known as Transcendentalism, an Americanized version of German Idealism. This found the only authentic reality in the world of the spirit, a realm that could be interpreted through reason. One of the most distinguished leaders of the movement in the United States was Ralph Waldo Emerson, a member of a long-established New England clerical family, who abandoned the Unitarian church in 1831. In 1836 his book *Nature* summarized his new Transcendentalist position, which he continued to expound over the next four decades, and from 1842 to 1844 he helped edit the magazine *The Dial*. Emersonian ideas stressed individual liberation, autarchy, self-sufficiency and self-government, and strenuously opposed social conformity. In the political sphere, Transcendentalist thought was progressive, leading its followers to support causes such as abolitionism and women's suffrage. Apart from Emerson, the best-known advocates of the position included Margaret Fuller, Henry David Thoreau and Bronson Alcott. Very different in origin but sharing a similar optimism was spiritualism, which in 1848 began an astonishing vogue that penetrated all classes of society. Its great popularity in part stemmed from its claims to provide scientific proof for doctrines about the continuation of human progress through the illusory veil of death.

Common in the religious thought of the time was a sense of utopianism, the idea that humanity could achieve a kind of perfection in this life, and not have to postpone that prospect until reaching heaven or the day of judgment. Perfectionist ideas were put into practice in a series of utopian communes and social experiments that sought to reform the human condition through new patterns of common property ownership, sexual relationships and (commonly) changes in diet. In the 1820s and 1830s these communities often followed the socialist models advocated by the European reformers Robert Owen and Charles Fourier. From the 1840s American prophets came to the fore. In 1841 a former Unitarian minister named George Ripley began a collective settlement at Brook Farm in Massachusetts, which attracted many Transcendentalists by its emphasis on simple living and a return to the soil. Still more radical was the colony established by John Humphrey Noyes on the principle that the Second Coming had already occurred, so that the saints should live according to new rules of sexual and social conduct. His group practised community of property and experimented with ideas of complex marriage and selective breeding. In 1847 the commune took up residence at Oneida in New York state, where it flourished into the 1880s. There were also several branch communities.

Among the most successful of the communal groups were the Shakers. They were founded in the 1770s but attained their greatest popularity between about 1830 and 1860, when perhaps 6000 members were scattered among 19 settlements. The sect was well known for its elaborate dance rituals, while among other remarkable features were belief in the total equality of the sexes and the observance of strict celibacy, on the ground that sin originated in the sexual act. Shakers adhered to other doctrines that would become the common currency of the radical fringe: they organized seances years before the rise of the spiritualist movement; their belief in spiritual healing foreshadowed the later ideas of Christian Science; and their ideas were based on the principle that the Second Coming was either at hand or had already occurred.

Other religious traditions of the day grew out of the belief that Biblical prophecies would be fulfilled both rapidly and literally, and that the United States would play a special role in God's prophetic plan. A well-known prophet in this respect was William Miller, a veteran of the War of 1812 whose theological studies convinced him that the end of the world was scheduled for 1843 (or possibly 1844). He attracted countless thousands of followers, a core of whom remained undismayed by the 'great disappointment' caused by the continuance of material existence. Apocalyptic notions survived in the new Adventist Churches, which took the lead in social and dietary experimentation. Millenarian ideas reached new intensity nationwide with the great revival of 1857.

The coming millennium and the Second Coming dominated Protestant thought, and often motivated political action. Rebellious slaves such as Nat Turner were fired by millenarian ideas, while in 1861 supporters of the federal union marched to war singing the popular song that linked the martyrdom of John Brown to a package of Biblical images about the end of the world and the coming of Christ. Revivalism promoted wide-ranging reforms in government and social services, instituting at least the goal of humane and reformative treatment in prisons, insane asylums and juvenile institutions, while both the temperance and the abolition movements were similarly inspired by visions of removing those structural injustices that impeded the coming of the earthly millennium and the reign of Christ on earth. The social reformers of this period usually shared a common intellectual baggage drawn from evangelical revivalism, millenarian thought and Temperance.

Millenarian enthusiasm was most marked in regions of western New York state that were so frequently licked by the fires of religious revival that they became known as the 'burned over district'. Not coincidentally, this region of religious excess was the primary base of one of the most remarkable religious movements of the age, the Church of Jesus Christ of Latter Day Saints, commonly known as the Mormons. The group was formed in the late 1820s in response to the angelic visions claimed by Joseph Smith, who announced that he had been mystically led to uncover the gold plates upon which were written the records of a Jewish civilization that had flourished in ancient America and had received visits from the risen Christ. The sources of this saga are controversial, but recent writers emphasize the many mystical influences on Smith and his circle, ideas drawn from occult, hermetic, Masonic and alchemical traditions, as well as folk magic and the lore of treasure hunting, curious notions that had survived in the religious underworld of southern New England.

Smith's new dispensation developed under the guidance of new revelations, upon the basis of which he and his followers began a westward migration in order to build a theocracy directed by a restored order of Biblical patriarchs, practicing the polygamy ordained in the Old Testament. Financial and other scandals resulted in several relocations, until the Mormon settlers built what would briefly become the largest city in the new state of Illinois, protected by a paramilitary force known as the 'Nauvoo Legion'. A virtual civil war ensued with local non-Mormons, 'Gentiles', and both Smith and his brother were assassinated in 1844. After a period of discord the sect found a new charismatic leader in Brigham Young, who led the Mormons on a further pilgrimage in quest of the new kingdom. In 1847 they settled in the Valley of the Salt Lake and founded the colony that would eventually become the state of Utah. By 1849 the Mormons were laying claim to a huge western territory of 'Deseret', including most of the southern Rockies. Sixty thousand Mormon converts reached Utah before the coming of the railway.

Though the Mormons undoubtedly attracted false accusations about their moral and sexual misconduct, their rule was indeed accompanied by violence against rivals and dissidents. For example, in 1857 Mormon paramilitaries allied with Indians to massacre over a hundred settlers travelling in a passing wagon train. Apart from this unsavoury quality, their practice of polygamy so appalled orthodox Christians that the Mormons were unable to achieve the legal status of a regular denomination until the end of the century, when a new revelation permitted the ending of the practice. Utah joined the union in 1896, but some polygamist families flourish to the present day.

Communitarianism, mysticism, occultism, food faddery, utopianism, sexual experiment, political radicalism: in so many ways the wave of experimentation in the 1840s closely resembled the circumstances of the radical 1960s. In both eras, there was a similar collapse of old assumptions and social guidelines, as well as a willingness to undertake daring ventures in such fundamental matters of life as family structure and relationships between races and within genders. Abolitionism serves as the closest parallel to the Vietnam War movement of the later period. Another point of similarity concerns women's issues, as the 1840s marked the origin of the continuous tradition of feminist politics in American life. In the fevered radical year of 1848, feminists Elizabeth Cady Stanton and Lucretia Mott called a women's rights convention at Seneca Falls, New York, which issued a declaration of principles asserting that 'all men and women are created equal'. Stanton thus placed the issue of women's political rights firmly in the political arena even before the Civil War.

CULTURE

Culturally, this was the period in which the United States declared its independence from Europe. The first American fiction writers to make a significant international mark were Washington Irving and James Fenimore Cooper, both of whom were active in the 1820s and 1830s. From about 1840 there was an outpouring of influential books, which constituted a distinctively American literature dealing with themes and settings peculiar to that country. Many of the works of that period would achieve classical status and attract European attention to what was obviously an emerging cultural power. Between 1845 and 1860, writers in their maturity included Herman Melville, Edgar Allan Poe, Nathaniel Hawthorne, Walt Whitman, Henry David Thoreau, Ralph Waldo Emerson, Henry Wadsworth Longfellow and others. Table 3.5 focuses on works regarded as having literary merit, but countless other works enjoyed bestseller status in their time, although they have since entered well-earned

Table 3.5   Major literary works published, 1845–60

1845	Frederick Douglass, *Narrative of the Life of Frederick Douglass*; Edgar Allen Poe, 'The Raven', and many other stories and poems
1846	Herman Melville, *Typee*
1847	Ralph Waldo Emerson, *Poems*; Longfellow, *Evangeline*
1849	Herman Melville, *Redburn*; Francis Parkman, *The Oregon Trail*; Henry David Thoreau, 'Civil Disobedience' (essay)
1850	Nathaniel Hawthorne, *The Scarlet Letter*; Ralph Waldo Emerson, *Representative Men*; Herman Melville, *White Jacket*
1851	Herman Melville, *Moby Dick*; Francis Parkman, *The Conspiracy of Pontiac*; Nathaniel Hawthorne, *House of the Seven Gables*
1852	Nathaniel Hawthorne, *Blithedale Romance*; Harriet Beecher Stowe, *Uncle Tom's Cabin*
1854	Henry David Thoreau, *Walden*
1855	Walt Whitman, *Leaves of Grass*; Henry Wadsworth Longfellow, *The Song of Hiawatha*
1857	Herman Melville, *The Confidence Man*
1858	Henry Wadsworth Longfellow, *The Courtship of Miles Standish*
1860	Nathaniel Hawthorne, *The Marble Faun*

oblivion, such as T. S. Arthur's then popular *Ten Nights in a Bar-Room* (1855).

The political crisis summoned forth several important books, including the autobiography of escaped slave Frederick Douglass, and Harriet Beecher Stowe's *Uncle Tom's Cabin*. Political satire may also provide the key to Herman Melville's enigmatic *Confidence Man*. Beyond fiction, Francis Parkman published some of the finest work on early American history. The new society had reached a stage of sufficient maturity to be fascinated by its roots, and to have no fear of exploring some of the darker aspects of that tradition: a point illustrated by the writings of Nathaniel Hawthorne on his Puritan ancestors. It was in these years that the statesman Daniel Webster ransacked early American history to construct a national mythology to reinforce the sorely threatened unity of the states: these were the years in which Plymouth Rock, Thanksgiving and Bunker Hill achieved the status of national ikons or rallying points.

America evolved a respectable tradition of painting as early as the 1770s, when Benjamin West, John Trumbull and John Singleton Copley had largely followed English examples in portraits and grand treatments of historical and political themes. By the 1820s an innovative American sensibility had emerged, expressed most frankly in the attitude towards landscape painting. Artists such as Thomas Cole were determined to explore American landscapes, rather than resorting to tired depictions of an imaginary Italy they had probably never seen. The 'Hudson River School' specialized in paintings of virgin landscape, usually fading off into apparently limitless space, these settings commonly being drawn from New York or New England. By the middle of the century, westward expansion had allowed American painters to develop a 'Rocky Mountain School', which depicted the radically different landscapes of that area, with the Grand Canyon as a favoured theme. In the 1840s George Caleb Bingham painted frontier themes such as fur traders and backwoods politicians. George Catlin painted the different American Indian tribes, perhaps sensing that his collection would soon gain great historical value as a portrait of a world that would soon be extinct. By the Civil War years American painting had massively diversified in theme and approach, and work of real quality was being done. This new self-confidence is best represented by Winslow Homer, who in the 1860s emerged as an innovative stylist whose work compare well with the best being produced in contemporary France.

PIONEERS: WESTWARD EXPANSION

While American society was developing, the scope of the new nation was growing dramatically. Around 1840 it seemed that the Mississippi would remain a natural western frontier, at least during the long phase in which Americans absorbed their new lands. While ultimately the United States would stretch to the Pacific, there was no reason to doubt Jefferson's estimate that subduing the whole continent might take several centuries. In 1845 there were perhaps 20 000 white Americans living west of the Mississippi, and the great plains were generally viewed as more or less permanent Indian territory, the 'Great American Desert'. Most white activity was focused not on settlement but on the fur trade, and catering to the European fad for beaverskin hats. In reality a new and still more explosive phase of westward expansion was about to begin. The annexation and settlement of the entire west were well under way before the Civil War, when there were already two American states with Pacific coasts. By 1870 the white population of the west was approaching one million, and it had reached four million by the mid 1890s. Mushrooming growth was indicated by the admission of new states (Table 3.6), which showed that not only had territory been acquired, but it had been settled, at least in rudimentary form. The number of states in the union almost doubled between 1815 and 1865.

By the 1830s much of the most attractive mid-western land had already been claimed, leaving a growing number of land-hungry settlers, while expansion of the southern plantations was tending to drive out small farmers. The potential for agricultural expansion was also massively enhanced by new technology, especially the mechanical reaper pioneered by Cyrus McCormick in the 1830s. Attention now turned to Missouri and Arkansas, and the city of St Louis became the gateway to the central plains. Few were prepared to risk the immense dangers of crossing the American heartland to reach the far west, at least until 1843 when John C. Fremont

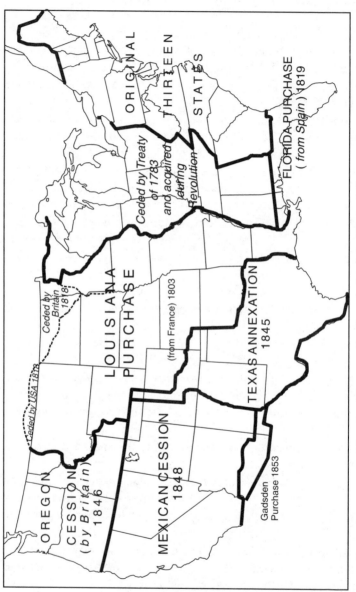

Map 5. The westward growth of the United States

Table 3.6   States admitted to the Union, 1836–64

	Year of Admission	Modern capital
Arkansas	1836	Little Rock
Michigan	1837	Lansing
Florida	1845	Tallahassee
Texas	1845	Austin
Iowa	1846	Des Moines
Wisconsin	1848	Madison
California	1850	Sacramento
Minnesota	1858	St. Paul
Oregon	1859	Salem
Kansas	1861	Topeka
West Virginia	1863	Charleston
Nevada	1864	Carson City

published a book describing how wagon trains might safely cross the Rockies, using the old trappers' route through Wyoming's South Pass. Once through the mountains, the emigrants would have their pick of the richest lands of California and Oregon Territory. From that time the Oregon, Santa Fe and California trails became key highways for westward migration, and settlers flooded into areas such as Oregon's Willamette Valley. By 1850 there were 13 000 non-Indians in the Oregon territory alone. Meanwhile the Mormons were building their kingdom in Utah. Between 1841 and 1867, 350 000 Americans migrated along the western wagon roads.

In 1845 the *Democratic Review* spoke of America's 'manifest destiny' to 'overspread the Continent allotted by providence for the free development of our yearly multiplying millions'. Divine guidance became evident in the next three years, with a series of land acquisitions that gave a legal framework for growth. The United States' chief competitor in the west was Mexico, which had earned its independence from Spain in 1821. By the 1820s Mexico's northern territory of Texas had settled by Anglo-Americans, who in 1835 launched a full-scale revolution. The Texan rebel forces were defeated and massacred at the battles of the Alamo and Goliad, but rebel victory at San Jacinto in April 1836 made Texas an independent republic. After repeated requests, Texas entered the American union as a state in 1845. The loss of this rich area stirred Mexican suspicions of their US neighbour, and their fears proved justified when the US administration announced plans to enforce a Texan boundary on the Rio Grande, far south of the traditional frontier. A US–Mexican war broke out in 1846, to great popular enthusiasm in the United States, which raised an armed force some 60 000 strong. US forces occupied New Mexico and Americans declared the creation of a rebel republic in California. As regular forces pushed into the heart of Mexico, atrocities multiplied on both sides. Mexico City fell in September 1847. By the Treaty of Guadalupe Hidalgo (1848), the United States acquired the territories that ultimately became the states of Arizona, New Mexico, Nevada, Utah and California. In 1853 the Gadsden Purchase acquired a further strip of border land from Mexico.

The other major revisions occurred after border tensions with Britain came close to causing all-out war in 1845. The two nations shared a long and ill-defined border, and boundaries were decided only gradually. Hostilities were aggravated by American sympathy for Canadian democratic movements, which reached dangerous proportions during the Canadian rebellion of 1837, and President Polk asserted the rights of 'the people of *this continent* alone . . . to decide their own destiny'. Maine and New Brunswick did not finally determine their borders until the British and American governments signed the Ashburton Treaty in 1842.

This was a trivial issue compared with the vast and profitable Pacific north-western region, which Britain and the United States had agreed to share under agreements signed in 1818 and 1827. In 1844 American expansionists demanded the cession of most of the later British Columbia, and a border at the latitude of 54° 40′ north: 'fifty-four forty or fight'. Britain in turn wanted a boundary on the Columbia river, giving it the modern state of Washington. Disputes were resolved by a treaty signed in 1846, which divided the claims at the 49th parallel. The US had now acquired something very close to the national boundaries it would retain until the 1950s, and the scale of these land acquisitions was staggering. Texas alone expanded the area of the United States by almost 400 000 square miles. The Oregon territory brought in another 280 000 the following year, while the Mexican cession added 530 000. Between 1845 and 1848 the size of the United States was increased by 1.2 million square miles, an area five times larger than France.

The already voracious appetite for new land was increased still further by the realization that the west was rich in minerals. In 1848, even before California had been formally acquired from Mexico, an American settler reported the discovery of gold at Sutter's sawmill in the foothills of the Sierra Nevada mountains. This signalled the beginning of an influx of people that in just twelve years would swell the non-Indian population of the territory from 14 000 to 380 000. California achieved statehood in 1850, by which point the brand new town of San Francisco had become a major western city. In 1852, Californian gold production peaked at four million ounces.

Between 1858 and 1875 successive rushes for gold and silver provided a massive impetus to western settlement, and the opening of many regions can be dated from the first discovery (or even rumour) of precious metals. After California, this is what occurred with the discovery of Nevada's vast Comstock lode in 1859, containing silver ore worth some $400 million. Colorado owed its foundation to the Pikes Peak gold rush of 1858–59, and subsequent silver discoveries to the end of the century. There were 100 000 settlers by the end of 1859, and the city of Denver was incorporated in 1861. Gold or silver fever infected Oregon in 1860, Montana in 1864 and the Dakota territory in the early 1870s. Often, exploration for precious metals would accidentally find immense resources of other minerals, for instance the copper found in Montana in the 1880s, and the zinc and lead of Idaho.

Each 'rush' tended to follow a broadly similar pattern, with wide-ranging effects on the given region. As large numbers of prospectors and miners were drawn in, so were the traders, business people and rogues who sought to serve or rob them. The white presence was reflected in the growth of towns and cities such as San Francisco, Denver and Portland, Oregon, which all emerged as major regional centres. Even by the minimal standards of contemporary urban America, such communities had little or no effective government, and such law and order as did exist was established at the rough and ready hands of vigilante movements. These were particularly active in San Francisco in the 1850s. On the other hand, boomtowns could easily bust when their mineral prosperity collapsed, a fate suggested by the many ghost towns that littered Nevada after the 'big bonanza' ended in 1878. Virginia City is the best remembered, a city of 30 000 people in the mid 1870s, that all but died over the succeeding decades. These rapid population shifts could also have dramatic political consequences. In 1853, for instance, the still new Oregon territory was subdivided to take account of the interests of new settlers concentrated around Puget Sound, giving rise to the territory (and later state) of Washington. A gold rush resulted in a further subdivision in 1863 and the creation of the new Idaho territory.

Improved technology brought the new cities and states of the west into ever-closer contact with the more developed regions of the east. In 1840 news could take five months to cross the continent. In 1860 the Pony Express provided an efficient system of relay riders, but this was almost immediately made obsolete by the coming of the transcontinental telegraph in 1861. From 1858 a transcontinental stagecoach line united St Louis with San Francisco. In 1862 President Lincoln signed a Pacific Railroad Act, under which railways would be built from east and west with the aim of linking the transportation systems of the entire Continent. Between 1865 and 1869 the Central Pacific Railroad proceeded east from Sacramento while the Union Pacific built west from Omaha. This was an epic endeavour, involving brilliant adaptation to apparently impossible conditions and the heroic labour of huge armies of immigrant labour: Irish in the East, Chinese in the west. In May 1869 the two lines met at Promontory Summit in Utah, and the states were united as never before.

RED AND WHITE

The headlong dash to build a continental empire was accomplished with little consideration for the existing residents, whether Mexican or Native American. As the area of white settlement grew, Americans of European descent were brought into contact with native groups who had hitherto avoided the blessings of civilization, and this contact was generally disastrous for the latter population.

While events of the 1820s and 1830s were catastrophic for the Indian populations of the mid-west, this seemed to have little relevance for the peoples of the great plains, for whom geography had surely provided an isolation that would keep them safe for centuries. However the social explosion of the 1840s created obvious tensions, as migrants and prospectors pushed forward into Indian lands. In 1851 tribal leaders from the northern plains were convened to sign a treaty at Fort Laramie, at which they agreed to confine their activities to certain areas. Though the lands acknowledged as tribal were vast, this event can retrospectively be seen to mark the beginnings of the reservation system on the plains. Enforcement was virtually impossible, and conflicts with settlers grew apace. Additional soldiers were brought in to keep the peace, and skirmishes erupted. The year 1854 saw battles of unprecedented severity, as the US Army began a pattern of taking revenge on recalcitrant tribes by sacking their villages. Often the communities punished were not even connected to the original provocation.

Matters deteriorated sharply with the Civil War, when regular soldiers were withdrawn and local militias rose up in their place. The 1860s were particularly violent in Arizona and New Mexico, where the tribes involved were the Apache and the Navajo. In 1862 abuses by reservation agents provoked a rising among the Eastern Lakota/Sioux of Southern Minnesota. Several hundred white settlers were massacred, in incidents accompanied by rape and the most extreme forms of torture and mutilation. This conflict poisoned white–Indian relations for a generation, and encouraged whites to take their revenge in like form against native villages. In 1864 the massacre of the population of a Cheyenne settlement at Sand Creek in Colorado was quite as brutal as anything perpetrated by the Lakota 'savages'.

SLAVERY

The vast new lands understandably encouraged Americans to believe in the apparently limitless resources of their new country. In the short term, however, westwards expansion threatened the destabilization of American political life, and of the hard-won compromises reflected in the constitution. Briefly, the new western lands would one day be organized as states, and when they were they might provide sufficient Congressional votes to abolish slavery by constitutional amendment.

Though slavery was obviously a southern characteristic, it by no means extended throughout southern society. Some of the concentrations of slaves could be enormous: in the 1850s, Colonel J. A. S. Acklen of Louisiana owned 700 slaves and 20 000 acres organized into six plantations and an elaborate hierarchy. As Kenneth M. Stampp remarks, such figures 'were central figures in the antebellum plantation legend', but they were also untypical.[3] Of six million whites in the southern states in 1850, only 347 000 owned slaves, and the vast majority of these owned just a few. Only 12 per cent of slave owners claimed twenty or more slaves, and about half the proprietors owned less than five. But slavery dominated some regions of the south, where there developed an advanced form of plantation agriculture closely tied to the British economic system in a classic colonial model.

As the abolitionists argued, slavery was like an addiction in that it never seemed sufficient for a given region to have just a few slaves. Where the system existed, it led to the formation of large bodies of slaves in a plantation or even an industrial economy. In no less than eight states, slaves comprised 30 per cent or more of the total population. Slaves approached or achieved numerical parity with the free population in South Carolina, Louisiana, Mississippi, Florida and Alabama, the core of what later became known as the Black Belt. The largest concentrations of slaves were as shown in Table 3.7.

Table 3.7   Slaves as proportion of the whole population, 1850

State	Percentage of slaves
South Carolina	58
Mississippi	51
Louisiana	47
Florida	45
Alabama	44
Georgia	42
North Carolina	33
Virginia	33
Texas	27
Tennessee	24
Arkansas	22
Kentucky	21
Missouri	13

Of the states listed here, all but Kentucky and Missouri joined the Confederacy in 1860–61

In addition to the slaves, there was a large number of free black and mixed-race people. By 1850 there were some 440 000 free people of colour, who constituted a significant share of the population of several northern and border states. Maryland had 75 000 free blacks, Virginia 54 000, Pennsylvania 53 000, and New York 49 000. It took no great prophetic skill to realize that if freed slaves were given political rights, then blacks would constitute a formidable electoral entity in perhaps a dozen states, at least five of which were likely find themselves under black political rule. Apart from the most radical abolitionists, few could contemplate such a far-reaching step.

Slavery became the distinctive badge that demarcated two rival regions, and from the 1820s the different areas acquired sharply different characters. As the northern states industrialized, they also became far more urbanized than the south, and were more likely to attract immigrants that gave them a far greater ethnic and social diversity. Economic schism led to political conflict. Anxious to promote domestic manufactures, the northern states generally favoured high tariffs to deter foreign and especially British industrial imports. This was anathema to the southern cotton lords, who depended on British mills as their chief market and benefited from the importation of cheap food and finished goods.

Tariffs occasionally rivalled slavery as an interstate grievance, and in 1828 southern leaders were appalled at a new tariff that stood to benefit New England at their expense. In 1830 there was a portentous public debate between northern Senator Daniel Webster and South Carolina Senator Robert Y. Hayne, the latter warning that the 'American System' was part of a war against the south, which was being treated much as England treated Ireland. In response Webster stressed the highest goals of national unity, making the largely novel argument that the federal union was indissoluble and dreading the day when the land might be 'rent with civil feuds or drenched, it may be, in fraternal blood'. By 1832 Vice President John C. Calhoun was advocating the extreme states'-rights doctrine that individual states could 'nullify' laws they deemed unconstitutional, and South Carolina shortly put this into practice by refusing to enforce the new tariff, even threatening secession. President Jackson responded with a law that allowed him to exert federal authority through the use of force if necessary, and asserting the principles of national unity in words akin to Webster's: 'Disunion by armed force is treason'. A compromise was reached, but the president later voiced his regret that he had not pressed the issue to the point where he could have had Calhoun hanged for treason.

ABOLITIONISM

Antislavery sentiment had grown steadily in the late eighteenth century through the work of religious bodies such as the Quakers. In the 1830s a new radical movement arose following the recognition that the slave system was not going to vanish simply of its own accord. The new abolitionists demanded instant rather than gradual reform, which could only be accomplished through federal action. In 1831 William Lloyd Garrison founded the newspaper *The Liberator*, with heavy support from free blacks. In the following decade black abolitionists emerged as a powerful force in their own right, as when Frederick Douglass founded the paper *North Star* in 1847. In 1839 Theodore Dwight Weld and Angelina Grimke published the book *Slavery As It Is*, which catalogued for a northern audience the worst horrors of the system.

Progress in gaining public support was slow, and racial antipathy in the north accelerated as former slaves settled in free communities in northern cities. Such areas were repeatedly targeted by the white mobs, as in Providence in 1831. A decade later rioters expelled the black population of Cincinnati, forcing them to seek homes elsewhere (they ultimately reached Canada). Anti-black sentiment is also suggested by the deep hostility to the abolition movement in communities with a southern population, or economically tied to the south. Abolitionists were regularly mobbed in the 1830s, and in 1837 an antislavery newspaper editor was lynched in Illinois. In New York, properties and churches belonging to abolitionists and blacks were attacked in July 1834. The headquarters of the movement in Philadelphia were burned in 1838.

Radical views gained new support in the climate of far-reaching social reform in the 1840s, when abolitionism became a basic tenet of progressive opinion. Antislavery activism was focused by the practical deeds of northerners, white and black, who assisted fugitive slaves to escape to new lives on the free soil of Canada, and a whole opposition subculture developed around this 'underground railroad'. Northern states became reluctant to help southern slavemasters and their employees to pursue their quite legal right to recapture escaped slaves, giving rise to dramatic challenges to legality. As in the 1760s, dissidents viewed the law and its enforcers as tools of tyranny, against whom opposition was a moral imperative. Abolitionist extremists freely exploited this view and spoke of the coming Second American Revolution. Garrison was drawing the logical consequence of his principles when he urged that the free and slave regions should divorce upon the most amicable basis now possible, through northern secession if need be. The slave issue caused tremors among the various religious denominations, several of which split apart on the issue in the mid-1840s. Presbyterians, Methodists and Baptists were all riven over the question of whether clergy or laity in good standing could continue to hold slaves. In most cases the northern and southern factions reunited after the Civil War, but the southern Baptists have retained their separate identity to the present day.

Abolitionism was a nightmare to southerners, for whom slavery was becoming not merely a source of profit, but a symbolic badge that differentiated them from the vulgar masses of the urban society of the north. From about 1830 also, the practical fact of slavery was justified by scientific theories that resorted to arguments of biological and historical necessity. To say the least, attitudes were hardening on both sides.

The survival of slavery was assured as long as it remained a matter for the states themselves, which would respect regional autonomy, but the real danger lay in the workings of the federal government. The constitution was deliberately intended to make it difficult for any one region or grouping to trample on the interests of a minority, and southerners were well aware of the danger that an early target of such an intrusive majority might be their own 'peculiar institution' of slavery. The constitution as it stood actually reinforced slavery through the strict defence of property rights and the enforcement of contractual obligations. However the constitution could be amended in any way the American public wished, even to abolish slavery altogether. Amendments had to be proposed on the recommendation of two thirds of both houses of Congress, or two thirds of the states, and the proposal would then require ratification of three quarters of the states. It was meant to be a difficult process, and in 1800 or 1810 it was unthinkable that free states would ever achieve a sufficient majority to overwhelm the slave states. But how long could this pattern prevail? The free states carved out of the west were soon likely to exceed the slave regions, probably by a majority sufficient to amend the constitution.

This perception had a major impact on US foreign policy, as southerners and their allies now saw excellent reasons to expand southwards, into lands presently held by Mexico. If annexed, these new areas would fall south of the Missouri Compromise line that delineated slave and free areas, and could thus expand the realm of slavery. The great success of this policy came in the mid–1840s. Texas and Florida were admitted as slave states, while the war with Mexico raised hopes of a US empire pushing into Central America. For this reason the Mexican adventure was bitterly criticized by northern reformers and abolitionists, whose support grew

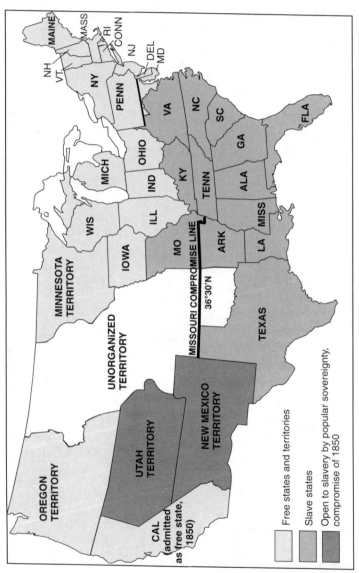

Map 6.   The compromise of 1850

once the initial patriotic fervour had subsided. There were even signs that the US government or private interests might be scheming to annex as slave territory the nations of Cuba (1854) and Nicaragua (1856).

These hopes proved illusory. During the Mexican war, Congressman David Wilmot introduced a contentious 'proviso', demanding the exclusion of slavery from any territories annexed in the war, and after long debate this was the *de facto* outcome of the controversy. Apart from Texas, virtually all the new territories were likely to be free, as indeed were all five states admitted between 1846 and 1859.

THE CRISIS OF 1848–60

The years from 1835 to 1860 are known as the 'antebellum' or prewar period, and the term well reflects the sense of irrepressible conflict that pervaded political life during these years. After the Mexican war, each new gain in the west further destabilized the regional balance. As John C. Calhoun remarked, Mexico was the 'forbidden fruit' for the American *status quo*, with 'political death' the penalty of eating it. The crucial issue now concerned the western territories, where the Missouri Compromise provided a clearly defined northern boundary for the institution of slavery. In the 1850s this rule was challenged by new arrangements that threatened to permit unlimited expansion. In this new phase of the crisis, the issue was less the elimination of slavery in its southern heartland, than its containment in the rest of the nation.

In 1849 California sought admission to the union as a free state, although most of its territory lay to the south of the Missouri Compromise line. The ensuing debate involved such oratorical titans of the age as Daniel Webster, Henry Clay and John C. Calhoun, whose statements showed the near-impossibility of achieving a long-term reconciliation. The scope of the debate had shifted from the specifics of the constitution to principles of divine law and natural justice, an intellectual territory where discussion is ultimately impossible.

California's statehood was granted, but only as part of a 'Compromise of 1850', under which the territories of Utah and New Mexico could become free or slave states as they chose. The south also received recognition of one of its greatest concerns, the difficulty of persuading northern jurisdictions to assist in the recapture of fleeing slaves. The solution was found in the invocation of federal power. Under a new Fugitive Slave Law, the slave status of an accused black was tried before a federal commissioner, without any of the rights normally involved in the trial of a free individual, so that race effectively predetermined guilt. Moreover all citizens were legally forbidden to assist the escape or rescue of a slave in flight.

A more painful assault on northern sensibilities was scarcely imaginable. In 1851 there were several incidents where northern crowds physically interfered to save fugitives from the hands of slave catchers, or even US officials. At Christiana in Pennsylvania, 38 were indicted for a riot in which a slave owner was killed while trying to reclaim a slave, but all were acquitted. Outrage was further stirred in 1852 by the furore over Harriet Beecher Stowe's novel *Uncle Tom's Cabin*, which depicted the brutalities of slavery and indicated the moral necessity to resist federal law in this area. In 1854 William Lloyd Garrison publicly burned a copy of the US constitution before a cheering crowd in Massachusetts, symbolically renouncing a government in the hands of the slave power.

In 1853 the issue was further complicated by the politics of transportation. A continental railway was seen as inevitable, but there was controversy between advocates of northern and southern routes, which would benefit different sections of the country. The northern route was favoured by key Democratic

Senator Stephen A. Douglas, whose scheme depended upon organizing the Kansas and Nebraska territories, which had been carved out of 'permanent' Indian territory. In order to win southern political support, Douglas's Kansas–Nebraska Act resolved that in these lands the slavery issue would be resolved by popular sovereignty. This now made slavery legally possible north of the Missouri Compromise line, and potentially opened the whole west to pro-slave interests.

'Popular sovereignty' forced both pro- and antislavery factions to secure local majorities who could determine the character of the new state of Kansas. By the mid 1850s, settlers of both opinions were avidly claiming their lands, and the ensuing conflicts constituted a virtual civil war, as when proslavery forces raided and burned the free-soil town of Lawrence. Atrocities were common. The free-soil activists or jayhawkers included extremists such as John Brown, who would shortly earn poetic immortality through martyrdom. In 1856 Brown was central to the Pottawattomie Massacre, when five proslavery leaders were executed for the murder of five free-soilers. By 1861 two hundred had died in guerrilla fighting. Violence even reached the floor of the US Senate, where in 1856 a militant southern congressman viciously beat Massachusetts Senator Charles Sumner with a cane in retaliation for his incendiary pamphlet 'The Crime Against Kansas'.

No less fierce than the physical battles of 'bleeding Kansas' were the legal struggles that would ultimately decide the future of slavery. For years abolitionists had tried to force the federal courts to define the legal position of slavery in the territories, and one such case eventually reached the US Supreme Court. At issue in 1857 was the status of Dred Scott, a Missouri slave who had been taken to the free lands of Illinois and Minnesota, the latter being part of the territory where slavery was banned by the Missouri Compromise. Was he free, and therefore exempt from later sale as a chattel? The Supreme Court could have taken several courses in this issue. It might have resolved either for or against Scott, addressing the specific legal questions of the case without entering into the constitutional matters involved. However the court chose the worst course possible, not merely denying Scott's claim to freedom, but arguing that Congress had no right to regulate or forbid slavery in the territories. As a non-citizen, Scott had no right to sue in court. Finally, blacks as a whole were dismissed as a degraded race, with no inherent rights beyond what whites chose to grant. This decision explicitly repealed the Missouri Compromise, and threatened to open the whole territorial west to violence as severe as that prevailing in Kansas.

Though stimulated by genuine moral outrage, abolitionist sentiment was now buttressed by real self-interest. If the slave system was so savage and so likely to drive its subjects to escape to the north, would that not presumably mean the entire United States would soon have a free black population, competing for jobs and presumably at lower wages? Moreover free northern labour was deeply concerned that southern slave owners might venture from plantation agriculture to the creation of slave mines or ironworks, producing at costs so low that no free concern could compete. The expansion of slavery threatened the high-wage economy upon which northern society was based and made it so attractive to European migration. In the west the potential spread of plantations made the territories unattractive to free farmers.

The growing crisis could not fail to have an impact on party politics. Already in 1848 a 'Free Soil' ticket had given former President Martin Van Buren more than 10 per cent of the popular vote in his bid to return to office. The Compromise of 1850 had strained the Whig Party, pitting the moderate faction of President Millard Fillmore against abolitionist Senator William H. Seward. Divisions caused the Whigs to suffer electoral disaster in 1852. The Kansas–Nebraska Act provoked antislavery militants to desert the existing parties to form a new grouping, which became the Republican Party. Though some former Democrats were present, by far the greatest damage was done to the Whigs, which soon ceased to exist as an organized group. While the party perished, large portions of its ideology survived into the new Republican Party through former adherents, including Abraham Lincoln himself. In addition to that of the Whigs, the Republicans also gained the support of many former Know Nothings, and a solid following of farmers and artisans attracted by the rhetoric of 'free labour'.

In 1856 Republican presidential candidate John C. Fremont heavily outpolled the Whig candidate but lost to the Democrat James Buchanan. Nonetheless it was a portent for future years that the combined strength of Whigs and Republicans exceeded that of the Democrats. The danger to Democratic power swelled during 1857, with a financial crisis that reverberated throughout the economy, and the impact of the Dred Scott decision. Meanwhile a nationwide religious revival fired evangelical and abolitionist sentiment. In 1858 the Democratic hero Stephen Douglas was challenged by Republican Abraham Lincoln in a contest for the Illinois Senate seat, and the two engaged in a critical and nationally publicized debate. Douglas attempted to portray Lincoln as a crazed radical whose election would mean war against the south and subversion of the Supreme Court; in return Lincoln forced his opponent to define his position on the territories in terms that lost him support in the south. Overall Lincoln reinforced the moral position of the Republicans, while widening the schism among the Democrats.

As the national elections approached, the likelihood of civil disorder grew. The threat became a certainty through the actions of John Brown, who decided to provoke a crisis by directly attacking slavery in its southern strongholds. With the support of northern abolitionists, he developed a bizarre scheme to establish liberated zones in the hills of western Virginia, and in October 1859 he led eighteen followers against the federal arsenal at Harper's Ferry, in what is now West Virginia. Though he never had any real prospect of inciting and arming a slave insurrection, his subsequent trial and execution in December 1859 gave the abolitionist cause an invaluable martyr and a rallying point. He also confirmed the worst southern fears of what they might expect at the hands of an abolitionist federal government. During 1860 these concerns were manifested in mob attacks on suspected abolitionists and organized boycotts against northern firms and goods. In Texas, fears of abolitionist plotting and slave revolt led to a general panic and a vigilante outbreak that resulted in the death of a hundred suspected dissidents.

Southern fears were decisive in the electoral politics of 1860. At the Democratic Party convention the south refused to accept the candidacy of Stephen Douglas, who they saw as too accommodating on slavery, choosing instead the extremist John C. Breckinridge. The split all but ensured a Republican victory. Hoping to avoid a national catastrophe, some former Whigs and Know-Nothings allied in a new 'Constitutional Union' Party, but it could not alter the result. In the event, Lincoln's Republican ticket received under 40 per cent of the 4.7 million votes cast, compared with over 47 per cent for the two Democratic candidates combined. While the Republicans could not claim a triumph in the popular ballot, they had 59 per cent of the electoral vote, which was ample to seat Lincoln in the White House.

Lincoln was by no means as dogmatic on slavery issues as many Republican leaders, to the point that his conciliatory remarks on the subject have caused real embarrassment to his countless later admirers. In 1858, he declared himself implacably opposed to 'the social and political equality of the white and black races . . . [to] making voters or jurors of Negroes . . . nor to intermarry with white people'. In 1862 he famously wrote that his overarching goal was to save the union, and if that could be done by freeing some, all or none of the slaves, he would do it: 'What I do about slavery and the coloured race, I do because it helps to save this union'. These subtleties were lost on the southern leaders, who believed they faced a simple choice between secession and destruction. Ultimately, they obtained both.

Much has been written about the causes of the civil war, but use of the word 'cause' provides a misleading emphasis. The real question is not why the union fell apart, but how this event was so long avoided, and why particular states seceded rather than others. In addition, why should the departure of some states be seen as an act of treason or war, rather than merely a reconfiguration of an admittedly temporary union? In both issues, slavery provided the decisive catalyst – as a cherished symbol of the way of life of one region but an abomination for the other: absolute principles were now in collision. The events of the 1850s appeared to show that slavery could not be confined to one area, and must either spread across the nation – or cease to exist altogether. That the problem was now phrased in such stark either-or terms goes far towards explaining why seven decades of constitutional union now began to disintegrate.

THE CIVIL WAR, 1861–65

The process of disunion was begun by the secession of South Carolina in December 1860. Effective federal action was delayed by the lengthy lame-duck presidency, in which the Buchanan administration – defeated in the November election by Abraham Lincoln – could do little and Lincoln was not due to take office until the following March. By the start of February six more states had seceded, including Florida, Georgia, Alabama, Mississippi, Louisiana and Texas, and the rebellious governments formed a new Confederate States of America, complete with its own president, Jefferson Davis. Even so, war was not quite inevitable until April, when Confederate troops fired upon the US flag at Fort Sumter in Charleston harbour. Within days Lincoln had called for troops and ordered a blockade of the south. Thereafter war was in progress. In May the scope of the conflict widened still further with the secession of North Carolina, Tennessee, Arkansas and, most critically, Virginia, which joined only

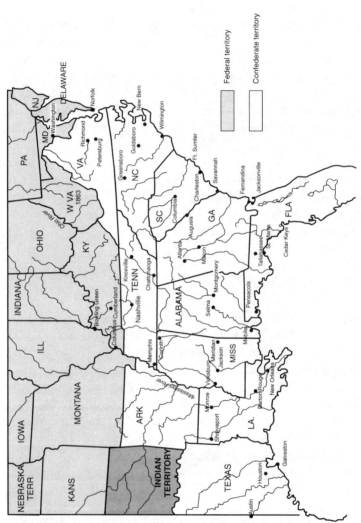

Map 7. The Confederacy at the close of 1861

after an intense legislative debate resulted in a majority of 85 to 55 for withdrawal. With the adherence of Virginia, the Confederacy now moved its capital to the city of Richmond.

By mid 1861 war fever was evident in both Union and Confederate territories, and neither side initially had difficulty in securing enough volunteers to form large-scale armed forces. By the end of the year the Confederate armed forces had some 600 000 volunteers. Enthusiasm was encouraged by the common sentiment that this could not be anything other than a brief war, to be decided perhaps by one giant confrontation. Such hopes were dashed by the first major engagement of the war, at Manassas in Virginia in July 1861. The Confederates put their Union foes to flight in this 1st Battle of Bull Run. This confirmed that the United States was facing no mere popular rebellion, but a full-scale war against a vast national entity, which would have to be systematically crushed.

Despite initial patriotic surges on both sides of the new frontier, neither of the new American nations was as united as it would like to claim. The loyalty of several border states was difficult to predict. It was by no means obvious which of the border states would eventually join the Confederacy, while the north faced secessionist rumblings from several other border states, including Kentucky, Maryland, Missouri and Delaware. Proconfederate factions in Missouri and Kentucky even sent representatives to the Confederate Congress. Maryland was critical, because if it withdrew from the Union, then Washington DC would find itself isolated in rebel territory, so secessionist advocates there were suppressed with a heavy hand. During 1861 it was an urgent priority for the Union to prevent the loss of further border regions.

The Confederacy also had centres of discontent, usually the more mountainous regions far removed from plantation agriculture, regions where slaves if present at all were engaged in domestic or farm service. The 'Constitutional Union' presidential candidate had won many counties throughout Virginia, North Carolina, Tennessee and Georgia, as well as a long snake of territories along the Mississippi river. There was Unionist sentiment through the Appalachian uplands of North Carolina, while the western upland counties of Virginia seceded to join the Unionist side in June 1861, and formed the state of West Virginia in 1863. In addition, both sides included ethnic and religious minorities who saw little purpose in the war, for which they felt they were being asked to pay a disproportionately heavy price. In the north the Irish, who constituted so large a part of the urban and industrial population, often demonstrated resentment at the burden of conscription.

Military strategy in the war was conditioned by the different economic structure of the two regions and their different international orientation. The north was vastly superior in population and industrial resources, with over three times the number of white men of military age. The north also retained control of the US Navy, laying the foundations for a natural 'anaconda' strategy of crushing the south by blockade while naval forces took vulnerable ports and coastal regions. One land army would press overland to split the Confederacy in two by opening the Mississippi route, and another force would invade Tennessee. A third was to march on the rebel capital of Richmond. It was a reasonable strategy, and one that ultimately worked, but its success was not self-evident. A northern campaign of attrition ran the risk of provoking war weariness in the north before southern willpower collapsed, and there was also a lively peace party in the north. The more extreme prosouthern elements were known as 'Copperheads', from the liberty pennies they wore as symbols. In a sense the south could win the war merely by not losing obviously or decisively, while the north would lose if it failed to win swiftly.

Foreign policy was critical. The ruling circles of England felt sympathy for the aristocratic ethos of the south, and moreover Britain needed southern cotton for its textile mills. France and Russia had no interest in promoting a strong United States, which could challenge their imperial designs, and there was a dangerous prospect of a long war being halted by 'humanitarian' intervention by the great powers, which would in effect secure southern independence. The naval danger was especially acute, as British and French ships could easily break the northern blockade if occasion arose. Conversely the European states were hampered by democratic and radical sentiment for the Union. For the first two years of the war, both north and south had to gear their policies to provoking or restraining such foreign intervention, which often appeared perilously close. In 1861 a Union warship seized two Confederate envoys from the British warship *Trent*, an insult to the British flag that technically amounted to an act of war. Diplomatic niceties were also ignored by the European powers, who permitted the Confederates to build warships and commerce raiders on their territory, most notoriously the *Alabama*, which caused havoc to US shipping before it was finally sunk in 1864.

Perhaps the most dangerous year for the union was 1862. Throughout the winter of 1861–62, northern efforts were concentrated on the creation of a mighty army of the Potomac some 150 000 strong, under the command of General George McClellan. McClellan's Napoleonic self-promotion was reflected in the naming of army formations after particular rivers, on the model of the French Army of the Rhine. His mission was relatively straightforward: to lead his army to an amphibious landing in the peninsula east of Richmond, and to proceed up the James and York Rivers to take the Confederate capital, following a suitably Napoleonic 'Peninsular Campaign'. He duly landed in March, but his progress thereafter was abysmally slow and prone to halting at the merest hint of enemy action. The general's tendency vastly to overestimate Confederate military strength indicated either extreme timidity or a deliberate desire to avoid battle. The latter interpretation is quite possible, as McClellan may well have seen himself as the likely reunifier of the country.

This campaign also signalled the emergence of a group of magnificent Confederate commanders, who had no difficulty in exploiting every weakness of their opponent. The most important was Robert E. Lee, who that summer thoroughly confused McClellan in the Seven Days Battle to defend Richmond, Virginia, after which the 'Little Napoleon' withdrew to the north. Meanwhile Confederate commanders Thomas 'Stonewall' Jackson and J. E. B. Stuart undertook brilliant diversionary raids in northern Virginia. This initiated a pattern that would often recur during the course of the war – relieving pressure on Richmond by launching an attack west of Washington that appeared to threaten the capital – and such a move seldom failed to cause the desired alarm in the Union camp. Henceforward much of the key fighting in the east would focus on northern Virginia, where over the next year Lee and his lieutenants generally outclassed the northern generals. In September 1862 Lee led an invasion of Maryland, which culminated in the bloody Battle of Antietam/Sharpsburg, causing over 23 000 casualties. Though Lee withdrew, he was still a formidable opponent and inflicted a devastating defeat on Union forces at Fredericksburg, Virginia, on 13 December.

Meanwhile the war was in full swing in the west, where the Union began 1862 with the capture of the two Confederate forts controlling the strategic Tennessee and Cumberland Rivers. The Federal forces here were commanded by Ulysses S. Grant, who early demonstrated a fighting spirit and determination that stood in marked contrast to his counterparts in Virginia. Grant won an expensive but critical victory at Shiloh near the Tennessee–Mississippi boundary in April 1862, and Memphis fell to the Union in June. In October the Battle of Perryville virtually ended the Confederate military presence in Kentucky. Meanwhile the northern fleet was fulfilling its mission of worrying at the Confederate coast, seizing New Orleans in early May 1862. By early 1863, Union forces marching down the Mississippi were close to linking up with comrades moving north from Louisiana, their proposed junction being the river port of Vicksburg, Mississippi, which endured a siege that summer. In the far west, Union armies thwarted a dangerous Confederate attempt to occupy New Mexico and Arizona.

The year 1862 also witnessed a naval battle between two steam-driven ironclads, the Union's *Monitor* and the Confederate *Merrimack*. Although this battle did not in itself have a great effect on the course of the war, the engagement instantly proclaimed the obsolescence of every other navy on the planet, and once more showed how the conflict was prefiguring the tactics and attitudes of warfare over the next century.

While federal achievements during 1862 fell short of unqualified success, the Union had at least averted the catastrophe that often seemed close at hand. Moreover the Union victory at Antietam was critical in averting European recognition of the Confederacy, and in proving to London and Paris that eventually, they would have to deal with a reunited nation that would remember how its transatlantic neighbours had acted in its time of national tribulation. In domestic policy too, military events permitted a decisive shift in war aims, and a refocusing of the moral justification of the struggle. Before Antietam there was the chance that a major southern victory could shake the loyalty of the border states, and perhaps splinter the union further. This had prevented the administration declaring the forthright and immediate end to slavery that was the natural consequence of its earlier ideology. The failure to condemn slavery alienated radical Republicans, and gave substance to southern claims that the real issue of the war had nothing to do with black freedom, but was rather a matter of states' rights versus excessive federal power. Days after Antietam, Lincoln issued a preliminary emancipation proclamation that threatened to free all slaves in rebel-held territory. Though the measure did not actually free any slaves, it began the process that would end in abolition. From a European perspective, taking the moral high ground in this way reinforced the practical impossibility of British or French entry into the war. Intervening to stop a war in an apparently impartial manner was one thing, but sending an army to fight on behalf of slaveholders was quite another.

One final consequence of emancipation may not have weighed much at the time, but it grew dramatically in significance as the war progressed. By 1863 the Union was short of manpower, and a rough and ready conscription scheme was introduced in March (the Confederacy had already taken this step in April 1862). Emancipation raised the option of recruiting thousands of willing soldiers in the form of free blacks and ex-slaves, though these were at first regarded with great suspicion. By the end of the war over 200 000 blacks had served in Union forces, and performed with courage and dedication: blacks represented about a quarter of the strength of the US Navy. Their zeal was reinforced by bitter hatred of the Confederates, who were notoriously brutal to black prisoners, and there were massacres, as at Fort Pillow in Tennessee (in 1864). At best, captured black soldiers could expect re-enslavement.

1863 proved to be the pivotal year of the war, in which the south lost the strategic initiative. As in the previous year, Lee followed up an important victory in northern Virginia with an invasion of the north. After defeating numerically superior US forces at Chancellorsville in May, Lee led his Army of Northern Virginia on an invasion of Pennsylvania, the initial goal being the rail junction at Harrisburg. This would allow the cutting of Union supply lines from east to west, and perhaps moving on key cities such as Philadelphia. The potential of this strategy is illustrated by signs of growing discontent and war-weariness in the north, which a major penetration into Pennsylvania might well have pushed to the point of explosion. In July 1863 New York city suffered one of the worst urban insurrections of the whole period. Though directly caused by grievances over the social inequities of the Civil War draft system, the fury of the largely Irish crowds focused on the blacks, for whose sake the war was apparently being fought. The number of deaths is unknown, but certainly ran into hundreds.

Lee's forces encountered defeat in the Battle of Gettysburg in July, in which 90 000 northerners encountered 75 000 Confederates, leaving a combined total of 40 000 casualties. Union fortunes were also in the ascendant in the west. The fall of Vicksburg in July opened the Mississippi and divided the eastern Confederate states from their allies in Arkansas and Texas. Union affairs in Tennessee were endangered by a grave defeat at Chickamauga in September, but Grant's victory at Chattanooga two months later secured most of Tennessee. The new year's campaigning season would inevitably see an invasion of Georgia or Alabama, and a decisive movement of Union forces towards the sea. In early 1864 it finally seemed likely that Lee had met his match when Grant became supreme commander of the northern armies.

That Gettysburg was so obviously a turning point makes it tempting to see the rest of the war as an anticlimax, in which the south merely postponed ruin, but this was by no means obvious to contemporaries. Robert E. Lee was as effective in defence as attack, and from mid 1864 the sieges of Richmond and Petersburg became a relatively static affair of trench combat. May brought the bloody but indecisive Battles of the Wilderness and Spottsylvania Court House, and in June the Battle of Cold Harbor near Richmond brought the Union one of its most traumatic losses of the whole war. In a disaster reminiscent of the suicidal frontal assaults of the First World War, Grant's army lost 6 000 casualties in a single hour. In one month, Grant's campaigns had cost the Union over 50 000 casualties, a record that could have induced a less resolute president to replace the general. Shortly afterwards the Confederate General Jubal Early and his forces attacked the outskirts of Washington DC.

In the summer of 1864 Lincoln was preparing advice for his successor as president on the understanding that he would assuredly not be reelected himself, hardly the actions of a triumphant warlord. His despair was broken only by the sensational news in September that General Sherman's forces, marching south from Tennessee, had captured the

Georgian capital of Atlanta, one of the key transportation centres of the confederacy. This foreshadowed the end of secession in Georgia and a further partition of Confederate territory. Lincoln was reelected in November, defeating Democratic candidate George McClellan. This time victory was indeed at hand, though the Confederate forces stubbornly held out until the following spring and mounted some desperate counterattacks. By 1865 the Union forces were perhaps one million strong, while the Confederates could muster only 200 000, a desperate situation that the south even considered solving through the enlistment of thousands of slave soldiers.

Savannah fell to Sherman in December 1864, days after a battle at Nashville destroyed the Confederate invasion of Tennessee. Richmond itself fell in April, and there was the brief prospect that guerrilla warfare might continue for years to come in the backwoods regions of the Carolinas. On 9 April, however, Lee surrendered to Grant at Appomattox courthouse in Virginia, and all Confederate resistance had ended by the middle of May. Union triumph was dimmed by the assassination of Lincoln on 14 April, by a group of Confederate agents and diehard sympathizers who had been operating in Washington through much of the war.

CONSEQUENCES

The most obvious effect of the war was the enormous loss of human life, in a war where the combatants on both sides were Americans. All told 530 000 died, including battle casualties and deaths from illness. To put this into context, American losses in this war were larger than those in the two world wars combined. Hundreds of thousands more were maimed, at a time when so much of effective medicine depended on the swift amputation of wounded limbs. Material destruction was also huge, especially in the south. Some areas suffered particularly badly, above all those regions of Georgia that Sherman's armies had subjected to a scorched-earth policy of mass destruction and plunder. Once-thriving cities such as Atlanta and Richmond were devastated. The destruction of industrial plant and railways virtually undid much of the progress of the antebellum years, and state finances were in chaos. The abolition of slavery alone amounted to a confiscation of real property worth billions of dollars.

Though the north also suffered materially, the political outcome of the war ensured it would also achieve long-term benefits. For decades southern Congressional strength had permitted the veto of various internal improvements and tariff protections, as well as new laws to foster western development, but secession meant that such obstructionism was no longer possible. In 1862 alone Congress passed a series of measures crucial to western expansion, including the Homestead Act and a Pacific Railroad Act. Federal lands were granted to support a network of new universities explicitly intended to promote the social improvement of the working classes. The potential for industrial expansion was vastly enhanced by the profitability of wartime production and military contracting, and there too the beneficiaries would be found in the north-east and mid-west. The economic and industrial policies of the Republican Party allowed them to secure a dominant position in American politics over the next 50 years, a power compounded by their role as the representatives of patriotism and national unity. The war thus accentuated the already substantial regional differences within the United States, and laid the foundations for the industrial expansion of the coming decades.

The consequences of the war were felt for many years afterwards, but in one way at least the effects were permanent, in that after Lee's surrender at Appomattox, secession was no longer a viable option in American politics. Before the war the common phrase was that the United States – plural – have or do something; afterwards, the correct phraseology was that the United States – singular – has or does. The country was now a unity, more than the sum of its parts, and that, in the simplest possible terms, is what the war was about.

4

. . . .

Cities and Industry,
1865–1917

By 1900 the United States had more than fulfilled Herman Melville's visions of half a century earlier. The nation was now a continental empire, its cities and industries were already as large as those of the greatest European powers, and its political might was being projected overseas in the form of a new colonial empire. In a sense 'the rest of the nations' were already 'in our rear'. In contrast to Melville's day, the issue of national unity was quite settled, with no need to consider endless delicate adjustments in the relationship between rival sections. There was much for the boosters and would-be laureates to celebrate, ample to justify projections of a new American century.

Far more so than in 1851, there were also voices of doubt and pessimism, grave questions about the changing meaning of Americanism. The urban and industrial nature of the country was a long established fact, but by 1900 the cities and industries had come to dominate American life, and both produced social worlds that were almost impossible to reconcile with republican ideals. The new America was marked by savage class conflict, extreme polarization of wealth, immiseration and endemic political violence. As the radical economist Henry George had argued in 1879, American progress seemed intimately and necessarily based upon poverty. While the ethnic diversity represented by the Irish and Germans was a familiar reality, a new European immigration threatened to destroy any vestiges of an American consensus. The popular ideologies of the day emphasized conflict, the clash of races and classes, the struggle of the strong against the weak. For many, the prospects for the new century appeared grim, even terrifying. If there was to be hope, it would be found in giving to government a role radically different from that envisaged by the nation's founders; and it is a measure of the desperation of the times that this was the course ultimately taken.

RECONSTRUCTION

With the end of the Civil War the United States faced unprecedented questions about the status of the territories that had been in rebellion. Several constitutional approaches were possible: the most benevolent view was that held by Abraham Lincoln and his successor, Andrew Johnson, who wished to reabsorb the former Confederate states into the union on the most generous terms possible. While most of their citizens had been in arms against the Union, practical necessity made it impossible to try each individual offender as a traitor who had utterly forfeited his civil rights. A reasonable compromise suggested that a state should be readmitted to full participation in the Union once a certain proportion of its citizens had taken the oath of loyalty to the United States, and thus entitled themselves to pardon. A relatively normal political life could resume. By the end of 1865, state governments founded on these principles were in place throughout the south.

This approach was too timid for the radical Republicans, led by Charles Sumner and Thaddeus Stevens. They felt that the existing reconstruction plans ignored the position of the former slaves, for whom it was morally imperative to design a political establishment that would secure their rights in perpetuity. This meant giving blacks all civil rights, including the vote, and tolerating no inferior status resembling slavery. In addition they were suspicious of the loyalty of the former Confederates, despite their new oath of allegiance. The radical stance implied that the secessionist states should be subjected to a thoroughgoing social revolution in which the once mighty would be forever cast down. Such a reversal could only be accomplished under close federal supervision, and presumably with the long-term presence of US troops and bayonets. The first steps in this direction were taken in 1865, with the passing of the 13th amendment to the constitution, which prohibited slavery or involuntary servitude, and the creation of the Freedmen's Bureau, to protect and advance black social interests.

Initially the restored southern states played directly into the hands of the radicals by placing former slaves under the auspices of the 'black codes', stringent regulations that gave freed blacks a status far inferior to that of true liberty or equality, and mandated labour service. In effect blacks as a community (rather than individuals) became the collective property of all southern whites. Extensive terrorist violence led to the death of several thousand freed blacks and their white sympathizers, and the new black schoolhouses were burned. In 1866 a pogrom against the blacks of New Orleans was halted only by the intervention of the US Army, and a similar rising occurred in Memphis. Arkansas was the storm centre in 1868, South Carolina in 1870, Mississippi in 1871. In Louisiana over 3 000 people, mainly black, were killed or wounded in battles and massacres in the decade after 1866; in Texas a thousand blacks were said to have been targeted each year between 1868 and 1870. The most notorious organization to emerge from this carnage was the Ku Klux Klan, a Confederate veterans' movement that originated in Tennessee during 1866 and rapidly acquired the status of a vast and lethal political movement across the entire south.

From 1866 the radicals dominated federal policies. The fourteenth constitutional amendment declared that anyone, black or white, born in the United States was a full citizen with all the appropriate rights, of which he or she could not be deprived without due process of law. (Though the language was meant to be unequivocal, the US Supreme Court more or less invalidated the measure as a safeguard for freedmen in 1873.) The measure also prohibited former Confederate officials from holding office again. A fifteenth amendment, proposed in 1869, forbade states to limit the right to vote 'on account of race, colour or previous condition of servitude'. In 1867 the Reconstruction Acts dissolved the southern state governments and reintroduced direct military rule, further specifying detailed procedures for new elections on terms that would encourage black participation. President Andrew Johnson vetoed these and other Congressional measures, but his veto was usually overruled, and in 1868 he became the first US president to undergo impeachment proceedings. Though the impeachment failed, Johnson was able to exercise little influence on the course of subsequent events.

The Reconstruction Acts created new regimes across the south, of a political and racial character utterly different from any of their predecessors. By 1868 there were 700 000 black voters in the south, as against 625 000 whites, a balance that contributed substantially to Republican electoral successes at the national level: black votes probably gave the presidency to Ulysses S. Grant in 1868. In southern mythology, this represented the worst of all possible worlds, a coalition of cynical northern adventurers (carpetbaggers) with southern traitors (scalawags), who conspired to manipulate ignorant black puppets, while all the time the natural and proper rulers of society were excluded from any participation. This dark age continued until the 1870s, when courageous white resisters succeeded in destabilizing and overthrowing the Republican dictatorships. History has been kinder to both carpetbaggers and scalawags, who in retrospect seem like well-intentioned individuals struggling to create a new and better south. The dismissal of Republican southern whites as traitors is based on the myth of the 'true' south as the land of aristocratic plantations, which ignores the poorer citizens, especially in the upland regions, who had been minimally connected to the slave economy.

Moreover the black office holders of those years were no worse than their white contemporaries, and only racist condescension supports the belief that they were acting in simple obedience to white puppet masters. Blacks represented a large proportion of the residents in all southern states, and were entitled to at least some representation in any fair electoral system. Moreover the political and cultural progress of the newly freed slaves was rapid, as was the speed with which they developed their own electoral networks, rooted in the black churches. Though governments in the reconstruction period (1865–77) spent heavily, they were trying to make up for the absolute lack of infrastructure to cope with the needs of black citizens in matters like education.

In this view, the real disaster was the rise of white revolutionary movements in the south, and the gradual collapse of federal support for mixed-race regimes. In 1874 several thousand supporters of the White League attempted an armed putsch in New Orleans, while attempts to defend the new regimes by arming blacks provoked even worse massacres. One by one the Republican governments in the south collapsed under the imminent threat of mob violence and assassination, to be replaced by regimes based on traditional white landowners and office holders, usually with records of Confederate war service. Tennessee and Virginia fell in 1869, North Carolina in 1870, and by 1877 the only survivors of the reconstruction regime were the state governments of Florida, South Carolina and Louisiana.

These fell victim to national partisan politics. In the presidential election of 1876, Democratic candidate Samuel Tilden won a convincing margin in the popular vote over his Republican rival Rutherford B. Hayes, but the picture in the electoral college was less straightforward. Tilden entered the negotiations with an electoral college lead of 184 to 166, and needing only one more vote for election. The presidency now turned on disputed returns from the three states that retained Republican administrations. In 1877 a bipartisan commission was established to settle the disputed election, which became transformed into a broader negotiation over the survival of reconstruction. The consequence was that Hayes was awarded the presidency, but only at the cost of withdrawing federal troops from the south, dooming the remaining Republican regimes. In 1878 the Posse Comitatus Act prohibited the future use of military forces in law enforcement. In 1883 the Supreme Court struck down the Civil Rights Act of 1875, which had guaranteed black access to public premises such as 'inns, public conveyances and places of amusement'.

The course of reconstruction aggravated southern rage at losing the Civil War and unified the white population behind the more extreme anti-black elements. The south remained solidly Democratic until the 1960s and the Civil Rights revolution, and even then it was some decades before many southerners could bring themselves to vote for the party of Lincoln and Sumner.

WHITE SUPREMACY

Lacking any capital, the great majority of former slaves were forced to become sharecroppers and small farmers, generally dependent on the white magnates of earlier years. Cotton production resumed its primary place in the southern economy, as the acreage allotted to this crop grew from four million in the 1830s to thirty million in the 1890s. However, even though reconstruction was over, the situation of the blacks was not unrelievedly bad, as the southern economy improved and diversified. By 1880, for example, the expansion of coal-fired iron smelting had provided Alabama with the basis for its new iron and steel industries in Birmingham, as well as increasing mine output. By the end of the century the state was growing rich from the production of steel, timber and textiles. Birmingham grew from 3 000 residents in 1880 to over 130 000 in 1910, a development of Chicago-like rapidity. Urban growth elsewhere in the south reflected a new prosperity. The population of Memphis rose from 23 000 before the civil war to around 100 000 at the end of the century, while other southern cities at or fast approaching this level included Nashville, Atlanta and Birmingham. The population of Louisville now exceeded 200 000. Much social mobility was now possible, so that northern commentators in the 1880s were startled at the relative cordiality of southern race relations. Blacks widely retained their voting rights, and they were actively courted by conservative Democratic politicians. In the Populist movement of the early 1890s, striking signs of interracial political cooperation caused real alarm among the economic elites. In 1894, Populists and Republicans combined forces to win control of North Carolina.

This relatively benevolent phase of black history ended in the last years of the century, in part because of a broad political struggle between Democratic conservatives and radical Populists, in an economic climate devastated by agricultural depression. Conservatives played the race card and revived fears of black domination, and former Populists were swept along by the new racial politics.

In practical terms, the political battles of the 1890s had their most direct effects on the rights of the black electorate, which was systematically deprived of the suffrage by discriminatory devices such as the poll tax and literacy tests. Between 1896 and 1904 the number of registered black voters in Louisiana fell from 130 000 to just 1350. The attack on black suffrage was accompanied by the spread of laws to create formal and complete racial segregation in all public facilities. These 'Jim Crow' laws were alleged to create 'separate but equal' provisions, and this interpretation was upheld by the US Supreme Court in the 1896 case of Plessy and Ferguson, over the furious minority objection of Justice John Marshall Harlan. However the Jim Crow era also marked the institutionalization of the caste system in the south, a rock-

solid stratification in which black social inferiority was enforced by casual violence and daily insult. Black servitude
was widely restored in the form of convict labour – which
often took the form of chain-gangs kept in order by white
guards – performing labour for private contractors: corporate public slavery in all but name.

Mid-century Abolitionists had asked rhetorically how
black Americans could suffer anything worse than slavery:
the years from 1890 to 1925 came close to providing an
answer. This was the height of lynch law in the United States,
an era in which mobs killed an average of one hundred
individuals each year. Most incidents occurred in the south
and involved black victims, usually for a perceived insult or
sexual threat against a white person. Early in the new century
such killings were frequently 'augmented' by torture, burning
or castration. As in any terrorist campaign, the aim was as
much to maintain fear among the general population as to
liquidate specific offenders. There were also collective outbreaks on the grim model of the reconstruction years, and in
1898 armed white vigilantes in Wilmington used terror to
root out the vestiges of black political power. In 1915, D. W.
Griffith's 'Birth of a Nation' used the potent new medium of
cinema to propagate an effective version of the racist myth of
southern history and reconstruction, in the process laying the
foundations for a rebirth of the Ku Klux Klan, which flourished into the early 1940s.

As black conditions deteriorated sharply in these years, the
prospect of northward movement appeared ever more tempting. While black communities had existed throughout the
nineteenth century in all northern cities of any size, mass
migration only began after 1900. The coming of the First
World War was a particularly important trigger here, creating as it did a vast labour shortage in northern munitions
factories. Four hundred thousand southern blacks migrated
to the north and west between 1916 and 1919, transforming
the ethnic structure and politics of cities such as New York,
Philadelphia, Chicago and Detroit.

There were different proposals for the best means to improve the desperate lot of southern blacks. From the 1890s the most visible black leader was the educationalist Booker T. Washington, who preached a gospel of self-improvement and hard work leading to evolutionary change, and who gained the support of conservative business leaders. His approach was epitomized by the Tuskegee Institute, founded in 1881, which aimed to provide a model of black higher education. As racial violence surged in the early part of the new century, this strategy appeared far too slow and moderate for other activists, for example W. E. B. DuBois, the first black to receive a doctorate from Harvard University. In 1910 DuBois was active in the foundation of the National Association for the Advancement of Colored Peoples (NAACP). Though radical and separatist solutions were scarcely conceivable in the political environment of these years, the first ventures towards the formation of black Muslim and pan-African organizations date from 1913. Nationalist currents flourished in the freer atmosphere of the northern cities, where in the 1920s the Jamaican-born activist Marcus Garvey aspired to the role of the messianic prophet who would lead all exiled Africans back to their mother continent. Also in this decade, the US Communist Party moved towards the eccentric solution of the 'Negro Problem' through the creation of separate self-governing areas within the Southern black belt.

THE WESTERN FRONTIER

The Civil War had caused a brief halt in the pace of westward expansion, but this resumed swiftly at the conclusion of war. In the second half of the nineteenth century the number of Americans living in the western states grew from 179 000 to 4.3 million, with a further increase to 9.2 million by 1920. Colorado's population grew from a mere 34 000 in 1860 to 500 000 by 1900. There were 1.5 million Californians by 1900, and the Golden State was set to play a major role in American politics in the coming century. In 1889 and 1890 the union admitted six northwestern states (Table 4.1) with a total area of some 540 000 square miles, over twice the area of France. It is a striking comment on the expansion of these years that such a vast development seemed so relatively routine and natural. By 1912 the admission of Arizona and New Mexico completed the political organization of the Continental US into what would become known as 'the Lower Forty-Eight' states, and the stars on the American flag took on a pattern that would remain unchanged until 1959.

American westward expansion was driven by the traditional motives of land hunger and the quest for mineral wealth. In 1862 the Lincoln administration passed the vital Homestead Act, which promised 160 acres of western land free or virtually free to anyone prepared to settle it, and by the end of the decade the already vast population movement was accelerated by the coming of the railroads. Efficient bulk transportation permitted the nationwide expansion of wheat

Table 4.1   States admitted to the Union, 1867–1912

	Year of Admission	Modern capital
Nebraska	1867	Lincoln
Colorado	1876	Denver
North Dakota	1889	Bismarck
South Dakota	1889	Pierre
Montana	1889	Helena
Washington	1889	Olympia
Idaho	1890	Boise
Wyoming	1890	Cheyenne
Utah	1896	Salt Lake City
Oklahoma	1907	Oklahoma City
New Mexico	1912	Santa Fe
Arizona	1912	Phoenix

and corn production, which in 1840 had been confined east of the Mississippi. By the 1880s production had spread through the great plains, and the corn belt stretched west through Iowa and Nebraska. The scale of the new area placed under cultivation was unimaginable to anyone accustomed to European conditions. Between 1870 and 1920 the total number of American farms grew from 2.7 million to 6.5 million, though the average acreage remained virtually the same at around 150 acres. Gold and silver rushes also continued both north and south of the Canadian border, and the ferocity of the pressure from would-be miners also strained other frontiers, especially those with the Indian nations.

In much of the west the social transformation was marked by the replacement of buffalo by cattle as the most abundant animal presence. In the late 1860s the cattle ranchers of Texas began moving their herds north to Kansas rail junctions at Abilene or Dodge City, from where they could be transported by rail to the cities of the mid-west. These great cattle drives and the attendant towns that grew up along their routes would become central to the emerging myth of the wild west, as would the whole structure of ranches and corrals, cowboys and roundups; but the age was short-lived – by the late 1880s much of the open land had been fenced in by homesteaders, using the newly invented barbed wire (1873). The ranch system expanded from Texas into high-plains states such as Wyoming and Montana, and west into Arizona, Nevada and New Mexico. The cattle ranches represented substantial business enterprises, with huge investments by European and specifically British capitalists.

The new west was celebrated as a heroic wilderness, a pristine frontier land of violence and outlawry, but in reality the conflicts of these years are better seen as typical of the conditions prevailing in other regions of the United States. Many of the outlaws, for example the Jesse James Gang, were survivors or heirs of the guerrilla conflicts that had torn through Kansas and Missouri before and during the Civil War. Union–Confederate memories also shaped the lengthy feud of the 1870s and 1880s between the Appalachian clans of the Hatfields and the McCoys. Battles associated with legendary names such as Billy the Kid and Wyatt Earp were essentially the same sort of factional struggles for economic or political power that also marked the elections in contemporary New York City or Philadelphia, or the industrial battles between eastern railroad corporations or canal firms.

The much-filmed Gunfight at the OK Corral, which took place in 1881, was in fact an incident in a continuing struggle between the Republican businessmen of Tombstone and the Democratic cattlemen, with the Earp brothers serving as the hired assassins of the former, much as the political machines of the east enforced their will through street gangs. The gun was by no means a western prerogative, and the west never produced violence remotely equivalent to that in, say, contemporary Louisiana or other parts of the 'wild south' during reconstruction. However there were some violent outbreaks of factional violence in the west, for example the Lincoln County War of 1878, when cattlemen were pitted against sheep farmers in New Mexico. In Wyoming in 1892 the Stock Growers Association, based in Cheyenne, mounted an invasion of Johnson County in Powder River country with the ostensible goal of ending rustling, but in reality to force the homesteaders into line. As in Lincoln County, hired gunmen were recruited to enforce the power of the ranchers. The resulting 'war' caused several fatalities and demonstrated the inability of the courts to convict powerful malefactors.

INDIAN CONFLICTS

The years between 1865 and 1880 represented both the crisis and the temporary solution of the 'Indian Problem' in the west, and especially the issue of the northern plains peoples: the Lakota/Sioux, the Cheyenne and the Arapaho. With the end of the Civil War, white settlers began pressing on the margins of Lakota/Sioux territory, as defined by the treaty of 1851. Further agreements in 1868 reduced this area somewhat to improve white access to gold-rich lands in the Dakotas, and even relatively moderate Indian leaders recognized they were being forced to choose between resistance and peaceful annihilation. In 1868 Chief Red Cloud of the Oglala Sioux led the plains tribes to a number of military and diplomatic victories that had the rare effect of actually closing one of the major western migration routes: the Bozeman trail, along which miners travelled to Montana.

This pause could only be temporary. White activity in the area increased with the building of the Northern Pacific Railroad in 1872, and the financial crash of 1873, which caused desperate western settlers to become resentful of any restrictions on their economic development. In addition the military commander in the west – the ironically named William Tecumseh Sherman – saw the confrontation between white and Indian in terms of the inevitable extinction of at least the Indian way of life, and probably the race itself. He certainly contemplated the 'extermination' of the Sioux. It was his deputy Philip Sheridan who made the immortal remark that the only 'good' Indians he had ever known were dead. Such leaders also recognized the crucial importance of the buffalo as the mainstay of the Indian culture, and that the extinction of the one might well result in the destruction of the other. They therefore encouraged the massacre of buffalo herds, already well under way in the decade after 1865 to meet the food needs of the railway construction crews. At the middle of the century there may have been sixty million buffalo, but four million were killed in 1871 alone. By 1883 their numbers had reduced to hundreds.

Matters reached a crisis in 1874 with the finding of gold in the Black Hills of South Dakota, an area regarded by the Lakota peoples as particularly sacred. Miners flooded in, quite illegally, and war naturally erupted. The US military commander was General George A. Custer, a magnificent self-publicist who already had a lengthy record of extreme brutality in earlier conflicts with Indians. Though a skilled cavalry commander, he was in this instance outclassed by the main Indian leaders, Sitting Bull and Crazy Horse. In June 1876 Custer's rash self-confidence led to the destruction of his command, some 225 men, at the Battle of Little Big Horn in Montana. The event was all the more traumatic for the American public as news of the disaster reached the eastern cities on 4 July, exactly when the nation was proudly celebrating the centenary of the Declaration of Independence.

Though the Custer affair was a temporary blow to national self-confidence, it was also a Pyrrhic victory for the native peoples, who now faced an enraged American people determined to suffer no further setbacks. Over the next three years the main Indian military formations were forced to surrender, and other tribes, such as the Nez Perce, were defeated. New treaties confiscated huge amounts of Indian lands on a 'sell or starve' basis. In 1877 the United States seized the western half of Lakota territory, including the Black Hills; a further grab in 1889 took eleven million more acres. The savage new mood also affected many tribes who had not the slightest role in the Custer affair, such as the Utes of Colorado and Utah, who were now driven to barren and remote areas with little concern whether they lived or starved. In 1886 even as formidable a foe as the Apache leader Geronimo was forced to surrender, ending years of bloody combat in the south-west.

This already dire picture grew worse in the late 1880s, with the decision to break up collective Indian landholdings, to be divided among individual landholders. Though justified as a policy to cure Indian idleness and promote thrift and self-reliance, the policy also involved a recalculation of the lands the native peoples would actually need. Once distributed, the Indian lands yielded a large surplus acreage, which was to be opened to white homesteading, even in what had once been designated Indian territory. In 1889 the Oklahoma territory was opened to the last great western land-rush, and over the next decade the region's population grew from 60 000 to

400 000. Native possessions in the 'Indian territory' shrank steadily, and the area was included in the eventual state of Oklahoma.

As so often occurs in times of inexplicable catastrophe, in 1889 Indian despair led to a remarkable millenarian movement, when a Paiute holy man named Wovoka began to have visions in which he was told of the coming of a messiah. In the new golden age the whites would be eliminated from the planet, and the buffalo herds would return in greater abundance than ever. To promote the millennium, the tribes must perform the Ghost Dance, which brought solidarity with ancestors watching over their peoples. During the next year the Ghost Dance religion spread swiftly over the plains, but at the end of 1890 the movement fell apart under army pressure. In December, 250 Indians were massacred at Wounded Knee in South Dakota, an event that can be taken to mark the end of the Indian wars.

While the West had been 'won' by about 1890, exploiting it successfully was a more complicated issue. Some of the new lands evolved highly successful economies, as ranching spread over several western states, and the Pacific north west developed a profitable timber empire. Western cities thrived: between 1860 and 1900 Denver grew from no residents to 134 000. As the hub of the Oregon region, Portland had 800 people in 1850, 90 000 in 1900 and 200 000 in 1910. Seattle exhibited a similar growth, based on its role in supplying the miners in the goldfields of Alaska and the Yukon: it had 1000 people in 1870, 80 000 in 1900 and 237 000 in 1910. Los Angeles was another classic boom story. In 1870 there were 5000 residents, but the city was then connected to the railway by two competing lines, the Southern Pacific and the Santa Fe, which competed fiercely for business. Fares plummeted and mid-western migrants poured in to boost the population to more than 100 000 by the turn of the century. In 1914 the completion of the port of San Pedro coincided with the new Panama canal, and made Los Angeles a leading Pacific port. By the 1920s the city was enjoying further stimuli: from oil, tourism, the film industry and new employment in aircraft factories. It soon rivalled San Francisco, that mushroom growth of an earlier generation.

Other areas of the west proved far less amenable, especially the high-plains country of the Dakotas, Kansas and Nebraska, which were first encountered in what proved to be the unnaturally good climatic circumstances of the mid century. As the rainfall levels deteriorated from the 1880s, farming there became harder, and agrarian protest movements reflected growing despair. The bitterly cold winters of 1885–86 and 1886–87 destroyed the livelihood of many ranchers. Nor was much of California naturally suited to the agricultural ambitions of its pioneers, and the water supply caused repeated crises. It took intense work and ingenuity to convert the ranches into farms, but the process was well under way by the end of this period. An urgent need for water was the factor that persuaded several southern Californian communities to accept annexation into greater Los Angeles.

In 1893 the historian Frederick Jackson Turner delivered a scholarly paper on the significance of the frontier in western history. He argued that the American character had been defined by the availability of an open and constantly receding frontier, which had also served as the real and symbolic boundary between savagery and civilization. That frontier was now closed with the settlement of Oklahoma, and the elimination of the distinction between settled and non-settled territory. 'The first period of American history' was thus at an end. The fact of closure permitted the romanticization of the west to reach a new fervour, suggested for example by the 1902 publication of Owen Wister's novel *The Virginian* and the early cinematic treatments over the next decade – 1903 brought the film, 'The Great Train Robbery'.

This frontier thesis has been of immense value to students of American history, for whom it can be invoked to explain countless aspects of American life and culture. However it is debatable whether or in what sense the frontier closed in 1890. Much of the most celebrated activity associated with the 'Wild West' was still to come, and indeed occurred in the new century, while the frontier remained very much alive in Canada and Mexico. In Texas the Spindletop oil boom of 1901 created a 'wildcatting' culture quite reminiscent of the mineral rushes of earlier years. Also, the frontier struggles of the 1870s had obviously left a mental mark on participants who survived for several decades afterwards. Regardless of one's attitude to the Turner thesis, unquestionably the 'winning of the west' did make a contribution to the shaping of American culture, and the transformation of the region into an integral component of the United States was bound to have a profound effect on the political balance during the coming century.

IMPERIALISM

By the end of the century the United States had developed a long domestic history of racial confrontation and territorial expansion, and both these came to influence its conduct of foreign affairs. Gradually and somewhat reluctantly, the United States became an imperial power and a military presence on a global scale.

The Civil War demonstrated the United States' ability to mobilize huge and deadly military formations, and this fact was not lost on potential rivals in the western hemisphere. In 1867, Russia chose to end its imperial ventures in North America by selling the huge territory of Alaska to the United States: 591 000 square miles for a price of around seven million dollars. The deal was rightly touted as a magnificent bargain by Secretary of State William H. Seward, though critics scoffed at the potential value of 'Mr. Seward's Icebox'. The British now decided that their position required urgent reinforcement, especially with Seward publicly declaring that the whole of North America 'shall be, sooner or later, within the magic circle of the American Union', and boasting that the new transcontinental railway potentially opened the whole Canadian West to future American annexation.[1] Several of Britain's North American territories were merged into a new Dominion of Canada in 1867, while the new country secured its western territories only by a prodigious effort in the next decade to build its own transcontinental rail line. Through the second half of the century there were periodic fears that sporadic American disagreements with Britain would lead to a military confrontation, for example in an 1895 quarrel over the boundaries of Venezuela. The potential for conflict was enhanced by the growing Irish presence in the United States, where anti-British rhetoric became commonplace in urban politics.

From the 1880s the growth of European imperialism caused mixed feelings among American elites. While some envy and hostility resulted from the overseas expansion of countries such as Britain and France, there was also a sense that the United States should bring its distinctive civilizing mission to the liberation of primitive peoples, to draw them under the enlightened and progressive wing of the American eagle. The first major opportunity to practice the new American imperialism was provided by the ramshackle and declining empire of Spain. In 1895 the inhabitants of Cuba launched a nationalist revolt that was suppressed with atrocities that the American press covered very critically, especially the popular papers of the Hearst and Pulitzer chains. Spanish 'concentration camps' were described in lurid detail. Tensions were rising by February 1898, when a mysterious explosion claimed the American battleship *Maine* in Havana harbour. Though the steam-powered warships of that generation were disaster-prone the American media immediately blamed enemy action and demanded an investigation, followed by suitable retaliation. By April the administration had approved intervention in Cuba, and war was declared. The subsequent conflict was extremely unequal and Cuba was soon in US hands. In May a naval victory in Manila Bay confirmed American control of the Philippines, and peace was brokered in August. Under the Peace of Paris, the United States annexed outright the possessions of Puerto Rico, Guam and the Philippines, and Hawaii was also claimed.

The whole affair seemed to have brought the United States into the ranks of imperialist powers with relatively little bloodshed: of the 300 000 American soldiers and sailors who served during the war with Spain, less than 400 died in battle (though 2000 more died of other causes). American military confidence was enhanced by such well-publicized heroics as the charge of the 'Rough Riders' at San Juan Hill in Puerto Rico. The unsavoury aftermath to this conflict has been all but forgotten. In 1899 the native peoples of the Philippines began a revolt that was not suppressed until 1902, after savage jungle fighting that foreshadowed the later conflict in Vietnam. Press coverage initially told little of the massacres and the destruction of villages by American forces, the torture and the butchery of guerrilla prisoners. These were counterinsurgency measures far bloodier than anything the Spanish had perpetrated in Cuba and the actions that were currently drawing such criticism of the British side in the Boer War. Nor did they suggest the scale of the fighting: by 1900 some 70 000 US troops were active in the islands. The final death toll is unknown and is complicated by the number of deaths in prisons and concentration camps, as well as losses due to starvation, but military casualties alone were appalling. All in all the number of Filipino dead certainly ran into the hundreds of thousands. As a US congressman remarked, 'They never rebel in Luzon any more because there isn't anybody left to rebel'.

Whatever its flaws, the Spanish conflict and its aftermath left no doubt of American standing as a world power, a status reinforced by the activist foreign policy of Theodore Roosevelt (president 1901–9). It was Roosevelt who acted as peacemaker in the Russo-Japanese war of 1905, and Roosevelt who in 1907 sent a 'Great White Fleet' on a world cruise to demonstrate the growth of American naval power. In 1902 Roosevelt invoked the Monroe Doctrine to persuade European powers to desist from a blockade of Venezuela. In its imperial guise the United States sought to dominate both the Pacific and the Caribbean, a role that necessitated a canal between the two bodies of water. In 1903 Roosevelt's administration leased from Colombia the land that became the Panama Canal Zone, and subsequently engineered a provincial rebellion to create the puppet state of Panama. The canal was completed between 1906 and 1914, at immense cost in human lives. The American fleet could now be moved easily and swiftly between the oceans, a facility that might be vital in the event of war with either Britain or its powerful naval ally, Japan.

The United States was able to treat most of the smaller nations of the Caribbean as *de facto* colonies, to be subject to occupation as and when the need arose, to protect US citizens or collect debts. Cuba and Panama were already virtual protectorates, while Puerto Rico was a colonial possession. In 1905 the US government took over the finances of the Dominican Republic, citing as justification a 'police power' said to exist under the 'Roosevelt Corollary' to the Monroe Doctrine. As international law, the idea was bizarre, but it offered a powerful precedent. US forces occupied Nicaragua in 1912 and again in 1926; they occupied Haiti from 1915 to 1934 and the Dominican Republic from 1916 to 1920. US forces also became involved in Mexico after that country entered its decade of revolution in 1910, but this vast country offered a very different prospect from the island republics, which had become so accustomed to the presence of US Marines. In 1914 a perceived insult to the US Navy led to the bombardment of the port of Vera Cruz. In 1916 General John Pershing led a major incursion into northern Mexico to punish the forces of Pancho Villa for an attack on American territory.

The new American empire had a cultural and ideological effect far beyond its commercial significance, and from about 1898 American thinkers became ever more imbued with the new racial science that was having such an intoxicating effect on their counterparts in Britain and Germany. One of the key advocates of 'Teutonic' racial theories in public life was Senator Albert Beveridge, a leading supporter of the Philippine venture. Such notions found a ready audience in a nation accustomed to generations of conflict with both blacks and Native Americans, struggles that had spawned countless negative stereotypes of the ' lesser breeds'. In 1916 Madison Grant published a popular text on *The Passing of the Great Race, or the Racial Basis of European History*.

Linked to scientific racism was the theory of eugenics, and the suggestion that social problems could be cured by promoting the breeding of the fittest and placing limitations upon inferior stocks. Eugenic ideas had a pervasive effect upon American social policy in the first quarter of the century, affecting areas as diverse as education, social welfare, criminal justice and juvenile delinquency, as well as the treatment of alcoholics, epileptics and the insane. The rise in popularity of intelligence testing after 1905 gave an allegedly quantitative basis for the American social pyramid, which proceeded downwards from white northern Europeans through Mediterranean and Slavic populations, and ultimately to blacks. These theories received apparent confirmation from the mass intelligence testing administered (shoddily) to military recruits during the First World War. Thereafter advocates of 'Anglo-Saxon' supremacy could claim that their position was fully justified by irrefutable data.

INDUSTRIALIZATION AND THE GILDED AGE

American industrialization reached full flood after the Civil War, in large part as direct consequence of that war. Apart from the obvious demands made on war industries, wartime contracting had allowed individual businessmen to accumulate substantial fortunes that could now be invested in other concerns. In addition the destruction of southern plantation interests permitted Congress to erect high tariff barriers to protect US industry. From the 1860s to the 1930s the legal and political environment of the United States was warmly friendly to industry, and opposed to even modest forms of regulation or restriction.

Two legal doctrines in particular served as the Magna Carta of unchecked capitalist development. One was the constitutional clause forbidding governments to 'impair contract', which was taken to mean there should be no official intervention in legal dealings between employer and employee, even in matters as basic as the setting of wages and hours. The other, remarkably enough, was the fourteenth amendment to the constitution, which notionally gave former slaves full civil and political rights. As interpreted by the courts in these years, the amendment gave virtually no protection to blacks, but bestowed the full rights of 'persons' on corporations in such a way that governmental regulation of business activities was viewed as an infringement of corporate civil rights. In 1905 the Supreme Court decided in the Lochner case that New York had no power to regulate the maximum working hours of employees. Legal attitudes were influenced by Social Darwinism, which in its vulgar form suggested that efforts to assist the poor and inadequate were not only useless, but a harmful interference in the proper course of social development.

From the 1890s onwards, reformist and interventionist state and city governments would meet almost total failure in their attempts to regulate business conditions in the interests of workers and consumers. In 1895 a Supreme Court's decision on declared income taxes unconstitutional; the same year, the Court refused to penalize a blatant violation of the federal anti-trust law. In the lower courts, meanwhile, tort law resolutely refused to acknowledge the new environment of the industrial world, so that it was virtually impossible to sue a corporation for even egregious misconduct resulting in the death or injury of a worker, or any destruction wrought on a neighbouring community. In industrial accidents, for instance, an injured worker could sue only the fellow-worker directly involved, and not the employer. Nor was any significant degree of restraint or regulation obtained from the criminal law, despite the often flagrant violations of legality in the age of the corporate 'robber barons'.

The last third of the nineteenth century was a time of buccaneering capitalism at its most flagrant, with figurative and often real wars that the media reported with as much zest as they did any border clash with Indians. Unusual only in scale was the great Erie war of the mid 1860s, in which Cornelius Vanderbilt sought to finalize his monopolistic hold on the transportation systems of New York state. He was opposed by the 'Erie Ring', three rival financiers all fresh from their dazzling successes in Civil War profiteering and blockade running: Daniel Drew, Jim Fisk and Jay Gould. The ensuing battle was fought out with massive bribery of courts, judges and public officials, as well as a large-scale manipulation of securities that would have been illegal in any society with even rudimentary mechanisms of financial enforcement. The two sides also freely employed bands of hired thugs.

From 1866 New York City was run by an extraordinarily powerful political syndicate known as the 'Tweed Ring', the destruction of which in 1871 brought corruption into the centre of political debate. Soon afterwards came the Credit Mobilier scandal of 1873. This firm had been created by the Union Pacific Railroad to fund the construction of its western railway line at vastly inflated prices, with shares freely distributed to US congressmen in order to discourage investigation. Even the US vice president was tarnished. President Grant's second administration (1873–7) was marked by a series of such affairs, which cumulatively demonstrated the intimate financial ties that bound office holders at all levels of government to corrupt businessmen. The profits to be made from such enterprises were astonishing, and Jay Gould died in 1892 leaving an estimated fortune of $70 million. The wars of the spoilsmen were fought out with an absolute disregard of the public good, and financial malpractice contributed to the parlous Wall Street Crash of 1869 and the panic of 1873. As Jim Fisk remarked, though: 'Nothing is lost, save honour'.

In the generation after the Civil War, the United States became the largest economy in the world, a process that can be illustrated by the rapid expansion of several different industries. US coal production stood at 14 million tons in 1860, an increase of more than 3000 per cent over the 1820 figure: production stood at 100 million tons in 1884. Bituminous coal production grew from 43 million tons in 1880 to 212 million in 1900, anthracite from 30 million tons to 57 million. The nation's first Bessemer steel plant was built at Troy, New York, in 1865, and over the next two decades the American steel industry was expanded by Andrew Carnegie. Steel production grew from a million tons in 1880 to 25 million in 1910. Pittsburgh became the heart of American heavy industry, with 34 separate iron and steel plants in the metropolitan area by 1904.

The production of copper (essential for electric cable) rose from 30 000 tons in 1880 to 500 000 in 1910. National growth was reflected in the developing rail network. The United States had 9000 miles of railway lines in 1850, 193 000 miles by the end of the century. By 1900, the railways represented about a tenth of the total wealth of the United States. Among newer industries, the United States soon led the world in oil production. As Andrew Carnegie wrote in 1886, 'The old nations of the earth creep on at a snail's pace. The Republic thunders past with the speed of an express'.

American industry also profited from the creativity of its inventors. For example Thomas Alva Edison, although often building on extensive work by predecessors, made crucial breakthroughs that permitted the practical application of such innovations as the gramophone (1877) and electric lighting (1879). In 1894 his Kinetograph laid the foundations of motion-picture technology. Alexander Graham Bell developed the telephone in 1876, and in 1903 the Wright brothers became the pioneers of powered flight.

From the 1880s American inventors played an important role in the development of the gasoline-powered automobile, and even more critically in evolving the mass production techniques required to produce cars in large numbers. One of the earliest successes was the Oldsmobile, which by 1903 could be produced at the astonishing rate of 4000 a year. Henry Ford built his first car in 1896, and the Ford Motor Company was formed in 1903. By 1907 Ford had created the production line system that allowed the manufacture of huge numbers of his Model T cars, 'tin lizzies'. Twelve thousand cars were produced in 1909, 19 000 in 1910. The figure grew steadily thereafter, to reach one million by 1920. Ford was also an innovator in his industrial practices, offering extremely favourable wages and hours to a workforce that was expected to reciprocate by accepting unprecedented industrial discipline and corporate loyalty. From 1911 the production process was accelerated by the new principles of 'scientific management' formulated by Frederick W. Taylor, 'Taylorism'. The concentration of the new industry in Detroit allowed that city to grow from 286 000 residents in 1900 to 466 000 in 1910.

Progress in manufacturing was parallelled by the growing sophistication of retailing, where American firms of the late nineteenth century perfected innovative techniques such as the mail order catalogue and modern advertising. By 1900 Sears Roebuck and Montgomery Ward were by far the largest retailers in the world. American business thrived on the growing commercialization of leisure activities made available to the urban masses. It was in the last quarter of the century that sport attracted large paying audiences, and baseball in particular became the national sport. In the 1890s newspaper magnates such as William Randolph Hearst pioneered the modern mass circulation newspaper, complete with publicity stunts to swell circulation, heavy use of advertising, and an alliance with demagogic politics. The number of daily newspapers in the United States rose from 574 in 1870 to 2600 in 1909, their circulation increasing from 2.6 million to 24.2 million.

At the opening of the twentieth century the United States' industrial might placed it alongside Britain and Germany as one of the three dominant powers on the planet. In coal and pig-iron production the United States already held first place, having surpassed the British, and in steel and iron ore it outstripped the Germans. The United States was producing 13.5 million tons of steel, 262 million tons of coal and 16 million tons of pig iron. Apart from industrial goods, the United States' natural resources made it a vast producer of precious metals, petroleum, wheat, tobacco and cotton at levels that challenged or exceeded such rich territories as Russia, Australia and India. In 1913 finished goods moved into first place in the list of US exports, ahead of crude materials and agricultural produce. The US share of international trade now stood at 11 per cent, close behind the British and German figures.

Industrial growth gave the opportunity for a fundamental restructuring of businesses in the direction of ever-larger corporations, soon to become giant cartels and monopolies. In a given industry, the largest firms would drive rivals out of business, and draw other concerns into alliance under the umbrella of trusts or holding companies. This was by no means a new development – in the Civil War the DuPont family had formed a 'Powder Trust' to control supplies of gunpowder and fix prices accordingly. But the process now accelerated. In 1890 James Duke combined the largest cigarette manufacturers into a new business empire, American Tobacco. American Telephone and Telegraph controlled the communications system

The oil industry provided a classic example. The world's first 'oil-rush' occurred in western Pennsylvania in 1859, and in the 1870s the trend towards monopoly proceeded apace under the guidance of former Civil War contractor John D. Rockefeller and his Standard Oil Company, founded in 1870.

Rockefeller entered into secret agreements with the railway companies, which offered discount freight rates to members of the cartel. Dissident firms were driven from business, occasionally through the use of violence and sabotage. By 1876 Standard Oil controlled some 80 per cent of American oil production, and in 1883 the Standard Oil Trust achieved a continental scale. As Rockefeller argued in 1905, 'The American Beauty rose can be produced in all its splendor only by sacrificing the early buds that grow up around it'. Rockefeller's power did not go unchallenged, his rivals being immensely powerful themselves, especially the Gulf Oil concern, which emerged after 1900 with the support of the Mellon banking family.

The process of trust building and corporate centralization reached new heights at the turn of the century, most notoriously with the US Steel Corporation of 1900, the first private economic entity to have a capitalization in excess of a billion dollars. Between 1898 and 1900, 149 combinations were formed with a total capitalization of $3.8 billion. This movement was supported by the great banks, above all the house of J. Pierpont Morgan, yet another war profiteer from the 1860s. In 1889 Morgan set up a banking cartel to corner federal gold reserves, which in the next decade gave him the power to haggle with the US president on terms of more or less equality. His control of credit also allowed him to dominate industries such as oil, steel and coal, and to finance the new conglomerations. In the 1890s Morgan money dominated four of the six vast railway systems, and by 1912 his bank and two others controlled corporations with a combined capital of $22 billion. Morgan died in 1913, leaving $130 million.

Corporate dominance extended to entire industries, and in several western states all economic activity was ultimately based on the railway, which exported produce and imported farm machinery, barbed wire and all the necessities of daily life. The railway corporations set fares and freight rates with unbounded discretion that allowed them freely to reward friends and harm or crush foes. In California, the Southern Pacific railway was known by the eloquent nickname of The Octopus.

In the last quarter of the century the accumulation of vast industrial and commercial fortunes was illustrated by the dazzlingly conspicuous consumption of the new American super-rich, by the glittering New York season and the building of 'cottages' (really, ostentatious mansions) at Newport, Rhode Island. In the 1880s there emerged a network of elite institutions appropriate to the new caste: summer resorts in New England, highly selective country clubs and private schools such as Groton. In 1883 the formation of the 'Sons of the Revolution' marked what historian E. Digby Baltzell terms 'the birth of the genealogical fad and the patrician scramble for old-stock roots': the *Social Register* was first published in 1887.[2] In these years the heiresses of the American nouveaux riches were desperately sought after by the blue-blooded but impoverished nobility of Europe, by English dukes and earls. The United States had created a powerful and well-recognized aristocracy complete with its characteristic institutions, the world of the Rockefellers, Mellons, DuPonts and Fords. On the positive side, these magnates practised philanthropy on a scale unparalleled in human history; but exactly how the existence of this overclass would mesh with the political ethos of a democratic republic would often be a source of bitter controversy in the next century.

MASS IMMIGRATION

As the rulers moved steadily further away from the ideals of an agrarian republic, so did the ruled. American industrial expansion was made possible by the ready availability of cheap labour in the form of the huge numbers of migrants entering the country from the 1860s onwards. From the 1880s

Table 4.2   US population, 1870–1920 (millions)

Census year	National population*
1870	38.6
1880	50.2
1890	63.0
1900	76.0
1910	92.0
1920	106.0

* After 1890, rounded to nearest million

the scale of migration constituted the largest population movement in recorded history. Between 1881 and 1920 there were over 23 million immigrants: 1907 was the peak year, with 1.2 million newcomers (Table 4.2). The great influx found a physical symbol in the immigration facility at Ellis Island in New York Harbour, opened in 1892.

This migration had a radical effect on the ethnic composition of the United States. Before 1880 the vast majority of immigrants came from the British Isles or Northern Europe, chiefly Germany; but after that point the emphasis shifted decisively to the peoples of southern and eastern Europe, including Italians, Poles, Hungarians and all the nationalities of the Austro-Hungarian Empire. In 1870 New York City had 80 000 Jews; by 1915 there were 1.5 million. By 1930 perhaps six million Americans were of Italian stock.

The migration affected most regions of the country to some extent, but the greatest impact was felt in the cities and industrial towns of the north-east and mid-west, where the new migrants took over the poorer sections that had previously been occupied by the Irish. The impact of immigration is suggested by the experience of the industrial state of Pennsylvania – by the 1920s about a fifth of its population was foreign born. In Pittsburgh more than one fifth was foreign born, the largest groups of non-English speakers using Yiddish, Polish, Italian or German. Similar concentrations of foreign-born populations were found in neighbouring industrial districts, smaller steel cities and mining towns. Some 50 Pennsylvania newspapers were directed at a specific ethnic group, written largely or entirely in the appropriate language – half of the foreign-language papers were aimed at Slavic nationalities. By 1910 only a third of the Rhode Island population was of native stock: one third were of foreign birth, and the other third had at least one parent born abroad.

As in the middle of the century, the difficulties of immigrant life were made easier by the political machines, which were happy to assist newcomers to find their way in the new land in exchange for electoral support. This apparent association between the new immigrants and political corruption was a powerful rhetorical weapon for traditional native-stock communities, for whom it confirmed all their worst racial and religious stereotypes. By the 1890s anti-Catholic fears were sufficiently intense to give rise to the American Protective Association, a vigorously Protestant and nativist group that between 1894 and 1896 dominated the politics of several states. Ethnic and religious tensions were also a boon for employers, who exploited mutual suspicion as a tool to prevent mass industrial organization. At least until the 1920s, privileged and managerial positions were the preserve of the old-stock populations, while the immigrants were confined to the more menial jobs.

By the turn of the century the character of urban life had radically changed, with the cities both growing and becoming far more diverse. In 1870 only about a quarter of the US population lived in settlements of over 2500 people; by 1917 the proportion was approaching half. By 1910, 50 American cities had 100 000 inhabitants or more. Between 1860 and 1910 the population of New York City grew from under one million to over four million, and to eight million in the 1920s. Chicago and Philadelphia both had more than a million people by the end of the century (Table 4.3).

Table 4.3   The leading cities of 'Gilded Age' America

	Population (thousands)	
	1860	*1900*
New York	806	3437
Chicago	109	1699
Philadelphia	566	1294
St Louis	161	575
Boston	178	561
Cleveland	43	382
San Francisco	56	342
Cincinnati	161	325
Pittsburgh	49	322
New Orleans	169	287
Detroit	46	286

Only cities with over 250 000 people in 1900 are listed.

This growth was made possible by new forms of mass transportation. In the 1830s the omnibus and the commuter railway appeared in New York, Boston and Philadelphia. From 1869 New York City pioneered a system of elevated railways, while Chicago used cable cars. Between 1890 and 1900 alone, the length of electrified railway line grew from 1 260 to 22 000 miles. Boston acquired an underground railway system in 1897, New York in 1904. Advances in building techniques also helped maintain these new population densities. The concept of skyscrapers appeared in the rebuilding of Chicago following its great fire of 1871, and the model spread elsewhere from the 1880s. These developments allowed an unprecedented concentration of people in areas such as Manhattan, which had 2.3 million people by 1910, and this takes no account of the surging population of the surrounding boroughs connected by underground and elevated railways. In 1898 the five boroughs were consolidated into the vast metropolis of New York City.

The character of the cities also changed, and neighbour-
hoods were often defined by language and religion. The new
cities were usually marked by violent extremes of wealth and
privilege, and the poorest areas suffered from unimaginably
acute forms of multiple social deprivation. By the 1880s the
population density in the slums of East Side New York was
perhaps double the figure of contemporary London. Disastrous public health standards in the nation as a whole are
suggested by the death rates, which were commonly 16 or 17
per 1000 in the first decade of the century, or double the
modern rate. Almost a quarter of deaths were attributed to
pneumonia, influenza or tuberculosis. Industrial accidents
were also extremely common. In 1904, for example, 27 000
workers died through job-related causes. Such figures confirm the remark of Lord Bryce (then a professor at Oxford
University and later ambassador to Washington) in 1893 that
'the government of cities is the one conspicuous failure of the
United States'.

LABOUR AND CAPITAL

Industrialization and urbanization naturally caused intense
social strains, all the greater in view of the glaring disparities
of wealth that existed alongside the egalitarian political structures of the democratic republic. From the Civil War onwards, industrial workers and farmers organized a series of
popular movements to promote greater economic democracy
and social justice, protests naturally being all the greater
during the regular economic downturns and crises. In the
immediate aftermath of the civil war the National Labour
Union emerged from a surge of unionization and labour
activism: in 1872, 100 000 workers struck in New York for
the eight-hour day. In 1869 industrial workers organized
themselves into the Knights of Labor, which had 700 000
members at its height in the mid 1880s; but the movement

faded thereafter, partly due to its reputation for violence. In 1886 the American Federation of Labor (AFL) was formed, drawing mainly on the skilled craft unions. Between 1883 and 1886 union membership rose from around 200 000 to a million, though that number had halved by the mid 1890s. By 1905 union membership stood around two million, perhaps half of whom belonged to the AFL.

Such movements met intense opposition from the state as well as from employers and powerful corporate interests. The courts' sympathy to vast and monopolistic economic structures emphatically did not extend to the interests of labour, and the United States lagged far behind other industrialized societies in recognizing the propriety of labour organization as such, or any form of collective bargaining. Judges sympathized with the paternalistic goals of employers such as George F. Baer of the Anthracite Trust, who declared that 'The rights and interests of the labouring man will be protected by the Christian men to whom God in his infinite wisdom has entrusted the property interests of the country'.[3]

Conversely, most legislatures raised no difficulties about employers forming their own paramilitary forces to control industrial populations and suppress strikes. From the 1870s Pinkertons' and other detective agencies offered comprehensive investigative and security services to the bosses, at a level of efficiency far higher than anything available from any public agency. Without a legal context, the interests of labour had to be expressed through force and extraordinary tactics that generally led to direct confrontations with the machinery of the state. As a consequence American labour disputes before the 1930s were marked by astonishing degrees of violence that often verged on civil war, and industrial conflict reached frightening dimensions in certain periods: 1876–7, 1885–6, 1892–4 and 1912–16.

There were many legendary struggles in these years. In the mid 1870s the anthracite country of Pennsylvania was the scene of a terrorist campaign orchestrated by the 'Molly Maguires', a secret Irish coalminers' organisation. The campaign was suppressed entirely through the private endeavours of the coal employers: all the state supplied was the courtroom and the hangman. In 1876 the centennial celebrations brought an outpouring of 'alternative' declarations of independence, illustrating the deep disenchantment with American society in its continuing depression. The Workingmen's Party of Illinois enumerated 'inalienable rights' that included 'life, liberty and the full benefit of their labor'. The National Woman Suffrage Association asserted that the first century of US history 'has been a series of assumptions and usurpations of power over women'.[4] Labour activist John F. Bray argued that the governments founded on the original declaration 'have failed to prevent the growth among us of the old aristocracies under new names'.

In 1877 the United States experienced a wrenching 'year of violence', which began with a series of strikes by railroad workers and then spread to other industries to create local general strikes during the summer. Protests spread through New York, New Jersey, Ohio, Illinois and Pennsylvania. Twenty-four were killed in battles with the militia in Pittsburgh, eighteen died in Chicago, ten in Baltimore, six in Reading: at least a hundred died during the course of the year. In St Louis a virtual commune was established – the nearest the US has yet produced to a workers' soviet – under the leadership of the Workingmen's Party. The cabinet seriously discussed a proposal to declare a state of insurrection in Pennsylvania, and calling for volunteers on the pattern of 1861. In several areas a critical issue was the loyalty of the state militia, who showed themselves unable or unwilling to oppose their fellow citizens on strike, and who even handed their weapons over to the crowds (the regular US Army was then committed to the Indian wars). This debacle caused the fundamental restructuring of the militias in the form of the new and more strictly military National Guard. Also from 1877, radical populist ideas spread rapidly in rural areas through the formation of the new Farmers' Alliances: within a decade there were 400 000 members. The fragility of public order in 1877 may well have contributed to the willingness of the political establishment to reach their great electoral compromise in this very year.

The mid 1880s produced a comparable explosion, with activism by the Knights of Labor and the Chicago-based Central Labor Union, and a victorious strike against the Union Pacific Railroad. In 1884 a riot over an attempted lynching in Cincinnati turned into a confrontation with class overtones, and 50 people were killed over a three-day period. In 1886 the number of strikes nationwide reached a historical high of 1400. In the same year radical theorist Henry George formed a coalition to run for the New York mayoralty on the working man's ticket.

Any potential revolutionary wave was diverted by the Haymarket incident in Chicago, where a demonstration by mainly foreign anarchists turned into a riot. Seven police officers were killed by a bomb, and four of the anarchists were executed, despite international protests. The outrage following this event crippled the cause of political radicalism for some years, but labour unrest continued, north and south. In 1887 black sugar workers struck under the auspices of the Knights of Labor, a movement that, unsurprisingly, was crushed with the greatest violence. In 1892 a wave of labour stoppages included a general strike in New Orleans. A steel strike at Homestead in Pennsylvania resulted in pitched battles between the workers and Pinkerton detectives hired by Carnegie steel, with perhaps twenty resultant deaths. This was also one of the first conflicts in which strikers faced a terrifying new weapon – the Gatling gun, which threatened mass destruction. In 1894 a strike at the Pullman Car Company near Chicago resulted in the intervention of thousands of federal troops, and the ruthless use of the federal courts to break the railway union. In all the conflict claimed some 34 lives.

One of the main storm centres of class conflict was the western mines, where between 1892 and 1917 the Rocky Mountain states endured a series of violent clashes, complete with assassinations, massacres, mass deportations and concentration camps. The tone of these years is illustrated by the great strikes of 1892, which in Coeur d'Alene, Idaho, led to gun battles of a scale sufficient to cause the governor to declare a state of insurrection and send in the National Guard. In 1899 federal troops in the same state rounded up hundreds of miners and held them for months in bullpens. In 1913–14 the storm centre was the coalmines of southern Colorado, where in April 1914 the National Guard used machine guns to perpetrate a notorious massacre at a miners' tent city near Ludlow. About 70 people were killed during the conflict, including many women and children. In Bisbee, Arizona, in 1917 a miners' strike was ended when vigilantes of a 'Loyalty League' rounded up 1200 workers and forcibly deported them into the desert on cattle trucks.

The main labour organization involved in these actions was the Western Federation of Miners (WFM), which naturally developed a radical and syndicalist bent. In 1905 the WFM participated with socialists and anarchists in the development of a new labour federation that aimed to unionize the workers ignored by the craft-oriented AFL. This was the Industrial Workers of the World (IWW), the 'Wobblies', who aimed at the syndicalist goal of 'one big union' to replace the class-based society that exploited labour. In this view, the union represented the future of social organization, gradually coming to fruition within the decaying framework of the capitalist order. From 1905 to 1919 the IWW made major advances in unionizing immigrant, unskilled and transient workers, while ignoring the colour barriers that were becoming so crucial a determinant of social advancement. It also concentrated on organizing women workers. Among its many battle honours were the strikes at McKees Rocks in Pennsylvania (1909), Lawrence in Massachusetts (1912) and Paterson, New Jersey (1913). The movement developed real strength in particular western regions, including the 'oil patch' of Texas and Oklahoma and the timber areas of Washington state.

The success of the movement excited great fear among the political elite, and repression was commonplace. In 1915 Wobbly leader and itinerant poet Joe Hill was executed on trumped-up charges in Utah. In 1916, at least seven died in a battle between Wobbles and vigilantes at Everett, Washington. The Wobblies were ultimately destroyed by two events in 1917: the declaration of war, which permitted the authorities to suppress most of their activities as German-inspired, and the Russian revolution, which diverted the energies of many radicals into the Communist movement. The IWW faded rapidly after 1919.

PROGRESS AND REACTION, 1877–1917

American national politics in this period were dominated by the Republican Party, which stood for the interests of industry and sound finance, manifested above all in the high tariff on imported manufactures. The party thrived on the mythology of the Civil War, and its image as the party of Lincoln and national unity. There was also an ethnic component, as in many states Republicans represented old-stock Americans against the newer immigrant communities, especially Irish Catholics, and the urban corruption they supposedly symbolized (though Republicans had their own spectacularly dishonest machines in cities such as Philadelphia). In the 1880s Republicans portrayed their Democratic rivals as the party of 'rum, romanism and rebellion'; that is, of liquor interests as opposed to prohibition, of Catholic-dominated political machines, and of the unreconstructed Confederate south.

Following the impeachment and political destruction of Andrew Johnson, the Republicans produced in Ulysses S. Grant a powerful figurehead, whose victory was assured by the disenfranchisement of so many natural Democratic supporters. In normal circumstances, 1876 should have brought a Democratic president to Washington, but the very tense circumstances of the final years of Reconstruction meant that conditions were anything other than normal, and Republican Rutherford B. Hayes obtained a questionable triumph. In 1880 the Republicans secured the presidency for James A. Garfield, but party schisms resulted in defeat in 1884. The Democratic successor was Grover Cleveland, who would again lead his party to victory in 1892. With this one substantial exception, Republicans maintained their hold on the presidency until 1912.

Republican hegemony survived a generation of pervasive scandals, and was not ended by the economic and labour crises of the 1870s and 1880s. From 1860 to 1908 many of the significant political debates occurred within the Republican family and between factions of that party, and dissident groups surfaced repeatedly. In 1872 liberal Republicans mounted a presidential candidacy against Ulysses S. Grant, and in 1876 Republican 'stalwarts' and 'half-breeds' divided over whether Grant should seek a third term as president. Political corruption proved the most persistently divisive issue. Especially after scandals such as that of Crédit Mobilier described earlier, Republicans divided over the workings of the spoils system and the quality of office-holders it produced. One potential solution was a civil service model for government, but attempts to promote a corruption-free bureaucracy were bitterly opposed, not least by those who benefited from the current environment. Nor did the Civil Service Law that was actually passed in 1883 have anything like the desired effect, as it only limited appointments in some federal offices. Throughout the 1880s civil service reform and clean-government issues continued to divide the old guard from the reformist 'mugwumps'. Like the liberal Republicans before them, mugwumps were willing to form coalitions with the Democratic opposition, a defection that helped give the 1884 contest to the Democrats (Table 4.4).

This apparent consensus conceals a great deal of unrest and partisan conflict. Republicans and Democrats ran neck and neck in popular support in every election from 1876 to

Table 4.4   Presidential election results, 1868–1916

	Winning candidate	Popular votes (millions)	Losing candidates	Popular votes (millions)
1868	Ulysses S. Grant (R)	3.0	Horatio Seymour (D)	2.7
1872	Ulysses S. Grant (R)	3.6	Horace Greeley (D)	2.8
1876	Rutherford B. Hayes (R)	4.0	Samuel Tilden (D)	4.3
1880	James A. Garfield (R)	4.5	Winfield S. Hancock (D)	4.4
1884	Grover Cleveland (D)	4.9	James G. Blaine (R)	4.9
1888	Benjamin Harrison (R)	5.4	Grover Cleveland (D)	5.5
1892	Grover Cleveland (D)	5.6	Benjamin Harrison (R)	5.2
			James Weaver (P)	1.0
1896	William McKinley (R)	7.0	William J. Bryan (D)	6.5
1900	William McKinley (R)	7.2	William J. Bryan (D)	6.4
1904	Theodore Roosevelt (R)	7.6	Alton B. Parker (D)	5.1
1908	William H. Taft (R)	7.7	William J. Bryan (D)	6.4
1912	Woodrow Wilson (D)	6.3	Theodore Roosevelt (Prog)	4.2
			William H. Taft (R)	3.5
1916	Woodrow Wilson (D)	9.1	Charles E. Hughes (R)	8.5

1896, and the Republican hold on the White House was an artifact of the American electoral system. Under the 'first past the post' model, a simple majority in any particular state gives the winning candidate all the electoral votes of that state, often producing distorted results. In 1888 Democrat Grover Cleveland achieved a somewhat higher proportion of the popular ballot than his Republican rival Benjamin Harrison, with almost 100 000 more votes out of the some 11 million cast. In the electoral college, however, Harrison defeated

Cleveland by the convincing margin of 233 to 168. The Democrats certainly outpolled the Republicans in 1876, and came close in 1880, though they ultimately lost both elections. They also won sweeping victories in Congressional elections, for example in 1874. Under a different system of representation (and assuming that vote counts were strictly honest on both sides) political power in the United States should have been equally divided between the parties throughout these years (see Table 4.5).

The electoral system also provides an inadequate sense of the underlying currents of radicalism, which gained new strength in the 1890s in the wake of the protracted crisis in the agricultural sector. In 1892 the new Populist movement ran a presidential candidate with one of the most radical platforms ever seen in a national race. Declaring that the nation was at the verge of 'moral, political and material ruin', the party advocated an eight-hour working day, an extension of public control over utilities and a graduated income tax. It

Table 4.5   US presidents, 1861–1921

	Time in Office	Party
Abraham Lincoln	1861–65	Republican
Andrew Johnson	1865–69	National Union
Ulysses S. Grant	1869–77	Republican
Rutherford B. Hayes	1877–81	Republican
James A. Garfield	1881	Republican
Chester A. Arthur	1881–85	Republican
Grover Cleveland	1885–89	Democrat
Benjamin Harrison	1889–93	Republican
Grover Cleveland	1893–97	Democrat
William McKinley	1897–1901	Republican
Theodore Roosevelt	1901–9	Republican
William H. Taft	1909–13	Republican
Woodrow Wilson	1913–21	Democrat

also called for the free coinage of silver, a deliberately inflationary measure that would benefit western farmers at the cost of eastern industry and finance, apart from its obvious appeal to the mining states of the west. To eastern Republicans, free silver and 'soft money' policies represented little less than blatant anarchism. Populist James Weaver of Iowa picked up over a million popular votes, 8.5 per cent of the whole, and even secured 22 electoral votes. One can only speculate what his performance might have been if the election had been held the following year, after the financial crash created so much misery and desperation.

The winter of 1893–4 was bleak, with perhaps 2.5 million unemployed and a total lack of social welfare facilities to begin to meet their needs. Strikes reached new heights, with an average of 1200 a year between 1893 and 1898, and the battles of Homestead and Pullman, described above, were among the most savage in the nation's history. In the spring of 1894 some 17 separate 'armies' of unemployed marched on Washington DC to demand relief and reform, the best-known of which was named after its sponsor, Jacob Coxey. Deep social discontent made inroads into the political mainstream in 1896, when populist ideas influenced the platform of the Democratic Party. William Jennings Bryan won the party's candidacy with an impassioned plea for free silver, and a protest against 'crucifying mankind upon a cross of gold'. He secured 47 per cent of the popular vote and did well in the south and west. However, he performed poorly in urban and industrial regions, 'the enemy's country', and carried no state north of Virginia or east of Missouri. Bryan again led the Democrats to defeat in 1900 and 1908.

The radical presence in the electoral system was indicated by the growth of the Socialist Party, which developed strongholds in many industrial communities. Eugene V. Debs carried the Socialist Party into the national arena with a series of presidential campaigns. He gained a mere 87 000 votes in 1900, but steadily improved his performance and in 1912 attracted a respectable 900 000 votes, or 6 per cent of the popular ballot. The party dipped in support in 1916, but Debs slightly increased his total in 1920. In that year he campaigned from prison, where he was serving a sentence for antiwar activities.

PROGRESSIVES

By the 1890s only the sheltered or optimistic could believe that American society in the new century would not require some kind of dramatic transformation, though there was no consensus about what that new direction might take. A spate of futurological works explored possible destinies, ranging from benevolent elitism to utopian socialism, but a disturbing number posited extreme violence between rich and poor, culminating in apocalyptic collapse. Popular works in this mold included Jack London's *The Iron Heel* and Ignatius Donnelly's *Caesar's Column*. The fears represented by such books did much to shape the thinking of the social reformers known as progressives, whose motivations were complex: while chiefly concerned about the horrors and injustices they witnessed around them, there was also a clear sense that social reform in the present might be the only means of averting turmoil or even civil war in another decade or two. Threats of violence were symbolized by the assassination of two American presidents – Garfield in 1881 and McKinley in 1901, the latter by an anarchist – but neither event represented an extensive conspiracy.

This sense of impending menace and revolutionary crisis helps explain the progressives' attachment to administrative solutions that entrusted powers to skilled experts at the expense of democratic participation. Mass democracy was fundamentally distrusted, and an efficient military model was infinitely preferable to flawed participation. Policing reform was central to progressive thought, as the existing urban forces were not only shockingly corrupt, but dangerously likely to sympathize with striking workers. Reform thus aimed to create strictly disciplined and military-oriented units, as far removed from direct political control as possible. This trend is suggested by the experience of Pennsylvania, one of the regions most prone to labour violence. In 1905 the state formed the State Police, a special constabulary modelled on the paramilitary unit that had suppressed the native revolt in the Philippines some years before. The 'colonial' quality of the mining districts could hardly be better illustrated than by the creation of this unit, which aggressively suppressed protests by immigrant labour and foreign militants. By 1920 the State Police model had been copied by most industrial states.

Though a few organized movements bore the progressives' name, the great majority of progressive activists operated as individuals or informal groupings, often working at the level of a particular city or state. Their activities were similarly diverse. One major element of progressivism was the exposure of abuses that required attention, for example in accounts of slum conditions such as Jacob Riis's *How the Other Half Lives* (1890), Stephen Crane's *Maggie: A Girl of the Streets*, and W. T. Stead's *If Christ Came to Chicago* (1893). The full flowering of exposé journalism came with the first decade of the new century. What Theodore Roosevelt called 'muckraking' was exemplified by work such as Lincoln Steffens' analyses of pervasive municipal corruption, in the articles eventually collected as *The Shame of the Cities* (1904), by Ida Tarbell's dissection of the Standard Oil monopoly, and the work of Ray Stannard Baker. Upton Sinclair's novel *The Jungle* mobilized public anger against the horrors of the meat-packing industry. Such investigations were echoed by official bodies, and in 1894 the Lexow Commission exposed the thoroughgoing corruption of the New York City Police Department.

The practical responses to social evils were diverse. In the political arena the story of the progressives is best observed through the experience of individual political leaders, especially a spate of reformers elected at the turn of the century: mayors such as 'Golden Rule' Jones in Toledo, Emil Seidel in

Milwaukee and Tom L. Johnson of Cleveland; and state governors such as Theodore Roosevelt in New York and (most notably) Robert LaFollette in Wisconsin. These leaders fought the dominant industrial interests, and aimed to reduce their influence in the political process by the promotion of direct primary elections and legislation against corrupt practices. New laws permitted voters to recall unsatisfactory legislators before their terms officially expired, while initiative and referendum laws allowed the electorate to pass desired reforms directly, thus bypassing state legislatures and the party machines that controlled them. The most progressive states, for example Wisconsin, revised their tax systems to place a fairer share of burdens on corporations, and introduced state income and inheritance taxes. It was an uphill struggle, but the enormous steps made are reflected in numerous new state laws regulating wages, hours worked, and health and safety provisions in the workplace, as well as providing compensation for injured workers. Private initiative also made important contributions, for example in the settlement houses erected by middle-class reformers in the worst slums in order to improve the physical and moral well-being of the residents. From the 1890s, Jane Addams' Hull House settlement in Chicago provided a widely imitated model for direct action and social service in the inner cities.

At the federal level the reformers found a friend in Theodore Roosevelt. Previous administrations had passed laws that theoretically enabled them to tackle abuses, notably the Sherman Anti-Trust Act of 1890, but they were rarely enforced with any seriousness. All this changed under Roosevelt, who engaged in well-publicized jousting with the most powerful trusts. In 1902 he ordered the dissolution of the Northern Securities Trust, formed by financial titans J.P. Morgan and E.H. Harriman to monopolize virtually the whole transportation system of the western states. The break-up had been successfully achieved by 1904, laying the foundations for a series of further campaigns. In 1906 the administration began the action that would soon cause the break-up of the Standard Oil Trust into smaller units, although even the new offshoots of the Standard Oil corporate 'family' were gargantuan in their own right (the three main successors became Exxon, Mobil and Socal).

In accordance with the progressive vision of the state as objective arbiter between capital and labour, Roosevelt broke new ground by intervening in a major strike as a genuine honest broker. In 1902 he overcame the employers' stubborn resistance to an anthracite strike by the simple expedient of threatening to use troops to seize the mines, an incredible departure from the violent anti labour policies of most previous administrations. In 1906 a Pure Food and Drug Act was passed, and a series of new federal regulatory agencies began to investigate areas of business practice that would once have been thought untouchable. From 1906 also, the Interstate Commerce Commission was given effective power to regulate railway rates, and a factory inspection system was proposed.

Roosevelt offered a dynamic and attractive model of reform, though in terms of actual achievements he was perhaps equalled by his successor, William H. Taft, who was a more effective trust-buster. It was during Taft's administration that Congress passed two vital constitutional amendments, each in its way fundamental to the progressives' agenda. These permitted the collection of taxes directly on income (the sixteenth amendment) and provided for the direct election of US senators (the seventeenth). However the Republican Party became increasingly split between liberal and conservative factions, which respectively looked to Roosevelt and Taft. In 1912 Roosevelt organized one of the most successful third-party candidacies in American history, the Progressive or Bull Moose Party, which took over four million votes and trounced the official Republicans.

While the split Republican cause only succeeded in securing the election of the Democrat Woodrow Wilson, Wilson was himself sympathetic to most progressive goals, and in fact his administration can be seen as marking the zenith of that tradition. Wilson's recent experience included a model governorship in New Jersey, in which he had sponsored laws introducing primary elections and regulating corrupt practices, and limiting the powers of the public utilities. As president he oversaw the introduction of a central banking system under a Federal Reserve Board (1913), which was correctly seen by its critics as marking a radical transformation of the relationship between business and government. The following year brought a new and far more effective antitrust law (the Clayton Act), and a Federal Trade Commission sought to eliminate unfair business practices. Between 1913 and 1916 the Wilson administration initiated wide-ranging reforms in areas such as child labour, industrial conditions and education. Wilson's bold innovations demonstrated the sweeping implications of the progressive model for federal powers. In terms of the scope of the national government, his regime looked forward to the New Deal of the 1930s as much as it echoed the precedent set by Federalist Alexander Hamilton in the 1790s.

WOMEN'S RIGHTS

One critical area of progressive reform was the extension of women's rights, an issue that had irrevocably entered the political agenda in the late nineteenth century. In 1869 the granting of the vote to black men had caused an upsurge of feminist radicalism, which involved at least an element of racist resentment and the assertion that white women were assuredly more qualified for suffrage than any former slaves. Two organizations were now founded, under the leadership of long-serving feminist activists Elizabeth Cady Stanton and Susan B. Anthony: the groups combined in 1890 to form the National American Woman Suffrage Association. Suffrage and feminist ideas were also advanced through reformist groups such as the Women's Christian Temperance Union (founded in 1874), which despite its name advocated a social agenda far broader than the simple question of drink.

The practical possibility of women's suffrage was advanced by its adoption in western states, usually in a desperate attempt to bring in a broader range and better quality of settlers, especially farming families. The Wyoming Territory was the first such jurisdiction, to be followed by the Utah territory in 1870, and in 1890 Wyoming became the first state whose women could vote. By 1914 women had full suffrage rights in the ten most westerly states. Expanding the system nationwide required a constitutional amendment, which was proposed in 1878 and reintroduced regularly thereafter. The issue was given new life by women's participation in the First World War, and after a series of extremely close votes the nineteenth amendment was passed by the Senate in 1919 and ratified by sufficient states in 1920.

The fight for women's political rights was parallelled by an equally difficult struggle for personal emancipation, which in the case of poor women especially required control over reproduction. Abortion was technically illegal in the early nineteenth century, but the activity continued despite occasional prosecutions of demonized 'abortionists'. Advertisements for abortion-related services were freely published. Though statistical evidence is difficult to interpret, the proportion of pregnancies terminated in the 1850s may have been similar to the present-day figure. Matters changed after the Civil War with the growing organization and assertiveness of the medical profession, which was determined to eliminate rivals such as midwives and abortionists. The American Medical Association (1847) was a major force in demanding legislation.

Criminal laws now acquired real force, reinforced by the moralistic and evangelical movements of the day. These were epitomized by Anthony Comstock, founder of the New York Society for the Suppression of Vice, who waged a fifty-year struggle against 'filth' in public life. In 1873 the Comstock Act prohibited the circulation of contraceptive information through the mails, and by the end of the century the availability of information on abortion and contraceptive technologies was severely limited. The Comstock regime was challenged after 1912 by Margaret Sanger, who was an ally of both Wobblies and socialists. Concerned with the lot of poor and immigrant women, Sanger tried to make contraceptive information freely available, activity that in 1916 resulted in her facing criminal charges. Her trial and imprisonment gave her the status of a martyr. In 1921 she formed the American Birth Control League, and in 1952 the Planned Parenthood Federation.

CULTURE AND RELIGION

The impact of the new social movements was apparent in literature. As in the 1850s, the last quarter of the nineteenth century produced an outpouring of important work, especially novels and poetry. Among the most significant novelists working in the 1880s were Henry James, Mark Twain and William Dean Howells (Table 4.6).

To put this into context, published in the mid 1880s alone were Howells' *Rise of Silas Lapham* and James' *The Bostonians*, while Twain's *Huckleberry Finn* can be regarded as a definitively American contribution to fiction and one of the greatest American novels. It also represents a common nostalgia for the freedom and mobility of the lost antebellum America. Apart from literature, American artists now made impressive contributions in the field of painting, where James McNeill Whistler, John Singer Sargent and Thomas Eakins were powerful innovators in the 1870s and 1880s. The Western paintings of Frederic Remington illustrated the emerging national mythology of cowboys, Indians and cavalrymen.

In the 1890s American literature was influenced by new concerns and literary styles, including a note of social radicalism and a related emphasis on realism. In very different ways, these ideas were represented in the fiction of Stephen

Table 4.6   Major literary works published, 1876–1907

1876	Mark Twain, *Tom Sawyer*
1879	Henry James, *Daisy Miller*; Henry George, *Progress and Poverty*
1880	Henry Adams, *Democracy*; Lew Wallace, *Ben Hur*
1881	Henry James, *Portrait of a Lady*; Mark Twain, *The Prince and the Pauper*
1882	William Dean Howells, *A Modern Instance*
1883	Mark Twain, *Life on the Mississippi*
1884	Mark Twain, *Huckleberry Finn*
1885	William Dean Howells, *Rise of Silas Lapham*
1886	Henry James, *The Bostonians*
1888	Bellamy, *Looking Backward*
1889	Mark Twain, *A Connecticut Yankee at King Arthur's Court*
1890–1	Emily Dickinson, *Poems*
1893	Stephen Crane, *Maggie: A Child of the Streets*
1894	Henry D. Lloyd, *Wealth Against Commonwealth*; Mark Twain, *Pudd'nhead Wilson*
1895	Stephen Crane, *The Red Badge of Courage*
1896	Emily Dickinson, *Poems 1896*; Harold Frederic, *The Damnation of Theron Ware*
1897	Charles M. Sheldon, *In His Steps*
1898	Henry James, *Turn of the Screw*
1899	Frank Norris, *McTeague*; Kate Chopin, *The Awakening*
1900	Theodore Dreiser, *Sister Carrie*
1901	Frank Norris, *The Octopus*
1902	Owen Wister, *The Virginian*; William James, *Varieties of Religious Experience*
1903	Henry James, *The Ambassadors*; Jack London, *Call of the Wild*
1904	Henry James, *The Golden Bowl*; Jack London, *The Sea Wolf*
1906	Upton Sinclair, *The Jungle*
1907	Jack London, *The Iron Heel*

Crane, Jack London, Frank Norris, Theodore Dreiser and Upton Sinclair. A new political sensibility shaped books such as Frederic's *Damnation of Theron Ware*, which among other things explores the intellectual barrenness of organized religion.

The strident ideological conflicts of the day had a strong religious dimension. Both reformers and reactionaries were motivated by their particular interpretation of the Scriptures and the Christian creeds, which were now debated at least as vigorously as any point of law or economic doctrine. The years after 1910, which in political terms marked the height of political 'Progressivism', are also known as the floodtide of religious 'Fundamentalism', two notions that obviously stood in sharp contrast to each other. Both in fact represented divergent reactions to common circumstances.

On the liberal side, the progressive ideas of social action and political reform were supported by advocates of the 'Social Gospel', represented by books such as Washington Gladden's *Applied Christianity* (1886) and Walter Rauschenbusch's *Christianity and the Social Crisis* (1907). Charles M. Sheldon's hugely popular novel *In His Steps* (1897) describes how a Protestant congregation decides to live according to their interpretation of what Christ would do in a particular situation. The answer is found in far-reaching reform and missions to the poor, in addition to the more traditional emphases on public decency and temperance.

While believers in social action might well have been strictly orthodox in their theological approach, Protestant Christianity of the day was marked by a powerful liberalism that challenged such basic beliefs as the divinity of Christ, his miracles and resurrection, and the literal truth of the Bible. The spread of Darwinian theory from the 1860s exercised an influence here, above all the notion that the world had evolved over many millions of years. If humanity arose gradually from a series of lower species, this left little room for the Creation and other events described in the Book of Genesis.

Ecclesiastical liberalism provoked a vigorous reaction among those already shocked by the spread of critical interpretations of the Bible in the universities and even the divinity schools. From the 1870s American Protestantism sparked a number of new movements and sects that were guided by a strictly literal interpretation of the Bible. Moreover the dominant theme of the new enthusiasts was premillennial, meaning that social reform was worse than useless, and might actually be a satanic snare. This theological position had important political consequences.

Millennial debates about the Last Times were ancient in Christianity. All agreed that the Book of Revelation described an era of harrowing disasters and misfortunes, as well as a glorious physical reign of Christ on Earth for a thousand years; but were the disasters to come first, or the glorious thousand years, the millennium? In the early nineteenth century many American Protestants agreed that the millennium would come first, to be followed by a brief time of troubles in which the devil would be conquered utterly. This post-millennial theory justified, even demanded, social activism, as removing atrocities such as slavery would promote the coming of Christ's kingdom. From the 1860s there was a general drift towards the darker and more pessimistic notion of premillennialism: the end of the current world-age was near, and it would be followed by the tribulation, a harrowing period of tyranny, famine, plague and massacres. Only after these horrors would the few surviving saints live to see the Messiah stand upon earth. There was little room in such a picture for social reform, especially when this meant alliance with those who spurned God's word.

Premillennial ideas spread under the influence of preachers such as John Nelson Darby, who popularized the notion of the 'Rapture', the sudden removal of the true saints from earth before the worst disasters occurred. These theories had become the evangelical norm by the end of the century, when the focus of discussion moved to the formulation of precise timetables of exactly which prophetic events would occur in what order, and how scripture foretold contemporary events or persons. Parallel to millennialism was a new interest in perfectionism, the idea that the truly reborn Christian could and must seek a higher spiritual state of sanctification. Debates on this theme within the Methodist churches produced yet another revival, in the form of the Holiness movement. The new and stricter churches explored ecstatic practices and faith healing, and engaged in excited premillennial speculation.

By the end of the century the Pentecostal movement asserted that individual Christians might receive the gift of speaking in tongues akin to that recorded in the Biblical Book of Acts. Pentecostal revivals originated in black churches, but soon crossed racial lines. As so often before, religious excitement was reflected in the sprouting of many new denominations between 1870 and 1914, including the Jehovah's Witnesses (millenarian), the Church of the Nazarene (Holiness), the Assemblies of God (Pentecostal) and the various subdivisions of the Church of God (Holiness/Pentecostal). Odder manifestations included the Appalachian sects which accepted the literal truth of Christ's promise that faithful believers would be able to handle serpents unscathed.

By the end of the century an insurmountable gulf separated the faith of the educated liberal social reformer and that of the literalist or Pentecostal believer, and the division was expressed in the notion of the 'Bible Belt', those regions of the south and west in which enthusiastic ideas were accepted unquestioningly. However it would be wrong to see this as a simple conflict of ignorance and education, as some of the literalists were scholarly individuals who formulated their arguments in a well-supported series of books and tracts. In 1895 the Niagara Bible Conference formulated 'fundamentalism', the idea that a core of doctrines must be defended as the essentials of Christianity. Between 1910 and 1915, books entitled *The Fundamentals* declared the minimum substance of beliefs for a true evangelical Protestant: the inerrancy of scripture, the virgin birth of Jesus, the substitutionary atonement, the bodily resurrection of Jesus, and the second coming. That they needed to defend these once universal doctrines also shows the distance travelled by liberal thought.

Religious distinctions became linked to ethnic and social hostilities, as evangelicals and fundamentalists saw themselves as beleaguered representatives of true Americanism against urbanization and immigration, and against the polyglot metropolises that came to dominate the nation from the 1880s onwards. Worse, the new cities were havens for Catholic and Jewish populations. The battle between the two cultures found its highest expression in the temperance movement, which sought to impose the values of the native Protestant countryside upon the ethnically diverse cities. Prohibitionist candidates actually ran in presidential campaigns from 1884 onwards, and were a regular fixture in state politics. The movement culminated in the adoption of a constitutional amendment, the Volstead Act, and by 1919 the United States was notionally dry. For feminists and fundamentalists, progressives and socialists, the answer to the ills of society was self-evidently to be found in the actions of government, and specifically the federal government.

Notes

1. Quoted in Pierre Berton, *The National Dream: The Great Railway 1871–1881* (Toronto: Penguin, 1989) p. 11.
2. In E. Digby Baltzell, *The Protestant Establishment: Aristocracy and Caste in America* (New York: Random House, 1964) pp. 113–15.
3. Quoted in Jack London, *The Iron Heel* (London: Journeyman Press, 1975) p. 46n.
4. These quotes are taken from Philip S. Foner (ed.), *We the Other People: Alternative Declarations of Independence by Labour Groups, Farmers, Woman's Rights Advocates, Socialists and Blacks, 1829–1975* (Urbana: University of Illinois Press, 1976).

5

War and Globalism, 1917–56

THE GLOBAL DILEMMA

Americans have long been troubled by the prospect of overseas entanglements. Opposition to the acquisition of imperial commitments in 1898 stemmed not merely from radicals and socialists but also from a wide range of religious, liberal and traditional minded groups. Moreover this was not a war that might have been expected to be expensive in American lives. Through the first half of the present century there was steady resistance to military endeavours in Europe, and American entry into both world wars was only accomplished after intolerable provocation. In peacetime also, US entry into international organizations was met with implacable resistance from quite broad political coalitions, overwhelmingly so in the case of the League of Nations. The prospect of the United States becoming a world power on the model of the despised imperial states of Europe appeared unacceptable from many points of view. However these were exactly the years in which the United States was forced to assume the role of a global power, and that role transformed the nature of domestic politics. Foreign affairs became central to internal debate; the executive gained unprecedented strength as the focus of the new imperial role; and the rise of the military caused a phenomenal expansion of the federal government. It can be argued that the growth of the defence and national security concerns of the American state has been the central reality of the nation's history in the present century.

There are many explanations for American willingness, however reluctantly obtained, to enter the world stage. Given the circumstances of world politics in 1917, 1940 and 1947, it is hard to see how such a role could have been resisted if the United States was not to find itself surrounded by the overwhelming strength of hostile powers espousing ideologies utterly at variance with American beliefs. Domestic issues merged seamlessly with international pressures in transforming American attitudes towards the wider world. In 1917 as in the 1940s, the confrontation with perceived foreign aggression became inextricably linked to campaigns to curb radical threats at home, so that the existence of foreign enemies, both German and communist, gave an ideological foundation for the establishment of a new conservative consensus at home. This linkage promoted acceptance of the new American role.

THE FIRST WORLD WAR

When the First World War broke out in 1914, American public opinion was strenuously opposed to participation. Radicals and socialists opposed entry into a struggle between rival capitalist cliques; liberals and pacifists hated the destruction caused by war, especially over a matter that had no obvious bearing on American life; many ethnic groups denounced any attempt to align the United States with countries they hated for reasons of their past or present misdeeds. German and Irish voting blocs were both committed to preventing any assistance to the British Empire. President Woodrow Wilson had no desire to risk his programme of domestic reform through an ill-considered military adventure.

Over the next three years, pressure to enter the war became unavoidable, largely because of the German campaign of submarine warfare against England. American ships were sunk, often intentionally, and American lives were lost. In May 1915 the sinking of the liner *Lusitania* caused a deterioration of German–American relations. The following year the German Navy stated frankly that the war could only be won if its U-boats adopted the tactic of unrestricted warfare against all ships in the blockade zone, regardless of nationality, and this measure was commenced in early 1917. Also at that time, the British released intercepted telegrams in which the German Foreign Ministry proposed a military alliance with Mexico, with the goal of restoring Mexican rule over Texas, New Mexico and Arizona. This 'Zimmermann Telegram' confirmed rumours that Germany was conspiring with Mexico and probably Japan to reverse much of the United States' nineteenth-century westward expansion. In April 1917 President Wilson declared war on Germany, though the lack of a national consensus is indicated by the Congressional vote in which six senators and 50 representatives opposed war, a figure that probably understates public qualms.

American entry into war was critical from a propaganda point of view. Allied forces on the western front would soon be reinforced by millions of fresh American soldiers, a prospect that counterbalanced the otherwise disastrous news of Russian withdrawal from the fighting. This was bitterly discouraging for the German forces. At the least, the prospect of American entry provoked the German offensives of 1918, the failure of which contributed to the disaffection that erupted throughout the Central Powers. In a military sense, however, the American role was strictly limited. In 1917 the regular US Army was a tiny force, and building and training the formations needed to intervene decisively in France would take years. The key American contribution was therefore planned for the campaigns of 1919 and perhaps 1920.

Initially US Commander John Pershing had to struggle to preserve the autonomy of the American Expeditionary Force, rather than having soldiers absorbed into French units. In 1918, independent AEF units won some significant engagements in the French sector of the western front. In the spring, Marines suffered heavy casualties at Belleau Wood, while other units blocked the German offensive at Chateau Thierry. By September a million Americans were participating in the Meuse-Argonne campaign, which broke the German lines. In all 4.7 million Americans served in the armed forces, which suffered 116 000 deaths, under half of which occurred in battle. This was far less than the damage inflicted on the other combatant powers: France, Germany, Russia and Austria–Hungary each suffered between one and two million dead, and the British Empire just under a million.

The impact of the war on American domestic life was out of all proportion to its military involvement. Partly because of the uncertain public attitudes to national policy, there was extreme hostility to the slightest expression of doubt or criticism about the course of the war. As historian David Kennedy writes, 'the war for the American mind' was the first and most decisive engagement in the American participation in this global struggle.[1] This aspect of the war had many fronts. In ethnic terms it devastated the German–American community, which for over a century had been one of the most esteemed immigrant groups, and had developed a lively cultural life throughout the nation. All German symbols were an obvious target: the renaming of sauerkraut as 'liberty cabbage' is a notorious example of the public mood. Orchestras ceased to play German music, schools abandoned the teaching of the German language. Hostility also extended to the other Central Power, Austria–Hungary, which was the home nation of millions of the Slavs and Jews who had entered the United States since 1880. Technically all were now enemy aliens.

The war uprooted the socialist and radical ideas that had spread so widely since the turn of the century, and which had thrived in the industrial crisis of the pre war years. Radicals and pacifists began a lively propaganda campaign against the war and the draft, but in June 1917 the federal government passed a draconian Espionage Act that severely limited any such criticism. This was enforced ruthlessly: by the post office, which refused to carry seditious literature in the mail; by local and state police, who raided socialist and IWW offices; and by private groups, who denounced any suspicious or 'un-American' behaviour, by which was commonly meant the slightest association with unorthodox or foreign ideas. Vigilantism was institutionalized through the American Protective League, which worked in intimate alliance with local employers and their existing structure of anti labour surveillance and espionage. Such groups were incredibly active and intrusive, arresting and interrogating thousands of possible radicals and draft evaders, and serving as a private arm of law enforcement.

For the authorities, the American war effort was constantly vulnerable to subversion by foreign and radical groups that were effectively German agents. The IWW was dismissed as 'this German-inspired, anarchistic organization'. In areas with a large concentration of foreign-born residents, official fears are well illustrated by the 1917 proposal to equip units of the Pennsylvania Reserve Militia with machine gun units specifically in preparation for mob violence or insurrection. In such encounters, 'machine guns are of inestimable value. The machine gun has acquired such a reputation for deadliness that its very presence frequently overawes a mob.'[2] The language is almost that of white settlers living outnumbered in an Asian or African colony.

THE CRISIS OF RADICALISM

The wartime panic directed against spies and saboteurs drew little distinction between socialists, syndicalists, pacifists and active German sympathizers, as all were believed to be equally hindering the American war effort. The identification of radicalism with foreign subversion continued undiluted when the German demon was replaced by the Russian–Soviet fiend, and the Kaiser gave way to Lenin as the ultimate puppeteer. As a socialist leader declared in 1919, 'The IWW and Bolshevism have replaced the Yellow Peril and Prussianism as the great menace.'[3] This perception received added impetus from the abundant representation of foreign-stock activists in the leadership of radical movements such as socialists, the Wobblies and (from 1919) the newly formed Communist Party of the USA. The repressive apparatus formed to defeat the Kaiser's supposed agents was now brought to bear on a new wave of 'un-Americanism'. The vigorous tradition of American radicalism suffered crippling blows between 1917 and 1920.

The year 1919 was marked by labour agitation quite as marked as anything in the nation's history, with massive strikes affecting not only traditional industries such as steel and coal, but also hitherto tranquil sectors of the labour market such as the police and even the theatre. Whole cities and regions were virtually shut down by strikes, and in some areas, labour conflicts resulted in massacres and civil strife. Seattle had a general strike, the Boston police walked out, and the steel strike in Pittsburgh was a traumatic affair. The coalfields of Pennsylvania and West Virginia now began several years of virtual guerrilla warfare. The nature of these struggles was soon transformed from issues of wages and standards of living to more poisonous ethnic and political battles, and a period of violent reaction now set in. It took different forms according to local conditions, but the recurring theme was the aggressive reassertion of traditional social and racial hierarchies. Wobblies in Washington state were massacred by rightist vigilantes in Centralia, and as so often the mobs were orchestrated through the newly formed veterans' society, the American Legion. Mobs attacked leftist demonstrations in New York, Boston, Detroit, Chicago and Cleveland, with violence reaching a peak that May Day.

Across the mid-west, 1919 brought some of the bloodiest race riots in American history, which usually involved pogroms of black communities by white mobs. The precursor to this outbreak was the pogrom of blacks in East St Louis in July 1917, when black strike-breakers were blamed for the failure of a labour protest. A hundred blacks died in the ensuing violence. Tensions increased during the following year, with fears that blacks would take the jobs of absent white servicemen; while black servicemen themselves were given a new determination by the relatively equal treatment they received in France and elsewhere. When strikes erupted in 1919, employers used black strike breakers in steelworks and coalmines, exacerbating racial tensions for years to come. As soldiers of both races were demobilized and the economic depression deteriorated, violence was inevitable. Forty died in Chicago, and large but uncertain numbers in Washington DC, Knoxville (Tennessee), Charleston (South Carolina), Omaha (Nebraska), and Texas. In Tulsa in 1921 there was a massacre of black residents after armed blacks attempted to defend a man from lynching. The scale of the violence deserves emphasis: in both Tulsa and East St Louis, black sections of the city were virtually eliminated.

Political reaction in 1919 was stirred by fears of leftist terrorism, by the dozens of mysterious bombings and bank robberies that appeared to be the first moves towards overt revolution by Bolsheviks or anarchists. In September 1920 a bomb placed in New York's Wall Street killed over thirty. Conservatives used the climate of violence to undertake a massive repression, and US Attorney General Mitchell Palmer ordered the arrest of foreign radicals – the detailed planning of the purge was entrusted to a young civil servant named J. Edgar Hoover. On the night of 2 January, 1920, 4000 were seized in mass raids across the United States, and hundreds were deported. There were also individual cases, such as the prosecution of two Italian radicals named Nicola Sacco and Bartolomeo Vanzetti for a robbery in 1920. The two were sentenced to death on questionable evidence, and the affair became a cause célèbre for radicals worldwide during the following decade. The two were eventually executed in 1927.

The implication of Palmer's raids was that radicalism was a foreign importation that could be excluded if sufficiently determined policies were adopted. The decline of industrial conflict from about 1922 appeared to show the truth of this perception, and the authorities could claim that the nation had been saved from red revolution.

Much of the repression from 1919 onwards involved extra-legal tactics and outright vigilantism, both by law enforcement agencies and private groups, on the model so ably established by the American Protective League. Courts rarely raised the slightest objection. Indeed a series of US Supreme Court cases now pared back the right of free speech to the point of near-oblivion. In 1919 the Schenck case upheld the right to suppress dissident speech when there was a 'clear and present danger', the exact definition of that danger being largely left up to the discretion of the authorities. In that specific case, the actions criminalized involved the distribution of antiwar pamphlets. The Whitney case in 1927 led to the conviction of a Californian woman whose crime was apparently confined to participating in radical discussions. Though not originally a political case, the Olmstead case in 1928 legitimised phonetapping, despite the protests of those who asserted a right to privacy. The court also showed itself sympathetic to the quite draconian measures legislated in the name of eugenics and the control of racially unfit.

THE 1920S: PROSPERITY AND CORRUPTION

With Germany in ruins and Great Britain exhausted, the war left the United States in an entirely novel position of world dominance. The United States was now a major military power, and the Washington naval treaty of 1922 gave its navy parity with the British fleet as the world's largest, although American strategic needs required far fewer ships than the far-flung British possessions. The tonnage of the American merchant navy grew sharply during the war, both in absolute terms and in comparison with the depleted British position. The United States secured economic hegemony with the great productive resources unleashed by the war effort. The US share of international trade grew to 15 per cent in the early 1920s, just ahead of Britain, while New York displaced London as the world's financial metropolis. The vast Allied war debt to the United States gave American administrations a potential diplomatic weapon of terrifying scale.

But military and financial muscle had to be combined with political will, and that was distinctly lacking. In 1918 President Woodrow Wilson's 'fourteen points' enunciated a detailed plan for the redrawing of European boundaries, together with a restructured system of collective security. Central to this was a League of Nations, which its more optimistic advocates envisaged as the seeds of a future world parliament. However the League would be meaningless without the participation of the United States, and Wilson grossly underestimated American opposition to this international entanglement. From the spring of 1919, League critics such as Senators Henry Cabot Lodge and William E. Borah were mobilizing support, and the politics of the following year were dominated by the president's desperate efforts to promote ratification. The Senate rejected the Treaty in November by 55 votes to 39. In 1921 the new Republican president Warren G. Harding (Table 5.1), formally announced that the United States would take no further part in the work of the League, an ultimately fatal blow to the whole scheme. In 1922 Harding withdrew the remaining American occupation troops in the Rhineland, and the following year the Senate rejected proposed US membership of the International Court of Justice. For the next two decades American society tried its best to isolate itself from the outside world, above all from the European plague-pits, which were the source of infections like Bolshevism and imperial diplomacy.

Table 5.1   US presidents, 1913–61

	Time in office	Party
Woodrow Wilson	1913–21	Democrat
Warren G. Harding	1921–23	Republican
Calvin Coolidge	1923–29	Republican
Herbert C. Hoover	1929–33	Republican
Franklin D. Roosevelt	1933–45	Democrat
Harry S. Truman	1945–53	Democrat
Dwight D. Eisenhower	1953–61	Republican

In 1920 the Republican presidential candidate, Warren G. Harding, ran on a platform of 'return to normalcy', which had enormous popular appeal. Though political slogans rarely bear close analysis, this was an unusually interesting example because of the question of which 'normalcy' was meant: though ostensibly calling for a return to pre-1917 conditions, it obviously did not include such normal manifestations of that era as the IWW, strikes, mass immigration and urban sprawl, but rather a return to an imagined 'normalcy' of social tranquility and ethnic homogeneity set somewhere in the historic past, perhaps before 1850. This conservative and indeed nostalgic phrase set the tone for the politics of the 1920s, which were marked by the ascendancy of rural and suburban Protestant values to an extent that would never be seen again. Significantly, the 1920 census was the first to show a majority of Americans classified as urban rather than rural, and more than a quarter of the workforce were now employed in factories. Harding's victory in 1920 secured the Republican hold on the White House for twelve years (Table 5.2).

White, Anglo-Saxon Protestant values were best exemplified by the victory of prohibition in 1919, a measure designed in contempt for the rival cultural and moral values of the

Table 5.2   Presidential election results, 1920–52

	Winning candidate	Popular votes (millions)	Losing candidate	Popular votes (millions)
1920	Warren G. Harding (R)	16.2	James M. Cox (D)	9.2
1924*	Calvin Coolidge (R)	15.7	John W. Davis (D)	8.4
			Robert M. LaFollette (Prog.)	4.8
1928	Herbert Hoover (R)	21.4	Alfred E. Smith (D)	15.0
1932	Franklin D. Roosevelt (D)	22.8	Herbert Hoover (R)	15.8
1936	Franklin D. Roosevelt (D)	27.8	Alfred Landon (R)	16.7
1940	Franklin D. Roosevelt (D)	27.2	Wendell Willkie (R)	22.3
1944	Franklin D. Roosevelt (D)	25.6	Thomas E Dewey (R)	22.0
1948**	Harry S. Truman (D)	24.1	Thomas E Dewey (R)	22.0
			Strom Thurmond (SR)	1.2
			Henry A. Wallace (Prog.)	1.2
1952	Dwight Eisenhower (R)	33.9	Adlai E. Stevenson (D)	27.3

* In 1924 Robert M. LaFollette ran on the platform of the Progressive Party.
**In 1948 there were four candidates. Apart from the Democrats and Republicans, Strom Thurmond ran on a States' Rights ticket, and Henry A. Wallace as a Progressive.

urban population. The effectiveness of the measure is controversial, and any long-term success was sabotaged by the doctrinaire insistence on banning beer and wine in addition to spirits. Alcohol consumption and related diseases probably did fall substantially, but at horrendous cost in terms of crime, disrespect for law, and political corruption. While American cities had always been governed by corrupt party machines and police, prohibition now made independent powers of racketeers who had hitherto enjoyed only a subservient role, whether Jewish, Italian or Irish. Organized crime syndicates acquired vast power that would in later decades be diversified into gambling, narcotics, prostitution and labour rackets. Gang wars became a source of public scandal, and gangland massacres in Chicago and Philadelphia in 1928–9 gave glaring proof of the failures of the prohibition experiment.

White Anglo-Saxon Protestant (WASP) and Temperance values inspired the Ku Klux Klan, which between 1921 and 1926 achieved dazzling success across the country, but especially in northern and mid-western states such as Indiana and Pennsylvania. At its height, around 1923–24, there were between four and eight million Klan members, including a strong female contingent. Though opposed to black and Jewish advances, the movement was primarily and fundamentally anti-Catholic, and drew heavily on the ideas and literature of the ultra-Protestant movements of the previous century. In industrial states, this ideology gave the movement a lively appeal among those skilled workers and middle managers who feared the competition of immigrant groups, as well as ordinary Protestant workers who had suffered from the importation of black or immigrant strike breakers. The Klan became a political fixture in many states, and absolutely dominated regions such as Indiana. Nativist sentiment reached a new height with the Immigration Act of 1924, which unashamedly focused its restrictive endeavours on the peoples of southern and eastern Europe, instituting quotas for various nationalities in terms of their relative strength in the American population as of 1890, before the recent migration wave. This measure virtually terminated mass immigration to the United States until the 1960s.

The Klan upsurge was politically critical for the Democratic Party, which rested on an unstable coalition between the Protestant countryside and the urban masses. By 1924 'rum and romanism' were pitted against the WASP heartland, causing chaos at that year's Democratic Party convention. The cities favoured New York's Al Smith, an urban Catholic who for the Klan and its sympathizers represented the worst in American life. It took 103 ballots to find an undistinguished compromise, who was resoundingly defeated by the Republicans that November. Radical and progressive forces were siphoned off by the candidacy of Robert LaFollette, who won one sixth of the popular vote nationwide. The Klan itself soon self-destructed amid gruesome scandals about the violence and corruption of its leadership, but the crosses blazed briefly once more in 1928, when the Democrats eventually summoned up the nerve to run Al Smith for president.

Distrust of new social directions was also apparent in the religious sphere, where the fundamentalists became embroiled in a bruising controversy with national repercussions. The state of Tennessee was one of several jurisdictions to have outlawed the teaching of the godless doctrine of evolution in its public schools. The law invited challenge, and a legal action was ensured when a young teacher named John T. Scopes flouted the statute. The ensuing trial in 1925 was brought into a realm somewhere between high drama and low farce by the gladiatorial combat between the two legal advocates, William J. Bryan for the prosecution and the socialist and secularist Clarence Darrow for the defence. The event was treated by the world media as a form of sporting match, in which the final score was extremely difficult to determine. Though Scopes was convicted, the fundamentalists were irredeemably tarred with the stigma of backwoods intolerance, and Bryan's reputation was destroyed. Sinclair Lewis's novel *Elmer Gantry* (1927) offered a definitive example of the dim view of fundamentalism held by the worldly and educated. On the other hand, laws such as those of Tennessee remained on the statute books for decades afterwards, and American textbook publishers had to exercise great caution on the delicate subject of evolution at least until the late 1950s, when Soviet successes in space caused Americans to fear that their science education might be falling badly behind that of international rivals.

In both business and politics the 1920s were marked by a distinctly easy-going disregard for ethics. President Warren G. Harding's administration was one of the most cheerfully corrupt of modern times, and scandal tainted several of his intimates from the 'Ohio Gang', at least two of whom committed suicide while under investigation. The Teapot Dome scandal arose when Interior Secretary Albert B. Fall was discovered to have secretly leased oil reserves in Teapot Dome, Wyoming, for personal gain, and Attorney General Harry Daugherty was forced to resign in disgrace. Conspiracy theorists even suggested that the convenient death of Harding in 1923 might have been accelerated in order to prevent further exposures. In business, the booming economy provided copious opportunities for sharks preying on gullible investors and real estate purchasers. The Florida land boom of 1925 ruined speculators while lining the pockets of confidence tricksters.

However economic conditions between 1923 and 1928 were generally good, and far more consumers were now able to acquire what had once been luxury goods, including cars, telephones and domestic labour-saving devices. As the automobile industry became a leading sector of the economy, production was increasingly dominated by a few large firms, with coordinated operations spread over a vast geographical area. By 1927 General Motors was the most powerful concern, followed by Ford and Chrysler, collectively the 'Big Three'. Though still a comparative infant, the aircraft industry grew steadily in the 1920s. From about 1915 manufacturers had often chosen to locate on the west coast: Boeing in Seattle, Lockheed in Burbank, Douglas in Santa Monica and Long Beach, North American in Los Angeles. During the 1920s, Southern California came to play a role in aircraft comparable to that of Detroit in automobiles. Air travel also established itself in these years. By the late 1920s aircraft were being used for bulk mail deliveries, and the first commercial airlines had been established. Within a decade, the industry was dominated by such familiar names as Transworld (TWA), United and American.

Aircraft symbolized speed, modernity and youthful heroism, images epitomized by the 1927 solo flight of Charles A. Lindbergh from New York to Paris. Together with the emerging skyscraper landscape of the great cities, aircraft represented the futuristic dream of a new society based on constant technological innovation and unlimited consumer prosperity. The Empire State Building was designed with a mast that was intended to assist the landing of commercial dirigibles, surely the luxury transportation of the future. Of course, when the building finally opened in 1931 it was in circumstances far grimmer than its designers had ever expected.

THE CRASH

The dream began to fall apart with the stock market crash of 29 October, 1929, followed by a wave of bank failures over the next year. Slumps were nothing new in American history, as every generation since the late 1830s had known slowdowns, with a major disaster roughly once every twenty years. It soon became apparent that 1929 was going to mark a wholly new scale of misery. Although the precise accuracy of the statistics left something to be desired, the scale of the disaster was apparent. Throughout the 1920s the national unemployment rate had usually fluctuated around 5–6 per cent, falling to a low of under 2 per cent in the good years in the middle of the decade. The rate then rose to 9 per cent in 1930 and had almost reached 24 per cent by 1932. In the worst days of 1933 nearly 13 million people were unemployed. By 1932 industrial production stood at 40 per cent of capacity, and the stock market was at one tenth of its pre-crash level.

The depression reached new depths in 1932, and there were signs of serious tears in the social fabric. Communist influence was growing among the unemployed, and hunger demonstrations and protests were becoming common in major cities. Homeless people formed tent villages known as 'Hoovervilles', in cynical tribute to the president, who repeatedly asserted that business confidence remained firm. Unemployed Councils adopted the simple slogan 'Fight – Don't Starve'. In March 1930 a demonstration of 35 000 marchers in New York City was disrupted by heavy-handed police action. In industrial areas, relief offices were targeted, and state authorities were painfully aware how close to exhaustion the relief funds were. The collapse of relief would mean starvation and food riots. In 1931 thousands of Chicago residents mobilized to prevent the eviction of tenants unable to pay their rents, a protest that led to violent struggles with police. Veterans' groups concentrated their attention on the issue of the cash bonus that Congress had promised them after the First World War. This sum was to be paid to the returning heroes in 1944, but militants now demanded that it should be paid forthwith, at the time of maximum need. In June 1932, 20 000 veterans of the 'Bonus Army' marched on Washington, where they formed a camp. In July they were dispersed by federal troops using bayonets and tear gas, led by General Douglas MacArthur. These violent scenes were uniquely disturbing to anyone who had watched democracies collapse in contemporary Europe.

Ruin was general. In agricultural regions of Nebraska and Iowa the Farmers' Holiday Association tried to force the government to support farm prices by withholding produce from the market, and their actions led to violent confrontations in 1932. Agrarian protests were also directed at preventing the foreclosure of farm mortgages and the consequent evictions. Farm conditions in other areas reached utter desperation in 1933–5, when drought and high winds compounded the effects of decades of soil erosion to turn the southern great plains into a dust bowl. Dust storms made life intolerable in a territory stretching from Texas to the Dakotas, and virtually destroyed the rural economies of entire states. Thousands of ruined farmers from Oklahoma and Arkansas trekked west to California in search of mere survival.

The crash accentuated long-developing regional tensions and structural changes within industries. In both mining and textiles, employers in the first quarter of the century had tended to shift their enterprises from the unionized and militant north to the more docile, low-wage south, a redistribution made possible by the rail network. The proportion of US cotton goods produced by the southern states rose from 6 per cent in 1880 to 30 per cent in 1910, and to almost 50 per cent by the mid 1920s. Southern competition was appalling news for textile states such as Rhode Island, which probably would have suffered an economic catastrophe in the 1930s even if the stock market had not gone under: the shakeout was aggravated by the great textile strike of 1934. Northern industry contracted accordingly, throwing thousands out of work. The miners of Pennsylvania were equally hard hit by the move to coalfields in Kentucky.

Obviously, economic crisis and the end of open immigration dramatically limited population growth, so that the US population of 1930 rose by only 14 per cent during the next two decades, by far the lowest rate in American history up to that time. Two hundred and fifty years of headlong expansion seemed to have come to an end overnight.

There were fears that a dictatorship might emerge from the growing chaos, and several demagogues emerged as likely candidates. Most spectacular was the governor of Louisiana, Huey Long, whose radical populist programme had already laid the foundations for a virtual monarchy in his own state. In 1930 he became a US senator, and his presidential ambitions were only cut short by his assassination in 1935. Long's counterparts and imitators included Art J. Smith, whose 'Khaki Shirt' movement was modelled on Mussolini's fascists, and who proposed a farcical March on Washington in 1933; and William Dudley Pelley, whose 'Silver Shirts' may have attracted 20 000 adherents in the west and mid-west.

Radio priest Father Charles Coughlin initially preached a Catholic social doctrine that denounced both capitalism and communism equally, but by the end of the decade he had become a crude exponent of conspiratorial anti-Semitism. In 1936 Coughlin allied with other extreme populists to mount a presidential campaign, but it proved lacklustre. However there were enough signs of impending trouble to justify concern. In 1935 Sinclair Lewis' novel *It Can't Happen Here* depicted a triumphant American fascist movement under its dictator 'Buzz Windrip', probably based on Pelley.

THE NEW DEAL

The 1932 presidential election occurred at one of the most dangerous points of American history, and its results were to be quite as revolutionary as the tumultuous contest of 1860. Franklin Delano Roosevelt gained power with a convincing popular majority, and began to take the political and economic measures so desperately needed to repair the society, and probably to save democracy itself. An immense amount was accomplished during the 'hundred days', the special emergency session of Congress that was called to pass sweeping reforms that would have been unthinkable in any context other than the present crisis. The first step was to rescue the financial system. A 'bank holiday' closed the banks long enough to end the immediate panic, while an Emergency Banking Relief Act and a Home Owners Loan Corporation provided for longer-term security. The year 1934 brought a Federal Farm Mortgage Corporation to finance farm loans, as well as a Securities Exchange Act (SEC) to regulate the financial markets and prevent renewed chaos like that of 1929.

The 'hundred days' also began the gargantuan task of dealing with mass unemployment and poverty, and there now appeared the first of countless regulatory and supervisory agencies to provide employment and begin the rescue of whole regions (Table 5.3). From their bewildering deluge of initials and acronyms, these bodies were collectively known as the alphabet agencies.

The programme involved a Federal Emergency Relief Act and a National Industrial Recovery Act (NIRA) to get people back to work, while a Public Works Administration oversaw vast public investments in buildings, roads, bridges and infrastructure. The Civilian Conservation Corps employed two and a half million young people to build roads and dams and plant trees on public lands; the National Youth Administration provided job training and part-time work for the young. Among the most daring schemes was the TVA,

Table 5.3   Major New Deal agencies, 1933–8

1933	National Recovery Administration
	Civilian Conservation Corps
	Tennessee Valley Authority
	Agricultural Adjustment Administration
	Public Works Administration
	Commodity Credit Corporation
	Farm Credit Administration
	Federal Deposit Insurance Corporation
	Federal Emergency Relief Administration
	Home Owners Loan Corporation
1934	Securities and Exchange Commission
	Federal Communications Commission
	Federal Housing Administration
1935	Works Progress Administration
	National Youth Administration
	National Labor Relations Board
	Social Security Board
	Rural Electrification Administration
1937	Farm Security Administration
	United States Housing Authority
1938	Federal Crop Insurance Corporation

the Tennessee Valley Authority, which began a vast programme of public works to provide jobs in that hard-hit
region by building federally funded dams to generate cheap
electrical power. In 1935 the national insurance programme
known as Social Security was introduced, together with a
Wealth Tax Act and the Works Progress Administration.
Among this whirlwind of reforms, the ending of prohibition
in 1933 looked like an afterthought.

The New Deal reforms were awe-inspiring in their ambi-
tion and scope, all the more so since they ran so directly
contrary to so much of the received wisdom of the proper role
of government in American national life, in areas such as the
power of the federal government and the sharing of responsibilities between Washington and the states. Generations of
conservative economic thought were swept away by the new
Keynesian paradigm, which saw massive government intervention as a key to recovery, incurring whatever short-term
deficits seemed necessary. In a few years the United States
became a far more centralized nation than ever hitherto, at
least in peacetime, and the scale of the national government
expanded enormously. For the first time, thousands of experts and technocrats now poured into government service,
creating a new meritocratic class whose origins were often
among the nation's newer ethnic groups. In so many ways, it
is difficult to avoid describing the New Deal less as a reform
package than a social and administrative revolution.

This was uniquely true in the area of labour relations, in
which the New Deal gave American workers the legal rights
that many of their European counterparts had enjoyed for
decades. The National Labor Relations Act of 1935 asserted
workers' rights to organize and bargain collectively, and
further established a bureaucratic mechanism to ensure that
employers complied with these principles. Naturally the Act
created an alphabet agency, the NLRB (National Labor
Relations Board). Over the next three years the labour
movement took full advantage of these opportunities and
expanded unionization through sections of industry that

hitherto had been beyond its reach. The main activists were associated with the CIO, the Committee for Industrial Organization, which from 1935 mobilized industrial workers largely ignored by the craft-oriented unions of the AFL.

The steel and automobile industries proved especially critical, and 1937 brought decisive strikes to unionize such bitterly antilabour firms as General Motors and the 'Little Steel' corporations. Many lives were lost, and labour acquired a new litany of martyrs with events such as the 'Memorial Day Massacre' in South Chicago, when five strikers were killed (though the loss of life was not large by nineteenth-century standards, the impact of the event was augmented by its representation on newsreel). The CIO enjoyed enormous success with its influential tactic of sit-in occupations, which prevented employers from breaking the strike by importing replacement workers. In 1937 alone there were almost 500 sit-down stoppages. Though heavy industry attracted the most media attention, the strike wave that reached its apogee in 1937 also affected countless other sectors, including southern sharecroppers and farm labourers, timber workers in the Pacific north-west, textile workers and department store employees.

By the end of the decade the CIO had enjoyed enormous victories, and the labour unions were firmly entrenched in the American economic scene, especially giant groups such as the steelworkers, miners, the teamsters (truck drivers) and automobile workers. By 1945 the AFL and CIO each had over six million members. The unions were occasionally assisted by the forces of government, both the federal New Deal administration and prolabour Democratic administrations such as that of Governor George Earle of Pennsylvania, who reversed a long precedent by using his National Guard to dragoon recalcitrant employers. The alliance of organized labour with the New Deal was infuriating for conservatives, who saw red revolution being imposed from above. Communist and syndicalist influence within the CIO was a source of provocation for more traditional union leaders, and in 1937 the CIO was expelled from the AFL. Although the political right considered that Roosevelt's administration was fulfilling their worst nightmares, it continued to be immensely popular. The 1936 election resulted in one of the worst electoral defeats in American history, when the Republicans managed to secure only Maine and Vermont; and while the 1940 election was a little less embarrassing for the right, the New Deal platform survived undamaged.

Mass popular support for the Roosevelt administration ensured that effective opposition would have to come not from the Democratic Congress but from the non-elected Supreme Court, long hostile to any form of official interference with property rights or contractual obligations: a concept that was extended to include virtually any government regulation of working conditions. Led by four implacable conservative justices, the 'Four Horsemen', the Court waged war on the New Deal, systematically striking down laws and agencies: the NIRA, the Agricultural Adjustment Act, a Municipal Bankruptcy Act, state minimum wage laws. Even the SEC seemed vulnerable, and in 1938, the powers of the NLRB were restricted. Normally a president facing an antagonistic court was expected to bide his time until enough justices died or retired to be replaced by more acceptable faces. The 1930s, however, were not normal times, and the weight of public support for the New Deal led Roosevelt to attempt a constitutionally risky remedy. In 1937 he announced a plan to raise the number of justices by six, to 'pack' the court, a suggestion that proved too much even for most of his supporters, and the measure failed miserably.

The New Deal had its greatest successes in Roosevelt's first term, with 1937 as perhaps the best year. Between 1930 and 1933 the gross national product of the United States had fallen from $99 billion to 77 billion – a figure that had more than bounced back to $113 billion by 1937. GNP per capita rose from $615 in 1933 to $881 in 1937, and to $954 by 1940. People also became significantly better off in material terms as the decade progressed, as measured by possession of material goods such as cars or telephones. In some ways the New Deal could only soften the worst effects of the crisis. Unemployment obstinately remained at an appalling 16–20 per cent for most of the late 1930s, and only fell below 15 per cent after the United States began its military rearmament programme in 1940. Even in 1937, unemployment only just dipped below eight million, and 1938 brought a brief but painful economic contraction. Ultimately, only war cured the problem, bringing the figure down to 1 per cent by 1943. Moreover the financial costs were immense: the federal debt grew from $22.5 billion in 1933 to $40.5 billion in 1939.

But even if Roosevelt could not boast complete success, the 1930s were in many ways a revolutionary era in American society. As government became vastly bigger, so did people's expectations of the appropriate role of that government, especially of Washington. As in the 1830s, a radical administration benefited from the expanded electorate, which resulted both from the enfranchisement of women and the overall growth of the population (Table 5.4). A typical presidential election in the 1880s usually involved some ten or eleven million ballots cast on both sides; the figure for the 1928 election was over 36 million; in 1948, about 50 million.

Table 5.4   US population, 1920–60

Census year	National population (millions)
1920	106
1930	123
1940	132
1950	151
1960	179

The New Deal had a particular impact on American agriculture, reinforcing long-established trends in rural society. While the depression initially wiped out many small farmers, the Roosevelt administration subsequently enhanced the position of larger operations through federal price supports. The movement towards fewer but larger farms was also promoted by advances in mechanization, which benefited those with sufficient capital to invest. There were 6.3 million farms in 1930, 5.4 million in 1950, 3.0 million in 1970. Total acreage under cultivation actually increased in these years, so that the average farm size had tripled since the late 1920s. The farm population contracted dramatically, from 30.5 million at the time of the stock market crash to under 10 million in 1970.

INTO WAR

From 1938, foreign affairs once again became central to American political life. The expansionism of Germany and Japan and the growing likelihood of war in Europe once more raised fears that the United States might find itself embroiled in overseas military entanglements. Roosevelt himself was a staunch opponent of fascism, and of the western leaders he may have had the most far-sighted vision of a grand strategy to confront and defeat the dictatorships. However antiwar sentiment in the United States was quite overwhelming, with a widespread sense that US involvement in the First World War had been disastrous and costly, all to benefit ungrateful allies who had largely reneged on their immense debts. In 1934 Senator Gerald P. Nye's investigating committee attempted to prove that American intervention in 1917 had been manipulated by a conspiracy of bankers and arms dealers, and in 1935 and 1937 Neutrality Acts attempted to make it virtually impossible for the United States to intervene in a European war. Moreover, by 1938 opposition to war was deeply entrenched among those large ethnic groups that either had a general sympathy for home countries now under dictatorial rule, or had historical reasons for opposing the western allies. Entry into war might force Roosevelt to confront a dangerous coalition of Germans, Italians, Irish, Ukrainians and others, possibly allied with a Catholic Church that viewed Bolshevism rather than fascism as its primary European enemy. From mid 1939 American communists and many leftists were also vehemently opposed to war, as a consequence of the Nazi–Soviet pact.

Between 1939 and 1941 Roosevelt had to pursue a careful strategy, repeatedly denying that he sought foreign entanglement, while providing the British and French with as much aid and support as could be given without creating a public scandal. The White House also used the media to focus attention on the American far right as a dangerous fifth column threatening to subvert the United States, and possibly resorting to sabotage in the event of war. Domestic fascists unwittingly cooperated with Roosevelt by holding increasingly daring rallies complete with swastika flags and torchlight rallies, and by boasting of the mass membership of groups such as the German American Bund, the (Coughlinite) Christian Front, the Italian Fascisti, the Silver Shirts and the Ku Klux Klan, all of which cooperated in a broad political front. Media exposés of such groups undoubtedly assisted the interventionists. Discrediting the fascists was all the more important in view of the refugee question. By the late 1930s millions of Europeans were seeking to go to the United States, many of whom were Jews. The prospect of a mass influx of Jewish refugees threatened to revive the immigration question that most had thought settled in 1924, and stimulated a wave of anti-Semitism and street violence against Jews in major cities. Linking anti-Semitism to treason and un-American activity was a step towards preventing worse violence.

Overseas events caused a rapid transformation in American attitudes. In November 1939 the best the administration could achieve was a revision of the Neutrality Act to permit belligerents to purchase munitions on a 'cash and carry' basis, a useful concession as long as Britain and France had the economic resources to take advantage of this. By mid 1940, however, all the Allied powers had been defeated with the exception of an embattled and impoverished Britain, which obviously needed assistance if the United States was not to confront a European continent wholly ruled by Germany. US public opinion was stirred to sympathy by the Battle of Britain, the first conflict in several years in which the Germans had met their match in either military or diplomatic terms; but even so, aid was slow in coming. In September the United States gave the British fifty ancient but useful destroyers, but only in exchange for long leases on naval bases in the western hemisphere. Roosevelt could legitimately claim this as a profitable trade, in which the United States finally achieved the naval supremacy in the Caribbean and elsewhere that it had dreamed of for a century. Only in early 1941 was the non-interventionist principle breached by the decisive Lend-Lease Bill, which employed the fiction that the huge quantities of weaponry to be sent to Britain were being amicably loaned, for return after use.

The US commitment increased over the following months, as naval cooperation with Britain became so close as to constitute a virtual state of undeclared warfare against German submarines in the North Atlantic. Domestically, the rearmament campaign and the introduction of peacetime conscription foreshadowed direct participation against the Axis, a probability reinforced by media reporting of the exploits of American pilots and American-made ships and aircraft in the Allied cause. The sense of military preparedness was heightened by regular training exercises, in which US aircraft 'bombed' strategic targets in and around major cities. Vicariously at least, the United States was in all essential ways a combatant power for most of 1941.

Throughout 1940 and 1941 the US public engaged in a passionate debate that involved issues more fundamental than at any time since the conflicts over slavery. Intervention was opposed by the America First Committee, an umbrella organization composed of conservatives in alliance with some liberals, religious leaders and pacifists. The AFC was much maligned at the time as a cover for pro-Nazi sentiment, and many of its analyses were discredited by subsequent events. But the movement as a whole raised critical questions that seem even more relevant in light of more recent historical developments: about the nature of executive power in matters of foreign policy, and the official use of propaganda and deceit to achieve what is believed to be a desirable political end. Much in the isolationism debate foreshadowed later controversies – Vietnam in the 1960s and Central America in the 1980s. The whole debate addressed such fundamental issues as the nature of the United States, the ethnic basis of political power, and the degree to which the nation had liberated itself from a European and specifically British political orientation. As the Bund's newspaper regularly declared, 'The USA is *not* a "British" Nation'. One did not need to be a crypto-Nazi to oppose any but a defensive war, nor to see Roosevelt's international policies as reckless buccaneering cynically designed to provoke a war, contrary to the overwhelming weight of public opinion.

America was finally drawn into the war by events in the Pacific, where the government was deeply concerned by Japanese expansionism in China and South-East Asia. As in Europe, the administration had offered covert aid to the Chinese war effort, including the use of American pilots, and, as in the Atlantic, there were outbreaks of real warfare: in 1937 Japanese aircraft sank the US gunboat *Panay*. Diplomatically, US pressure increased as the Japanese pushed further into China and Indo-China. The commercial treaty between the nations was abrogated in mid 1939, and over the next two years the United States imposed economic restrictions, including the crucial weapon of oil supplies. By July 1941 the United States had frozen Japanese assets in the United States, imposing a virtual embargo on all trade, including oil. This step made it all but certain that Japan would have to seize oilfields to fulfill its strategic needs, while ejecting the United States from the Asian theatre.

THE SECOND WORLD WAR

On 7 December, 1941 Japanese forces attacked the main US naval base at Pearl Harbor in Hawaii, causing immense damage to battleships, but providentially missing the aircraft carriers that would prove decisive in the coming months. The United States immediately declared war, and the dilemma of whether to go to war against Germany too was ended when Hitler declared war on the United States.

For the first few months America's chief military concern was stemming the ferocious Japanese advance across the Pacific, which had resulted in the capture of the Philippines, Malaya and Burma, and presented a serious threat to Australia. A lively invasion scare on the American west coast resulted in the mass arrest and deportation of Americans of Japanese ancestry, an act later judged to be illegal and racially discriminatory. America regained the military initiative in the naval war in the Battles of Coral Sea (May 1942) and Midway (June), and then began the long series of island-hopping campaigns to reconquer Japanese-held territory in the south Pacific, through the Marshalls, the Carolines and the Marianas.

Though fought in small areas, several of these island battles were among the bloodiest of the whole war and caused heavy casualties among the US forces. The Marine Corps alone was to lose a total of 20 000 men in the course of the war, almost as many as in all its other wars before or since. Among the most important Pacific battle honours were Guadalcanal (1942), Tarawa (1943) and Saipan (1944). By 1944 American forces had secured general supremacy at sea and in the air, which allowed reconquest of the Philippines. In 1945

US forces won the two critical battles of Iwo Jima (February–March), and Okinawa (April–June), which together gave
American aircraft the landing strips necessary to maintain a
bombardment of the Japanese home islands, and to prepare
for an invasion should that become necessary.

Despite the heavy involvement in the Pacific, US commanders had made the early decision that Germany remained the
chief military enemy, and that the major military thrust
would be in Europe. This was a contentious decision, and
once more raised isolationist arguments about the nature of
US political goals: was the United States in the war to defeat
the Japanese aggressor, or to serve once more as the puppet
of British imperialists and communist slavemasters? The
European orientation was complicated by debates with the
British over how soon a massive Allied force might be landed
in Western Europe. Initially the Americans wanted to organize such a stroke as soon as possible, in 1942 or 1943 at the
latest, but the British were nervous at the prospect of heavy
casualties in a ground war that could produce carnage of
First World War proportions. The British preferred a Mediterranean strategy to knock out Germany's allies, accompanied by an air offensive in which Anglo-American bombers
would destroy German cities and industries. Ideally this
phase might last long enough for the Soviets to break the
back of the German army.

Britain enjoyed some success in these negotiations, and the
United States was persuaded to support amphibious landings
in French North Africa (1942), Sicily and then Italy (1943–4).
Meanwhile American forces were building up in Britain itself
in preparation for the ultimate move across the Channel. This
culminated in the D-Day landings of 6 June 1944, in which
American, British and Canadian soldiers participated. By
August the Axis forces in France had been decisively defeated, and Allied forces advanced into the Low Countries.
After a brief setback in the German Ardennes offensive that
winter, American forces led a breakthrough across central
and southern Germany in spring 1945, and in fact went far

beyond the limits originally planned for them when the occupation zones were originally designated.

Following the German surrender in May, American attention turned to the defeat of Japan, which continued to resist despite deadly air attacks that killed hundreds of thousands. Invasions were planned, with estimated US casualties ranging from an optimistic 40 000 to a more realistic figure five times that size, to say nothing of Japanese fatalities. Allied commanders were also worried about Japanese revenge against the large numbers of American and Allied prisoners in the event of invasion. Moreover, while the Japanese had expressed interest in a negotiated peace, their proposed terms suggested a lack of realism about the depth of their defeat. These factors encouraged the US administration to use the new atomic bomb, which was first successfully tested on 16 July in New Mexico, and the destruction of the cities of Hiroshima and Nagasaki in August forced the Japanese to surrender.

Over 16 million Americans served in the armed forces between 1941 and 1945, of whom 292 000 died in battle and 114 000 from other causes. On the home front, the removal of so large a proportion of the young male population had an enormous effect on economic and social life. Their places in the workforce were largely taken by women, three million of whom were employed in war production. Between 1940 and 1944 the proportion of women in the workforce grew from 27 per cent to an unprecedented 35 percent. Black workers also found themselves with vast new opportunities, accelerating the migration from the south to the north and west, and from the countryside to the cities. This naturally increased expectations for social justice and enhanced political aspirations (see below).

The gigantic US war effort had a lasting effect on the structure of American society, including a geographical shift of power to the western states, which played so critical a role in war production. The west-coast aircraft firms became major employers after 1940, initially supplying Britain, and then the American war machine. Lockheed was already employing 50 000 people before the United States entered the war, and the workforce approached 100 000 by mid 1943. Californian shipyards were swiftly turning out 'Liberty Ships', while the ports of San Francisco, Los Angeles, San Diego and Seattle were all embarkation points for the Pacific war. Though the late 1940s were a difficult period for the defence industries, the Korean War and subsequent tensions provided a renewed stimulus, which chiefly benefited the west and south. Lockheed, for example, bought a large new plant at Marietta in Georgia, while General Dynamics was headquartered in Missouri. Texas was the heart of the aerospace industries from the late 1950s.

The shift to the 'Sunbelt' has been one of the central events of American history in the current century, a movement of population and influence comparable to the post-1840 'winning of the west' in its social and political impact. The change is exemplified by California, where the population increased by 50 per cent during the 1940s, to reach 10.6 million. Western cities flourished. Los Angeles ended the war with 1.5 million people, San Francisco with 800 000, Seattle with more than 400 000, San Diego with 300 000. Between 1945 and 1960 this trend was reinforced by increased prosperity in the nation at large, which expanded the range of leisure options available to middle-class people. Tourism and a taste for retirement in the sun contributed to the rapid growth of states such as California, Arizona and Florida, and the expansion of urban centres such as Miami and Las Vegas.

In the international sphere, the United States ended the war as the greatest economic and military power on the planet, indeed in human history, and it was from that time that the word 'superpower' entered the language as the only term adequate to express its supremacy. Apart from its nuclear monopoly, the United States was the only combatant power not to have had serious damage wrought on its national territory, and it had by far the strongest financial structure. Though older world empires were still notionally intact, the only power with any potential to challenge the United States in the short term was the Soviet Union, and at that time the Soviets were of course cherished allies.

CONFRONTING COMMUNISM

The years from 1945 to 1949 marked a turning point in American history. After the peace with Japan, there was a natural temptation for the nation to withdraw from overseas commitments and concentrate on domestic reconstruction. Although the Soviets remained a formidable rival, the United States' belief that it held an indefinite monopoly on the atomic bomb might well have promoted isolationism, a fortress mentality. In reality the reverse occurred, and the United States entered into international commitments on an unprecedented scale.

Shortly after the coming of peace, US politics came to be dominated by a profound sense of fear about external aggression and internal subversion. This was partly a response to domestic political conflicts and the unresolved debates of the New Deal, aggravated by the upsurge of labour unrest that crippled large sections of industry in 1946. In the first half of that year, some three million workers were on strike. For conservatives, the Democrat administration was dangerously tinged with socialist ideas scarcely removed from communism itself, and these notions were all the more dangerous because of their strength in organized labour. The 1946 mid-term elections returned a vigorously active Republican eightieth Congress that set about passing draconian anti-union laws that would re-shape labour relations for decades to come.

But domestic considerations took second place to international tensions. Between 1945 and 1948 relations with the Soviet Union were first soured and then poisoned by the consolidation of communist rule in the countries of Eastern Europe. By 1947 the new Soviet bloc included Poland,

Rumania, Bulgaria, Hungary, Albania and the occupied zone in Germany, as well as (less firmly) Yugoslavia. The year 1948 brought the traumatic fall of Czechoslovakia. The customary domestic constituency for anticommunist interventionism was now strengthened by new elements, both ethnic and religious. The communist military threat in Europe was a source of special concern to the Catholic Church, which had already lost such loyal territories as Hungary, Croatia and Poland, and stood in imminent danger of being driven from France and even Italy. In the United States the Catholic leadership emerged as a stridently anticommunist advocate, a role in which it was supported by many of the immigrant groups that had come to dominate the politics of major American cities: Irish and Italians in many regions of the country, Hungarians, Slovaks and Poles through much of the industrial north-east and mid-west.

The United States was forced to take on a direct role following the abdication of the policing role formerly played by other traditional powers, especially Britain. This became apparent in Greece, where a guerrilla war was raging. In early 1947 Britain declared it could no longer continue to support the anticommunist cause without US assistance, and threatened to withdraw its forces. In response President Truman declared his 'doctrine', which pledged American support for 'free peoples who are resisting attempted subjugation by armed minorities or by outside pressure'; and American military aid began to arrive in Greece that August. Also in 1947, a National Security Act proposed the radical restructuring of American defence, creating a National Security Council and a Central Intelligence Agency (CIA) to offer the intelligence coordination that had so conspicuously been lacking before 1941. At the same time the United States began a vast programme of European reconstruction under the title of 'Marshall aid', which eventually poured billions of dollars into laying the foundations of the postwar economic miracles across Western Europe.

In sum, the developments of 1947 heralded a major change in US policy, the creation of a 'national security state' in peacetime, with the obvious implication that preparations were being made to combat further Soviet advances through diplomatic and intelligence means where possible, and military means where necessary. American leaders were determined to avoid a repetition of the 1930s, in which dictatorships had been able to proceed more or less unchecked, to the point where the only way of stopping them involved all-out war. The new policy was soon apparent in France and especially Italy, where US resources were employed to prevent communist victories during 1948. The United States' strategy included the encouragement of moderate anticommunist wings within socialist parties and unions, and the creation of new Christian Democratic parties on the right.

Soviet–American relations had now come perilously close to open warfare, which seemed likely to erupt over the Soviet closure of land routes to Berlin in June 1948 in an attempt to eliminate this island of Western influence in the communist zone. The city was saved by the Berlin airlift, in which supplies were flown in to the city for over a year, but tension remained high. In 1949 the United States formed the NATO alliance, a departure from its earlier reluctance to join international coalitions in peacetime. Perceptions of the scale and nature of any future conflict were radically altered by two events later in 1949. In September the Soviets detonated their first atomic bomb; and in October the Chinese communists secured a hold over the whole of mainland China, establishing the People's Republic. Each of these phenomena caused horror in the west. For Americans, there was now the possibility that New York or Washington might become nuclear targets to be eradicated as thoroughly as Hiroshima, a vision made far worse by the evolution of the even more terrifying hydrogen bomb. (The United States exploded the first such weapon in May 1951, the Soviet Union followed suit in

August 1953.) The loss of China to communism not only added several hundred million new 'slaves' to the emerging world empire, but simultaneously destroyed the American dream for a benevolent empire in that part of the world, a civilizing mission that would spread an advanced evangelical Protestantism to a people deemed hungry for the gospel.

KOREA

Fears of Armageddon reached new levels in June 1950 with the outbreak of war between communist North Korea and the pro-Western south, and an apparently unstoppable communist invasion. This was commonly seen as the early phase of a general communist push against the West, and similar actions were thought likely in other frontier regions, including Germany. It was thus a matter of desperate urgency to prevent the fall of South Korea, where the United States was able to construct a broad coalition technically under the flag of the United Nations. Though there were major contingents from many European and Asian nations, the UN army was overwhelmingly dominated by American forces, and American commanders ran the war with only formal acknowledgement of the UN dimension. Between 1950 and 1952 the strength of the US military grew from 1.5 million to 3.6 million.

The early phase of the war was disastrous for the UN, with communist forces sweeping over most of the south by early September, forcing the allies into a small pocket based on Pusan in the extreme south-east of the peninsula. The UN commander in chief, Douglas MacArthur, then devised a daring counterstroke involving a large-scale amphibious assault at Inchon, in the North Korean rear. The operation (15 September 1950) was a brilliant success, generally ranked among the greatest military feats in American history. The course of the war was transformed: the communist forces

retreated far north of their original border at the 38th parallel. UN forces pressed forward, taking the northern capital of
Pyongyang in October. However the United States became
overconfident and ignored diplomatic messages warning of
Chinese intervention if they drew too close to the borders of
the province of Manchuria. True to their government's word,
a huge Chinese army invaded Korea in October, rapidly
driving the UN forces back to the 38th parallel. In January
1951 a new Chinese offensive resulted in the temporary loss
of Seoul.

At that point political realities came into conflict with the
military dynamics of the war. General MacArthur vocifer-
ously advocated an escalation of the struggle to include
China itself, proposing an invasion of mainland China by
the Nationalist forces expelled two years before. He also
raised the nightmare prospect of using nuclear weapons
against Chinese bases in Manchuria, an action that would
have forced Soviet participation and resulted in all-out global
war. Moreover his public advocacy of these positions, his
public criticisms of President Harry S. Truman, and his more
or less open diplomacy with the Nationalists all posed grave
questions about civilian control of the military. The nuclear
issue in particular caused severe tension with US allies such
as Britain, and there was at least the possibility that the crisis
would fragment the UN coalition. In April 1951 Truman
demanded MacArthur's resignation, over the protests of Republican warhawks, who flirted with the idea of a MacArthur
presidential candidacy in the coming year.

By mid 1951 all the major combatants had made clear that
they were ready to discuss a ceasefire, having gained all they
were reasonably likely to. However protracted diplomatic
arguments meant that the struggle dragged into a long and
bloody stalemate, with a war of attrition for bare hills that
were little more than reference points on the maps of the
strategic planners. The war was also becoming internationally unpopular. Though few outside the far left believed the
widespread communist charges that the UN forces were using

biological warfare, there was firmer evidence of maltreatment of northern prisoners, and scandals followed bloody outbreaks in southern prison camps. In 1952 the indecisive war became a central election issue, when the Republican presidential candidate Dwight Eisenhower promised that if elected he would go to Korea in order to break the impasse. A ceasefire was declared after his election in 1953, with the restoration of the 38th parallel as the *de facto* border between the two countries. The US participation in Korea had involved 5.7 million servicemen and women, 34 000 of whom had been killed in battle.

While in the decade after Korea the United States was not involved in a further 'hot' war, there was continuing tension with the communist powers, which were perceived as direct successors of the wartime Axis: as Hitler had had his Oriental partners in Japan, so the Soviets found their accomplices in China. This perception reinforced the United States' determination not to back down in the face of aggression, and to extend the collective security agreements that safeguarded Europe. In Asia, Chinese and thus Soviet manipulation was seen behind each political crisis. The collapse of the French position in Indo-China in 1954 led to discussions of American involvement, and possibly of nuclear intervention. Later that year the United States became the core of the new South-East Asia Treaty Organization, SEATO, an oriental echo of NATO. In 1958 the United States sent the Seventh Fleet to help Nationalist China (Taiwan) resist an attack by the People's Republic on some disputed islands. Europe also remained on a hair-trigger, a situation aggravated by the aggressive Western propaganda machines aimed at the people of the communist bloc. Yet another war scare erupted when the Hungarian people rebelled against communist rule in 1956, but despite the threatening words of the American radio stations, NATO tanks did not roll eastward. The conflict between East and West had attained a kind of stability, however tenuous.

THE ANTI COMMUNIST PURGE, 1946–56

Confrontation in foreign policy had repercussions at home, especially the multiple shocks of 1949–50: the Soviet A-bomb, the fall of China and the Korean War. Coming as the culmination of years of communist triumph, such a series of catastrophes was clear proof that American endeavours must have been undermined by sinister forces, by spies and traitors, and the quest for culprits now began in earnest. Though the anticommunist purges of those years are generally known as 'McCarthyism', they were well under way years before Senator Joseph McCarthy of Wisconsin first achieved celebrity in 1950, and in fact occurred chiefly under the Democratic administration of Harry Truman between 1946 and 1953.

The first and most obvious casualty was the Communist Party. In July 1948 the party leadership was found guilty of trying to overthrow the government, an innovative prosecution because they were chiefly accused of circulating books and pamphlets that discussed and advocated such a line, rather than taking direct steps to that end. In the Dennis case of 1951, the US Supreme Court held that even such discussions could properly be regulated, and that the government was under no requirement to wait until a coup was in active preparation. By 1951 many US states had banned the operation of the party in their jurisdictions and placed numerous burdens on members, including the removal of welfare benefits. Most states also instituted loyalty oaths for public employees, requiring them to swear that they supported no subversive causes or activities. Civil servants, teachers and others were summarily fired on the strength of alleged communist ties, or even on 'reasonable suspicion' that such links existed. State legislatures usually passed such measures by an overwhelming majority, as few politicians were prepared to go on record as defending red activism. Including the long-drawn-out legal procedures and appeals, the war on the local operations of the Communist Party lasted into the mid 1950s. Official action was reinforced by mob violence and vigilantism, often organized through veterans' and Catholic groups.

The official justification for such heavy-handed tactics was that leftists represented a fifth column equivalent to those that had assisted the Nazis in the early days of the Second World War, and who were already preparing to support world communism through sabotage and espionage. The quest for spies found its most visible target in Alger Hiss, a State Department official who had allegedly formed part of a clandestine communist ring since the late 1930s. Hiss's trial lasted from August 1948 to January 1950 and fanned popular fears about traitors in high places. Among the public at large, the search for traitors was undertaken under the powerful auspices of the House Committee on Un-American Activities, which severely limited both the right to free speech and traditional protections against self-incrimination. Armed with the testimony of a legion of professional informers and alleged defectors, the committee targetted particular regions or industries, and identified supposed communists in terms of their participation in liberal or leftist groups, which were described as communist front organizations. These groups included clubs and organizations that had been perfectly reputable or even aligned with earlier US policies: for example bodies supporting the Soviet Union during the Second World War. One useful source of 'subversives' was the list of individuals who had supported the left–liberal presidential candidate Henry Wallace in 1948, for instance by signing nominating petitions. Though participating in a proper electoral procedure, Wallace supporters thus branded themselves as potential traitors.

Denying a charge of communist affiliation was dangerous in itself, as an informer could easily be produced to contradict this, showing that the person accused was guilty of perjury. The only way to avoid this was to refuse any answer that might self-incriminatory, that is to 'take the fifth amendment', but this made the respondent look as if he or she had something criminal to hide. Once accused, innocence was extremely difficult to establish except through the unpalatable tactic of becoming an informer oneself, and publicly naming names. A network of private agencies sprang up, often composed of former FBI agents, who would investigate a given firm at the request of its management in order to root out subversives, and to 'clear' those who showed themselves sufficiently cooperative. As in any witch-hunt, the process of accusation was cumulative and self-sustaining. Once marked as a communist, a person was entered upon the record books of these private vigilantes, who would be consulted by any potential future employers. Being blacklisted meant forfeiting all hope of employment. Removing passports ensured that most suspects could not save themselves by emigrating.

The purges went through several stages, but victims that suffered particularly badly included radical unions such as the Electrical Workers, who were severely damaged in a campaign partly orchestrated through Catholic union activists. The film industry was attacked in the hearings of 1947–48, an event that has since attracted much notoriety because so many of the victims made public their stories during the subsequent decades. Those in education were hard hit, both university professors and teachers' unions, and charges of red subversion in schools caused an atmosphere of extreme paranoia as different institutions raced to cleanse themselves of possibly suspect material in textbooks and assigned readings.

In February 1950 Senator Joseph McCarthy delivered the first of a series of speeches that elevated the panic to new heights. McCarthy warned of 'a final all-out battle between Communistic atheism and Christianity'. He claimed to have detailed lists of communist activists in the State Department and elsewhere who had delivered China to communism, and his intelligence was sufficiently precise to give the exact number of these traitors. His irresponsibility and disregard of the truth were allowed to go unchallenged by a media and political establishment terrified of incurring the red smear themselves. In January 1953 McCarthy took over over the Permanent Subcommittee on Investigations, which now reached new heights of malice and publicity seeking. In October McCarthy began the investigation that would cause his downfall: the hearings on traitors within the US Army. His excesses had long caused concern, and the army case brought the committee and its investigators, like Roy Cohn, against establishment figures who were willing and able to fight back. Television played a major role in exposing his tactics, and a mass audience was thus able to see the humiliation inflicted on McCarthy by counsel Joseph Welch. In March 1954 the Eisenhower administration denounced McCarthy and Cohn, who were duly condemned by the Senate that December. Though this is often taken as marking the end of the purges, many of the worst persecutions remained in progress, and the laws called forth by the panic remained on the books into the 1970s or beyond.

THE NEW STATE

The series of wars and internal security scares transformed the state, hugely increasing the size of government and its involvement in everyday life. The growth was so enormous as to make the national security state of the 1950s a fundamentally different creature from the rather limited federal enterprise of the Woodrow Wilson era. War was the crucial factor throughout. In 1860 the federal government was drawing in only $56 million annually, a figure that had increased to $334 million by the end of the civil war in 1865. In those four years the US government spent more than the total spent until then since independence. The First World War marked an even sharper growth in state activity, receipts rising from $683 million in 1915 to $3.65 billion in 1918. Government expenditure in the late nineteenth and early twentieth centuries averaged around $3–400 million dollars annually; the figure for 1918 was $12.7 billion. Public expenditure on this scale required innovative financial methods, and income tax became increasingly common despite initial doubts about its constitutionality. In 1913 the sixteenth amendment to the constitution secured the legality of this device, and contributed to the massive expansion of the federal state in the twentieth century. The same year, the Federal Reserve Act gave a new security to the banking system, under the auspices of the national government.

The New Deal and the subsequent wars further expanded state operations. In 1929 the federal government laid out some $3 billion, a figure that had risen to almost $9 billion by 1939. This appeared trivial when set aside World War Two expenditures, $95 billion in 1944 alone. Peace brought retrenchment, but to levels far higher than anything contemplated even in the New Deal, and Korea turned the ratchet several notches further, even allowing for the effects of inflation. Government expenditure in the peacetime year of 1960 was over $90 billion, half of which was destined for the military.

Government employment grew accordingly. In 1940 the federal government employed 1.1 million people, compared with the 3.4 million working for state and local government. By 1945 the number on the federal payroll had reached 3.5 million, as against 3.2 million others. The total number of government employees rose from 4.5 million in 1940 to 8.8 million in 1960 and 15 million in the mid-1970s. Though other factors were also at work, the changing scale of government is reflected in the development of the national capital. During four years of civil war the population of Washington DC doubled to 120 000, a growth spurt that was paralleled in 1917–18 and again after 1941. There were 450 000 people by 1918, 800 000 by the late 1940s. Though the city itself has subsequently declined in scale, the wider metropolitan area has boomed, notably the Maryland and Virginia suburbs. Today Greater Washington has some four million people.

The growth of the federal state was also reflected in the expansion of the military, in a country that historically had been suspicious of a permanent army. Throughout the 1930s the combined strength of all US military forces rarely exceeded 450 000, fewer than the armies of even middling European powers. This naturally was transformed in the conditions of total war prevailing in 1944–5, when some 12 million men and women were in service. This number fell again in peacetime, but after the Korean War the United States never again allowed its military to contract to the pre-1941 scale. The armed forces were 2.5 million strong in 1960, and not until after 1990 did the level fall below two million.

Americans' dislike of federal police powers far exceeded their hostility to a large military, and in 1900 the federal government had little more at its direct disposal than a small Secret Service. Thereafter the growth of federal police agencies was rapid. In 1908 the Justice Department set up a Bureau of Investigation, which in 1924 became the Federal Bureau of Investigation. The FBI expanded dramatically under its director, the master self-publicist and bureaucratic infighter J. Edgar Hoover. Throughout the FBI grew on the strength of public panics over alleged crime waves and moral dangers: the pioneering 'Mann Act' of 1910 gave the agency jurisdiction over interstate crimes, in this case white slaving. In 1933 a panic over kidnapping caused a new infusion of powers and resources. Spies were also a vital foundation for growth. From 1936 the Roosevelt administration gave Hoover permission to investigate subversion by domestic communists and fascists, and this role grew with the red scares of the 1940s.

Outside the FBI, federal policing agencies were growing within the Treasury Department, where in Roosevelt's first term Treasury Secretary Morgenthau proposed an amalgamation of several small forces into one imposing unit. The Narcotics Bureau, Customs, IRS Intelligence, Secret Service and Alcohol Department would form a superagency that critics denounced as an American counterpart to the OGPU or Gestapo. The scheme failed. After the Second World War, similarly, opponents fought hard and successfully to prevent the FBI from acquiring the foreign jurisdiction that passed to the new CIA, showing a continuing concern with the prospect of an overmighty intelligence agency subverting democracy from within. But by the 1950s the federal government did indeed have at its disposal the range of policing and intelligence forces that would once have characterized a European power, rather than a democratic republic.

As the ever-larger American state focused national energies on foreign threats, so power within that state concentrated in the hands of those areas of government charged with the responsibilities of war and peace, above all the president in his role as commander-in-chief. The imperial presidency was buttressed by the workings of the media, which made the president the visible face and symbol of government, and in the 1930s made Roosevelt appear a personal friend and refuge against a deeply hostile outside world. After the New Deal and the Second World War, the presidential office retained much of that charisma, and became the linchpin of government to a degree that would have troubled the founders. Not until the 1970s did a president so overreach himself as to cause any reversal or diminution of that trend.

THE AMERICAN DILEMMA

War and its related social changes had a particular impact on American race relations. In 1944, in the middle of the Second World War, Gunnar Myrdal's influential book *The American Dilemma* analyzed American racism and pointed to the growing dangers of racial conflict. The problem had reached an acute stage, not because black Americans were undergoing any novel form of discrimination or violence, but because rising expectations had intensified resentment against structural injustice. Racial subjugation in the south was as bad in the interwar years as at any point since the fall of slavery, but many blacks had fled to the cities of the north and the migration reached floodtide during both world wars. In

1910, 90 per cent of American blacks lived in the south, but by the early 1960s about half lived in the north. The 'typical' African-American of the 1950s and 1960s was as likely to be northern as southern, and was far more likely to be urban than rural. Northern and mid-western blacks were less likely to accept any form of racial discrimination, especially when the political culture of the Roosevelt era placed so much emphasis on the raising up of the formerly downtrodden.

Blacks moved *en masse* from the Republican Party (the 'Party of Lincoln') to support the Democrats, and become a critical part of the New Deal electoral constituency. They were also heavily involved in the industrial activism of these years, and the insurgent unionism of the CIO. Rewards were naturally expected, the primary demand being a federal commission to ensure fair employment practices and the elimination of job discrimination. While Roosevelt was sympathetic, he was reluctant to appear too radical on race issues for fear of losing the Democratic southern states, upon which his regime depended.

Frustration among the mainstream black leadership was accompanied by growing anger in urban communities such as Harlem, which in 1935 exploded in a novel type of race riot that foreshadowed future events: instead of a white-on-black pogrom, this was a popular insurrection against whites and their property. Ill feeling was exacerbated by the Second World War, a conflict against fascist and racist regimes abroad, which the United States entered with its own thoroughly segregated armed forces. The irony was not lost on the blacks, who demanded 'double V': victory over Hitler abroad and Jim Crow at home. At home the administration now came under pressure from black union leaders such as A. Philip Randolph to fight discrimination, with the threat that otherwise Washington would become the scene of a massive civil rights protest that would be an international public relations catastrophe. Roosevelt acceded with an executive order requiring equal employment. Deteriorating race relations were illustrated by traumatic rioting in Harlem and

Detroit in 1943. These events caused real concern, with the added element that it would not be too long before millions of black war veterans returned to American shores, with a firm expectation of just treatment in return for their military contributions.

The pace of reform accelerated under President Truman, whose direct observations of racial injustice in Missouri made him more willing than Roosevelt to undertake political risks in this area. In 1946 the Committee on Civil Rights recommended new legislation against discrimination in jobs and voting, as well as the long-sought federal anti lynching law. In 1948 Truman issued an executive order desegregating the US armed forces. Also important symbolically was the appearance of the first black player in major league baseball in 1947, as Jackie Robinson joined the Brooklyn Dodgers and forced open the first crack in the segregated world of sport and popular culture. Though the pace of change now seems painfully slow, it was too rapid for southern conservatives, who in 1948 bolted the Democratic Party to run a States' Rights candidate for president. Though 'Dixiecrats' won only 1.2 million votes, they took four states in the deep south.

Though federal administrations could achieve much by piecemeal action, lasting change could only be achieved through the courts and an attack on the framework of legal discrimination that maintained the subordinate status of southern blacks. In the 1890s the US Supreme Court had upheld Jim Crow laws, but matters were changing in the Roosevelt years, with a wave of more liberal appointees. In 1932 the Court decided the first of many cases expanding the legal rights of defendants in criminal trials, in this instance requiring that a black defendant on trial for his life must have adequate legal representation. It was a small start, but over the next two decades the Court heard a steadily growing number of cases about discriminatory political practices in the south. In 1953 the United States acquired a new chief justice named Earl Warren, whose political career in California had demonstrated little sympathy for radicalism, and he had been involved in implementing the discriminatory policy under which a hundred thousand Japanese Americans were deported after Pearl Harbor. However Warren had also been affected by the race rioting of 1943, and he now supported policies of desegregation. The critical decision came in the 1954 case of Brown versus the Board of Education, which condemned 'separate but equal' education as a violation of equal opportunity, and ordered the ending of segregated teaching 'with all deliberate speed'. The Civil Rights revolution had begun.

CULTURE

Both social change and political controversy had an impact on the cultural life of the interwar years. The novels of the 1920s (Table 5.5) often reflected postwar disillusionment and a cynical suspicion of the new orthodoxies of American life, no less than its materialism. Fitzgerald's *Great Gatsby* and the novels of Sinclair Lewis both epitomize these trends. The crash of 1929 gave rise to a critical examination of the pre deluge world, and an exploration of ways in which America might recapture its original ideals. The tone was often pessimistic: in 1935, Lewis' *It Can't Happen Here* warned of an imminent American dictatorship, while Steinbeck's works addressed the sufferings of the poor driven from their homes by the economic collapse. For many writers of the 1930s, social activism brought them close to the organized left and specifically the Communist Party, especially under the impact of the Spanish Civil War. Some soon reacted against this and swung to the far right. Dashiell Hammett, Lillian Hellman and Dorothy Parker remained friendly to the left; Dos Passos, Wright and Hemingway were either excommunicated by the party or went forcibly into opposition.

This was a great age for American fiction, both in terms of high culture and in genre writing such as science fiction and detective stories, where American authors produced work of

Table 5.5   Major books and plays, 1922–40

1922	Sinclair Lewis, *Babbitt*
1925	F. Scott Fitzgerald, *The Great Gatsby*; Sinclair Lewis, *Arrowsmith*
1926	Ernest Hemingway, *The Sun Also Rises*
1927	Sinclair Lewis, *Elmer Gantry*; Willa Cather, *Death Comes for the Archbishop*
1928	Thornton Wilder, *Bridges of San Luis Rey*
1929	William Faulkner, *The Sound and the Fury*; Sinclair Lewis, *Dodsworth*; Ernest Hemingway, *A Farewell to Arms*; Thomas Wolfe, *Look Homeward, Angel*
1930	William Faulkner, *As I Lay Dying*; Dashiell Hammett, *The Maltese Falcon*; John Dos Passos, *42nd Parallel*
1931	Eugene O'Neill, *Mourning Becomes Electra*
1932	Ernest Hemingway, *Death in the Afternoon*; John Dos Passos, *1919*
1934	F. Scott Fitzgerald, *Tender is the Night*; Lillian Hellman, *The Children's Hour*
1935	Sinclair Lewis, *It Can't Happen Here*; Robert Sherwood, *The Petrified Forest*
1936	William Faulkner, *Absalom, Absalom!*; John Dos Passos, *The Big Money*
1937	John Steinbeck, *Of Mice and Men*
1938	William Faulkner, *The Unvanquished*; Thornton Wilder, *Our Town*
1939	Lillian Hellman, *The Little Foxes*; Raymond Chandler, *The Big Sleep*; Steinbeck, *The Grapes of Wrath*; Eugene O'Neill, *The Iceman Cometh*; Thomas Wolfe, *The Web and the Rock*
1940	Ernest Hemingway, *For Whom the Bell Tolls*; Richard Wright, *Native Son*; Thomas Wolfe, *You Can't Go Home Again*

the highest quality, that would have an impact worldwide. In poetry, American authors of the 1920s now assumed an unprecedented leading role through the work of Ezra Pound and T.S. Eliot, while other key figures included William Carlos Williams, Robert Frost, Wallace Stevens and Carl Sandburg. From the late 1920s American painting entered an era of major achievement, with work by Ben Shahn, Georgia O'Keeffe, Charles Demuth, Edward Hopper and Grant Wood. Under the New Deal, artists and writers benefited from the support of the federal government under schemes such as the Federal Writers' Project.

American culture achieved a global status if not dominance in those years through the spread of popular cultural forms, especially films and music. By 1920 the American film industry was already the most active in the world, and this hegemony increased in the 1930s after the advent of the talking picture and the influx of refugee talent from the European dictatorships. Though such opinions must be subjective, one year – 1939 – saw the release of several films that would be included in any list of the best pictures ever made, including 'Gone with the Wind', 'The Wizard of Oz', 'Gunga Din', 'Ninotchka', 'Mr. Smith Goes to Washington' and 'Stagecoach'. The new industry was dominated by East European Jewish magnates, many of whose families had entered the United States in the great migration at the turn of the century. In music too, the sounds heard on radios and gramophones worldwide had often been recorded in the United States by American artists, or else reflected traditions that originated in the United States, usually among black Americans: ragtime, jazz, blues and big band music, and dances such as the Jitterbug.

After the Second World War American popular culture received a severe blow from the anti-leftist purge, which caused the removal of numerous talented screen actors, directors and writers. On the positive side, the United States was the favoured destination for many European artists fleeing dictatorship and wartime devastation, so that by the early

1950s New York had clearly assumed the role of a global art capital. In literature too, the early 1950s saw the emergence of a new generation of impressive novelists, including James Jones, Norman Mailer, Saul Bellow and J. D. Salinger. In popular culture, a new emphasis on a youth culture alienated from the assumptions of parents was suggested from 1953 onwards by the rise of rock and roll music, and of films such as 'The Wild One' and 'Rebel Without a Cause'. Though superbly packaged in commercial terms, figures such as Elvis Presley and James Dean became icons of social and generational rebellion. They also assumed this role throughout Europe and indeed much of the globe, where American imagery struck a powerful chord. As in politics, American popular culture sought to transform the world into its own image.

Notes

1. David M. Kennedy, *Over Here: The First World War and American Society* (New York: Oxford University Press, 1980) pp. 45–92.
2. Quoted in Philip Jenkins, 'Spy Mad: Investigating Subversion in Pennsylvania 1917–18', *Pennsylvania History*, 63 (1996) pp. 204–31.
3. Reading (PA) Socialist leader James H. Maurer quoted in ibid.

6

· · · · · · ·

The Modern Era,
1956–96

FACING WEST FROM CALIFORNIA'S SHORES

As in each previous era, in the last four decades the United
States has continued to transform itself with incredible rapidity. Though only two states have been added (Alaska and
Hawaii, both in 1959), the nation's centre of gravity has
continued to move steadily to the south and west. From
the 1950s, one of the decisive facts in American life was the
drift away from the north and mid-west to western and
southern regions, from the 'Rustbelt' to the 'Sunbelt'. The
proportion of Americans living in the statistical regions
known as the south and west rose from 46 per cent in 1960
to 56 per cent in 1990.

From the 1840s to the 1960s American urban centres were
concentrated in the north-east and mid-west, and the urban
hierarchy was dominated by centres such as New York,
Chicago, Boston and Philadelphia (Table 6.1). All declined
in the 1960s and 1970s, losing people both to the suburbs and
to other regions. By the 1990s, nine of the nation's fifteen
leading cities were situated in the south: Los Angeles, San
Diego, San Jose and San Francisco (California); Houston,
Dallas and San Antonio (Texas), Phoenix (Arizona) and
Jacksonville (Florida).

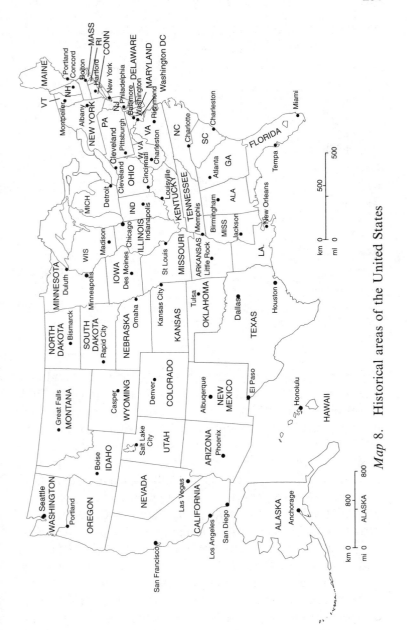

Map 8. Historical areas of the United States

Table 6.1   America's leading cities, 1950–90 (population in millions, and rank order)

	1950		1990	
New York	7.90	(1)	7.30	(1)
Chicago	3.60	(2)	2.80	(3)
Philadelphia	2.10	(3)	1.60	(5)
Los Angeles	2.00	(4)	3.50	(2)
Detroit	1.90	(5)	1.00	(7)
Baltimore	0.95	(6)	0.74	(13)
Cleveland	0.91	(7)	0.50	(24)
St Louis	0.86	(8)	0.40	(33)
Washington DC	0.80	(9)	0.60	(19)
Boston	0.80	(10)	0.60	(20)
San Francisco	0.78	(11)	0.70	(14)
Pittsburgh	0.67	(12)	0.40	(40)

The seeming decline of the cities of the north-east and mid-west is somewhat misleading, as the figures shown in Table 6.1 measure only the core city areas rather than the broader metropolitan statistical areas to which residents usually fled. Table 6.2 illustrates the current urban framework, using as basic units the sprawling complexes of core and suburban areas into which the traditional cities evolved. This table confirms the significance of upstart areas of the south and west that are currently marked by the most dramatic urban growth, and Table 6.3 shows the national population growth. Newer cities such as Seattle also tended to set the social fads and fashions for the rest of the nation: in a sense, popular culture in the 1990s flowed east rather than west.

American ethnic geography was reshaped in these years by a process some have called the 'Browning of America'. For most of the history of the nation the 'racial' question, for all its complexities, had essentially revolved around two groups:

Table 6.2   Urban complexes, 1990

Metropolitan area	Population (millions)
New York/Northern New Jersey/Long Island (NY–NJ–CT)	18.1
Los Angeles/Anaheim/Riverside (CA)	14.5
Chicago/Gary/Lake County (IL–IN–WI)	8.1
San Francisco/Oakland/San Jose (CA)	6.3
Philadelphia/Wilmington/Trenton (PA–DE–NJ)	5.9
Detroit/Ann Arbor (MI)	4.7
Boston/Lawrence/Salem (MA)	4.2
Washington MSA* (DC–MD–VA)	3.9
Dallas/Fort Worth (TX)	3.9
Houston/Galveston/Brazoria (TX)	3.7
Miami/Fort Lauderdale (FL)	3.2
Atlanta MSA (GA)	2.8
Cleveland/Akron/Lorain (OH)	2.8
Seattle/Tacoma (WA)	2.6
San Diego MSA (CA)	2.5

* MSA = Metropolitan Statistical Area

Table 6.3   US population, 1960–90

Census year	National population*
1960	179
1970	203
1980	223
1990	249

*rounded to nearest million

black and white. In 1930 the nation comprised 110 million whites, twelve million blacks, and 600 000 'others', meaning Native Americans and Asians. From the 1960s onwards the 'otherness' of America developed apace (Table 6.4), largely due to the Immigration Act of 1965, which repealed the European-biased 1924 Act. Between 1971 and 1993 some 15.5 million people emigrated to the United States, equaling the scale of the migration at the turn of the century. By 1995 the foreign born constituted nearly 9 per cent of the US population, a figure higher than at any point in the previous fifty years. In addition Hispanics were now recognized as a separate category (though they could count as either black or white for the purposes of the census). Ethnic assertiveness contributed to a rapid growth of those identifying themselves as American Indian or otherwise 'Native'.

The changes were dramatic: in 1990, 22.4 million Americans were counted as Hispanic and 7.5 million were Asian, mainly Chinese, Japanese, Filipino, Vietnamese and Korean. The projections for 2025 suggest 57 million Hispanics and 25.5 million Asians, so that the two groups, which together represented 12 per cent of the population in 1990, will grow to almost a quarter by 2025. Even these projections are subject to radical revision in the light of as yet unforeseen refugee influxes. American politics is moving from a black and white affair to a multicoloured reality, which is already having a revolutionary effect on every aspect of life, initially in certain states, but ultimately throughout the nation. Geographical and ethnic shifts are already conditioning overseas attitudes, so that Los Angeles and Seattle look to the Pacific Rim, just as Miami has become the regional metropolis of the Caribbean and Central America.

In international terms, the move south and west greatly enhanced US sensitivity to the likelihood of communist or otherwise hostile regimes acquiring power in eastern Asia or Latin America, a constant political theme of this period. Meanwhile European entanglements appeared less attractive than at any point since the 1930s.

THE COLD WAR

Demographic changes would have their impact on political life, but for much of the period American thinking was dominated by the more basic question of whether the nation would survive in any recognizable form, or fall victim to a war that would annihilate most of the population and subject the survivors to a Stone Age existence.

Until the late 1960s American foreign policy was shaped by the confrontation with communism. Though the nature of the nuclear standoff remained relatively constant from the early 1950s to the late 1980s, there were periods of high international tension when it seemed likely that actual conflict was only days or hours away. Following the twin crises of Suez and Hungary, the Soviet success in launching the unmanned satellite Sputnik in October 1957 appeared to demonstrate both superiority in space technology and the ability to attack the western hemisphere by orbital missiles. American horror at this prospect was heightened by a series of embarrassing failures to rival Soviet space achievements in the next three years, and in 1961 the Soviets won the race to

Table 6.4   The changing ethnic balance (millions)

Racial group	1960	1990	2025 (projected)
White	159.0	209.0	262.0
Black	19.0	30.5	48.0
Other	1.6	9.6	28.8
including:			
Native American/ Alaskan Native	N/A	2.1	3.3
Asian/Pacific Islander	N/A	7.5	25.5
Total	179.0	250.0	338.0

* 'Other' groups were not counted separately in 1950.

put a man into orbit. Catching up in the space race dominated the administration's thinking in the following decade,
and the Cold War added fuel to the drive that ultimately
placed Americans on the moon in 1969.

Nuclear tension reached a new plateau between 1959 and
1962, with international crises erupting over control over the
city of Berlin, and the newer issue of Cuba. In January 1959 a
corrupt Cuban dictatorship was overthrown by revolutionary
forces headed by Fidel Castro. After some initial uncertainty,
Castro identified with the Soviet cause and the USSR gained
its first close ally in the western hemisphere. This was catastrophic for the United States, which feared Cuba's influence
as a role model for other Latin and Third World peoples, and
dreaded having a Soviet military base so close to its national
territory, which would allow the communists to compensate
for the inferiority of their long-range weapons systems. The
United States broke diplomatic relations with Cuba in January 1961, and in April the CIA sponsored an invasion of
Cuba by anti-Castro exile forces, which met disaster at the
Bay of Pigs.

This inclined the Russian leadership towards overconfi-
dence, and in October 1962 the United States revealed that
the Soviets were installing nuclear missiles in Cuba. President
John F. Kennedy demanded their withdrawal and ordered a
naval blockade of the island. For some days a world war
seemed unavoidable, either as a consequence of the Soviets
attempting to breach the blockade, or of the US leadership
acceding to military demands for an immediate invasion of
Cuba. Disaster was narrowly averted, and the two governments reached a pact whereby the missiles were withdrawn
and the United States pledged not to invade Cuba. Covert
moves against the Castro administration continued for decades, and anti-Castro gangs continued to operate, becoming
ever more deeply involved in the shadowy underworld of
narcotics and international terrorism.

The US nuclear arsenal expanded dramatically during
these years, from under 5000 warheads in 1959 to over

20 000 by 1963 and peaking at some 30 000 in 1966–7. (The Soviets probably did not reach even the 5000 figure until the mid 1960s.) Apart from the deadly intercontinental ballistic missiles housed in the American west, smaller tactical weapons proliferated among the US forces on land, sea and air, so that US military strategy was committed to an early escalation to nuclear war in any confrontation with Warsaw Pact forces. Even so the state of military preparedness was a constant source of nervousness in these years, and the Democratic candidate John F. Kennedy successfully used the supposed 'missile gap' against his Republican opponent in 1960, taking office in 1961 (Table 6.5).

Even the aggressive military and diplomatic stances of US administrations were woefully inadequate to those hardline conservatives who felt that war with the Soviets was imminent, while presidents such as Eisenhower and Kennedy were communist stooges. Throughout the 1950s and 1960s, ultra-right, anti communist views were mobilized through extremist groups such as the John Birch Society and the (paramilitary) Minutemen, who believed that communism had already subverted large sections of the American political elite. By 1964 the far right influenced broad sections of the

Table 6.5   US presidents, 1953–97

	Time in office	Party
Dwight D. Eisenhower	1953–61	Republican
John F. Kennedy	1961–63	Democrat
Lyndon B. Johnson	1963–69	Democrat
Richard M. Nixon	1969–74	Republican
Gerald R. Ford	1974–77	Republican
James E. Carter	1977–81	Democrat
Ronald W. Reagan	1981–89	Republican
George Bush	1989–93	Republican
Bill Clinton	1993–	Democrat

Table 6.6   Presidential election results, 1956–96

	Winning candidate	Popular votes (millions)	Losing candidate	Popular votes (millions)
1956	Dwight D. Eisenhower (R)	35.6	Adlai E. Stevenson (D)	26.0
1960	John F. Kennedy (D)	34.2	Richard M. Nixon (R)	34.1
1964	Lyndon B. Johnson (D)	43.1	Barry Goldwater (R)	27.2
1968	Richard M. Nixon (R)	31.8	Hubert Humphrey (D)	31.2
			George Wallace (Ind.)	9.9
1972	Richard M. Nixon (R)	47.2	George McGovern (D)	29.2
1976	James E. Carter (D)	40.8	Gerald Ford (R)	39.2
1980	Ronald Reagan (R)	43.9	James E. Carter (D)	35.5
			John Anderson (Ind.)	5.7
1984	Ronald Reagan (R)	54.3	Walter Mondale (D)	37.5
1988	George Bush (R)	48.9	Michael Dukakis (D)	41.8
1992	Bill Clinton (D)	44.9	George Bush (R)	39.1
			Ross Perot (Ind.)	19.7

Note: Third party candidates are only listed when they obtained more than 5 per cent of the total popular vote in any given year.

Republican Party, whose presidential candidate, Barry Goldwater, could proclaim that 'Extremism in the defense of liberty is no vice'. To the media Goldwater appeared far removed from the political mainstream, and his campaign resulted in electoral annihilation; but he still won some forty per cent of the popular vote (Table 6.6).

The Cuban missile crisis proved that Kennedy could be as vigorously anti-Soviet as any of his critics. However the perilous proximity of actual war had caused real panic in political circles no less than among the public, and a general desire to withdraw from the brink was suggested by international agreements such as the Nuclear Test Ban Treaty of 1963. Thereafter conflict with the communists and those perceived to be communists (by no means the same thing) would continue, but through intervention in local brushfire wars and 'low intensity operations', usually in the Third World. American forces were involved in several military interventions aimed directly or indirectly at thwarting supposed communist advances, including Lebanon in 1958 and the Dominican Republic in 1965. American policy sought to contain communist progress in the Third World as it emerged from under the colonial domination of nations such as Britain and France, a task made all the more dangerous by the shining examples of China and Cuba. This involved not only covert action in the form of destabilization and the subversion of governments perceived as leftwing, but also direct activity by American advisers. The United States played a role in the demise of leftist regimes in the Congo (1961), Iraq (1963) and Indonesia (1965).

US involvement in geopolitical conflicts came to focus on South-East Asia, as the Kennedy administration was alarmed by communist guerrilla movements in Laos. From 1957 guerrilla activity increased in South Vietnam, orchestrated by the local Viet Cong communists in tight alliance with the North Vietnamese government. Rebel movements such as the Viet Cong and Pathet Lao were rarely evaluated in terms of local conditions, but were rather seen as tools of world communism, and specifically of China, which would become a nuclear power in its own right in 1964. American military thinking was shaped by a 'domino theory', which saw communist victory in Laos and Vietnam leading to the subversion of neighbouring states, which would in turn fall like dominoes, until the cumulative process overwhelmed such huge prizes as India and even Australia.

During 1963 Vietnam rather than Laos became the primary arena of conflict. Anti government protests there generated a massive political crisis that threatened to lead to the collapse of South Vietnam, which was now buttressed by US aid. The United States sent military advisers to organize the South Vietnamese armed forces, as well as modern military equipment for their use. CIA operatives undertook vigorous covert campaigns. In August 1964 a spurious attack on two

American warships in the Tonkin Gulf in the China Sea off Vietnam encouraged Congress to pass a resolution allowing the president 'to take all necessary measures to repel any armed attack against the forces of the United States and to prevent further aggression', a vague document that provided legal justification for the vast escalation of the war that now began. In February 1965 US aircraft began the bombing of targets in North Vietnam, and in March the first regular ground troops arrived to defend the base at Da Nang. While this scarcely marked the beginning of the Vietnam War, which had in fact been under way since 1946, it meant that the American phase of the struggle could now begin.

It is tempting to see US foreign policy in the 1950s and 1960s as an uninterrupted story of confrontation with communism, varied only in the degree of nuclear brinkmanship at any given time. However, by the standards of large sections of the right wing, by 1963 President Kennedy had become dangerously soft on communism. He had agreed never to invade Cuba, he was expressing concern about the degree of direct US involvement in Vietnam, and he was actively sympathizing with the black civil rights struggles, which the right viewed as a simple tactic of communist subversion.

This context is significant for Kennedy's assassination in Dallas, Texas, on 22 November 1963, an act that has given rise to much speculation. The Warren Commission, which investigated the murder shortly afterwards, attributed sole responsibility to a lone gunman, acting out of warped personal motives. Others have postulated wider conspiracies, including as possible culprits the Soviet and Cuban governments, or elements of the American military and intelligence communities. Though bitterly controversial, conspiracy theories endure to the present day. One common interpretation places the blame on the anti-Castro Cuban community in Miami and New Orleans, and conceivably on groups with low-level intelligence ties. Lone gun or conspiracy, the assassination and the president's removal probably did have long-term consequences for policy, delaying détente with the Soviets for another decade and preventing encouraging signs of a reduction of US involvement in Vietnam. For this reason alone, the Kennedy assassination sits alongside the Cuban Missile Crisis as one of the critical moments of the Cold War.

RACE AND CIVIL RIGHTS

International tensions are often accompanied by increased authoritarianism or social repression on the domestic front, but the Cold War years in the United States were in many ways a period of extreme liberalism. The years from 1954 to 1965 marked the 'civil rights revolution', activism that was moreover made possible only by the support of the federal government and the judiciary. While much of the political elite tended to be genuinely liberal in these areas, international factors also played a role, in that one could hardly seek to win the friendship of former colonies if the United States was stigmatized worldwide for racial discrimination and violence. Enlightened conservatives recognized that desegregation would benefit the global anti communist crusade.

The movement against legal segregation had made massive strides since the early 1940s, with the Supreme Court playing a vital role (see Chapter 5). The Brown decision contributed to a spreading protest movement across the south, which found a symbol in 1955 when Rosa Parks of Montgomery, Alabama, refused to yield a bus seat to a white passenger. Blacks boycotted the public transportation system, under the leadership of Baptist minister Martin Luther King. Over the next decade there were many such protests and boycotts to challenge legal segregation as widely as possible, effectively demanding that the authorities either renounce discrimination, or resort to repression on a scale that would create national and international embarrassment. 'Freedom rides' brought in groups to demand service at segregated eating facilities as incidents involving interstate travel automatically brought the issue into the federal arena, and thereby into the jurisdiction of federal courts. King was one of several individuals and groups who emerged to organize the movement, alongside the Student Non-Violent Coordinating Committee (SNCC, or 'Snake'), the Congress of Racial Equality (CORE) and the older NAACP. All were committed to non-violence and Gandhian civil disobedience, a tactic that was not only morally correct, but also politically essential in order to win public support and avoid alienating northern voters.

The campaign met predictable opposition, as it was in effect offering a fundamental challenge to the most firmly rooted structures of southern politics and society, and the alliance with white radicals brought back ancient nightmares of interracial sex and miscegenation. In 1957 the governor of Arkansas mobilized the National Guard to prevent the court-ordered desegregation of the Little Rock public school system, a decision overcome only by President Dwight Eisenhower's use of federal troops to enforce the law. In the following years many southern states and legislatures expressed forceful opposition to what was dismissed as federal tyranny, and some ostentatiously revised their state flags to incorporate the old Confederate banner. In 1962 the prospect of a black student being admitted to the University of Mississippi was greeted with a lengthy campus riot, which was eventually suppressed by federal troops and the National Guard, now under federal control. Countless vigilante and terrorist groups formed, most notably the reborn Ku Klux Klan. Many individual acts of mobbing and violence were directed aga'nst civil rights protesters. In 1963 organizer Medgar Evers was assassinated in Mississippi, and four children were killed in the bombing of a black church in Birmingham Alabama. The following year the 'Freedom Summer' campaign was accompanied by many more attacks and murders, which drew worldwide condemnation and undoubtedly increased the support of non-southerners for sweeping legal reforms.

The civil rights movement reached its peak between 1963 and 1965. August 1963 brought a mass march to Washington, at which Martin Luther King delivered an impassioned speech that is still regarded as one of the high points of American political oratory. In 1964 President Lyndon Johnson succeeded in passing a sweeping Civil Rights Act that prohibited discrimination in public facilities and employment. However black voters were still widely excluded from the franchise by various ostensibly non-racial voter tests, and only the federal Voting Rights Act finally permitted blacks to secure their gains by a long-term restructuring of the political system. Once again this measure was obtained in direct response to southern repression, specifically the riot that erupted in Selma, Alabama, where police used brutal violence against civil rights protesters. Though the event was shocking enough in its own right, this was one of the first times that televised images galvanized opinion in many countries within hours of its occurrence, and the pictures of southern police turning dogs and water-cannon on black children was unforgettable: it would also be a mainstay of leftist and communist propaganda for years to come. By August 1965 the United States had a federal Voting Rights Act, the consequences of which would reshape southern politics. While millions of blacks were now effectively enfranchised, President Johnson also recognized that in signing the Act he was allowing the Democratic 'solid south' to pass to the Republican Party, at least for a generation.

BLACK POWER, 1966–71

By the mid-1960s the civil rights movement had accomplished many of its original legislative goals, though the social changes that these were hoped to accomplish would take decades longer. But at this point of apparent victory there was a sharp intensification of racial conflict in the United

States, this time chiefly concentrated in the northern cities. From 1964 many cities experienced rioting in protest against the perceived callousness and casual violence of the police towards the black community. Thereafter the rioting of the 'long, hot summers' became a fixture of urban life. Notorious outbreaks occurred in 1965 in the Los Angeles ghetto of Watts, and in Newark and Detroit during 1967, while the 1968 murder of Martin Luther King provoked an uprising in Washington DC. Thirty-four people were killed in Watts, 26 in Newark and 43 in Detroit, where heavily armed federal soldiers were brought in to control the city. These notorious manifestations were very much the tip of the iceberg, and in 1967 alone, 75 cities experienced rioting.

Early explanations of these events often lay the blame on outside agitators or communist manipulation, but investigations by a distinctly conservative Presidential Commission headed by Illinois Governor Otto Kerner told a different tale. This group saw the riots as quite spontaneous in nature, and found the causes in unemployment, poor housing and improper police practices. To note the most obvious statistic, blacks then made up about 10 per cent of the population, but constituted almost a third of those living below the poverty level.

The urban crisis reinforced President Johnson's determination to make social spending a national priority, to employ New Deal tactics to build a 'great society'; and fear of unrest persuaded other more conservative politicians to accept these policies as a means of preventing worse chaos. Social welfare expenditure by federal and state authorities rose dramatically, from 11.7 per cent of GNP in 1965 to 20 per cent in 1975. In 1965, such spending accounted for 42 per cent of total government outlays; by 1975 this had risen to 57 per cent, by far the largest proportion of which came from federal moneys. And there were successes to be claimed. Between 1965 and 1974 the number of people believed to live below the poverty level fell by 42 per cent. Though a national health insurance scheme proved politically impossible, Medicare

(1965) became a vast and popular programme providing universal coverage for the elderly.

For many blacks these reformist efforts were at best trivial, at worst part of a continued conspiracy to deceive and subjugate the underclass. There was a rapid growth of support for black nationalist opinions, which favoured black separatism rather than integration, and which stressed the self-determination and even armed self-defence of black communities. These ideas were expressed in the slogan 'Black Power' popularized by Stokely Carmichael and other activists from about 1966. By this time, Martin Luther King had become ever more marginalized in the black leadership. In some cases radicals were bitterly anti white, a fact that caused shock and incomprehension among white liberals. The most visible example of this strand was the Black Muslim movement, formed in the 1930s as a minor religious sect that taught a theology in which all whites were devils, the misbegotten creations of an evil scientist. The group gained support in urban ghettos in the 1950s, and won national visibility through the oratory of a charismatic leader who took the name Malcolm X (for most members, X symbolized the lost African name that had been replaced by a white surname in the slave era). Malcolm X himself became alienated from the Muslim leadership, and took up a revolutionary socialist stance that abandoned the violent racist hatred of whites. He was assassinated in 1965, but his speeches and writings inspired a generation of black activists.

In 1966 the Black Panther Party was founded in Oakland, California, where its armed and uniformed cadres fulfilled every traditional nightmare of city and federal law enforcement agencies. Making superb use of public relations and exploiting white liberal sympathies, the group became a national phenomenon by portraying itself as the authentic voice of an outraged and exploited black community. It also developed an armed wing, which became increasingly involved in terrorism after the mainstream of the party was destroyed by police activity in 1969–70. Racial struggles also revolutionized the American prison system, where thousands of inmates were radicalized by black nationalist rhetoric. By the late 1960s, especially in California, prisons such as San Quentin and Soledad had become revolutionary finishing schools, and inmate writers such as George Jackson emerged as prophets of the radical movement, black and white. Jackson's suspicious death in 1971 was the catalyst for inmate protests, which culminated in a rising at Attica prison in New York state. Over 40 guards and prisoners died in the ensuing clash.

SOCIAL CRISIS

Increased racial tensions were only one element of a spreading social and political crisis that was intimately linked to the continuing war in Vietnam, which reached its ferocious height between 1966 and 1968. In all, 8.7 million served in the US forces during the war, far more than in any American conflict except for the Second World War. The absolute height of direct American participation came in early 1969, when the number of US military personnel in Vietnam reached 543 000. The war would ultimately claim the life of some 58 000 Americans, plus an undetermined number of Vietnamese and others, mainly civilians. Two million is a not unreasonable estimate for the total death toll. The war caused immense physical and social damage through bombing, defoliation and the disruption of traditional cultural patterns through the relocation of villages. Moreover this catastrophe was undertaken for no apparent gain, and the prospect of victory seemed to recede ever further as military involvement increased. Americans encountered the classic problem of guerrilla warfare, that an irregular army wins such a struggle by simply continuing to exist, while a regular force loses by achieving anything short of total victory. The continued activity of the communist forces could not be

disguised by torrents of optimistic 'body count' estimates and
the alleged destruction of Viet Cong units.

In January 1968 the communist forces launched a desperate offensive to coincide with the Vietnamese New Year
festival of Tet. The Tet offensive was ultimately beaten back,
but not before the attackers had tried to storm the US
embassy in Saigon and briefly seized the city of Hue. Militarily, the communists suffered a severe setback, but in propaganda terms their victory was near-total. The offensive
showed the falsity of optimistic American claims about imminent victory, and suggested just how many more soldiers
would be needed to make any significant progress. Meanwhile international outcry against the American bombing
offensive was straining relations with most of America's allies
in Europe and elsewhere. In contrast to wars such as Korea,
from the outset this was an overwhelmingly American operation lacking the figleaf of token forces by key European allies
such as Britain, an absence that could not be disguised by the
more limited presence of troops contributed by regional
powers such as Australia and South Korea.

By 1968 domestic opposition to the war was reaching a
new plateau. Again in contrast to previous wars, President
Johnson was determined that the military draft should operate as fairly as possible, so that conscription reached deep
into the homes of the middle class as well as those of the poor
and minority population. This occurred at a time when the
baby boom was coming of age, and there was an explosive
youth culture removed from the social mainstream through
involvement in various forms of alternative lifestyles: new
forms of political and religious thought, radical experimentation in music, dress and personal appearance, and extensive
use of illegal drugs. The year 1967 brought the 'Summer of
Love' and the mass popularization of the hippie movement.
The centrality of the drug culture to this phenomenon
brought vast numbers of young white people into sharp
conflict with the law and established institutions, and promoted sympathy for outlaws, criminals and rebels.

Antiwar protest found an enthusiastic home in college campuses, and campus demonstrations and sit-ins became commonplace in the spring of 1968. Violent conflicts with police became ever more frequent, as did active draft resistance and the destruction of draft cards. All this, moreover, was occurring in the lead-up to the presidential election that November. American forces in Vietnam itself were demonstrating signs of disaffection, suggested by racial violence and drug use, by localized acts of mutiny and violence against officers. A collapse of morale and discipline is indicated by atrocities against Vietnamese civilians, such as the notorious massacre of several hundred villagers at My Lai in March 1968.

Following the Tet offensive, President Johnson began to resist military demands for additional ground forces, and in March 1968 he ordered the suspension of bombing attacks on the north. Johnson also announced his withdrawal from the 1968 presidential race, heralding an unusually bitter and divisive election season. Over the following months an assassin's bullets would claim the life of presidential candidate Robert F. Kennedy, the most prominent advocate of the peace faction within the Democratic Party.

Political tension reached a flashpoint with the Democratic convention in Chicago, when a demonstration by antiwar protesters was broken up by the Chicago police in what was termed a 'police riot'. The event was all the more traumatic as it occurred before the news cameras assembled to observe the increasingly irrelevant proceedings within the convention hall. Moreover, many of the assaulted protesters were white, middle class and articulate, and thus able to win the sympathy of many previously neutral viewers. The violence in Chicago and elsewhere was polarizing. For conservatives, the protesters were almost literally committing treason against the nation and its soldiers, who were facing death on the battlefields of South-East Asia. In addition, antiwar protest became assimilated with other types of violence rending the nation, including ghetto riots and rising street crime, mainly committed by blacks. Rightist sentiment found expression in the third-party movement organized by former Alabama Governor George Wallace, who gained almost ten million votes in the presidential elections that November, carrying five southern states. This movement drew southern and labour support that would normally have gone to the Democrats, whose candidate Hubert Humphrey lost narrowly to Republican Richard M. Nixon.

The antiwar movement was further radicalized by the events of 1968. The SDS movement split over the next year, with Maoist and other ultra-left factions vying for control of the remnants. One wing ultimately went underground as the 'Weatherman' movement, which launched a terrorist campaign in 1969–70 (the group took its name from a rock song by Bob Dylan). However the few dozen bombings attributed to Weatherman were paltry in comparison with the thousands of physical or violent actions committed in those years as part of the antiwar protest, ranging from gasoline bomb attacks and arson to serious bombings.

The disaffection prevailing in those years is suggested by the rhetoric of the antiwar movement, which adopted the black usage of 'pigs' to refer to police and government officials, while the government these lackeys served was dismissed as 'Amerika', a term that implied both Germanic authoritarianism and the racist 'K' of 'Klan'. By 1970 Weatherman statements were asserting that the violent antiwar resisters were 'an underground . . . fighting Amerikan imperialism . . . [who] use our strategic position behind enemy lines to join forces in the destruction of the empire'.[1] Antiwar militants carried the Viet Cong flag in demonstrations, deliberately seeking to enrage and challenge conservatives. The movement reached its height following the US invasion of Cambodia in April 1970, after which virtually all the nation's college campuses were affected to a greater or lesser degree by strikes and protests, and four students were killed in a confrontation with Ohio National Guardsmen at Kent State University. The convergence of political and racial violence between 1967 and 1971 resembled some of the bloodiest years of American history, including the mid 1870s and 1919–20.

By that stage many who would have condemned the extreme revolutionary rhetoric of groups such as Weatherman wholeheartedly agreed that the war had to be ended urgently, and peace sentiment had a special appeal to religious and civil rights organizations. In the autumn of 1969 several hundred thousand people participated in mass demonstrations in Washington and elsewhere. Disaffection within the political elite was suggested by the Pentagon Papers case of 1971, in which a government analyst leaked to the press a large number of documents revealing the decision-making process that had led to the current state of affairs in Vietnam. Most of the major news media were now clearly in opposition to continued military involvement.

The mainly white antiwar protesters attracted the bulk of media attention, but in these critical years there were many other groups who shared a comparable disaffection with American society, voicing a rhetoric of generalized structural oppression, often deriving from Marxist and New Left theories, but with an apocalyptic hatred of the American military–industrial machine. Black groups were particularly active and influential.

By the late 1960s, calls for 'Black Power' had stimulated other movements that similarly saw themselves as victims of historic group oppression. Hispanic activists in California and elsewhere formed 'Beret' movements modelled on the black Panthers, and advocated the rights of Chicanos (Mexican Americans). 'Red Power' was a convenient summary of the revived American Indian movement, which undertook spectacular protests and confrontations with federal officials. These culminated in the seizure of premises at Wounded Knee, site of the brutal 1890 massacre that formed the symbolic end to the frontier military conflicts of the previous century. For some weeks in 1973 it was suggested half-jokingly that Richard Nixon might be the first American president in this century to have a full-scale Indian war on his hands.

Apart from ethnic movements, what might be described as '68'ism' was also manifested in the women's movement, the reborn feminism that would form one of the most important social strands of late twentieth century America. The movement had its origin in the middle of the decade with the publication of works such as Betty Friedan's *Feminine Mystique* (1963) and the formation of the National Organization for Women (NOW); and the idea exploded in the political atmosphere of 1968. Kate Millett's *Sexual Politics* appeared in 1970. The new feminists campaigned especially on sexual issues that could scarcely have been broached in the public debate of earlier eras, including the right to abortion. Rape played a central part in the movement's rhetoric, as an integral component of a system of sexual terrorism intended to subjugate all women, a direct parallel to lynching in black history. By the early 1970s a substantial number of radical feminists had moved towards 'separatist' positions, and women's political organizations developed substantial lesbian caucuses. Feminism had an immense cultural influence through its impact on the media and the academic world. The movement had a sufficient impact to transform language, through the spread of 'gender-neutral' terminology.

Discontent with traditional concepts of gender and sexuality produced the 'gay rights' movement, an assertion of homosexuality as a normal and acceptable lifestyle. The crucial moment here was a riot at New York's Stonewall Bar in 1969, when homosexual protesters fought back against a long-standing pattern of police harassment. As with feminists, gay rights activists emerged in the 1970s as a powerful political presence in some areas, with consequent legal changes.

Finally, the late 1960s produced the ecology movement, which began to protest against the pollution of the environment by industrial society. Perhaps the best propaganda for this idea was the celebrated photograph of the Earth taken from an Apollo spacecraft, which depicted the magnificent blue-green beauty of the planet, but also suggested its fragility and its isolation in the hostile wastes of the cosmos. Though it rapidly became a cliché, this single image did much to promote the daring concept of 'Spaceship Earth' as a single vessel whose inhabitants shared a common duty to preserve its well-being. The year 1970 witnessed the first annual Earth Day celebration. In the new decade, environmental ideas grew in popularity with media focus on ecological disasters such as the massive pollution at Love Canal, and the nuclear near-catastrophe at Three Mile Island in Pennsylvania in 1979.

WATERGATE AND THE CRISIS OF THE AMERICAN STATE

By 1971–2 the reform of the draft system and the scaling down of US activity in Vietnam sharply reduced the scale and bitterness of antiwar protest. Significantly, public protests at a US invasion of Laos in 1971 were pallid compared with the Cambodian uproar the previous year. President Richard Nixon also achieved some remarkable diplomatic successes, including his visits to China and the Soviet Union in early 1972. The traditional arch-enemy of communism now emerged as a diplomat on a global scale, promoting policies of détente with the USSR and negotiating to reduce the number of strategic nuclear weapons.

However it was at this point that the American state was assailed and nearly overwhelmed by a political crisis that grew directly out of the earlier controversies. Though it is best remembered as a bizarre burglary scheme, the Watergate scandal was in fact an offshoot of the intelligence community's response to the antiwar movement. Throughout the 1960s, law enforcement agencies had enjoyed vast discretionary powers in observing, bugging, infiltrating and sabotaging leftist and liberal movements. The FBI was by far the most active, with its vast Counter Intelligence Programme, COINTELPRO, which was particularly directed against black organizations. There was also intense activity by city Red Squads, and by other federal agencies, including the CIA, although this was legally prohibited by its charter from operating within the territory of the United States.

The tumultuous protests of the late 1960s caused deep concern within the Nixon White House, thoroughly dissatisfied with the intelligence efforts of other agencies, especially since the antiwar protesters were accused of links with foreign intelligence agencies. In 1970, the White House established a special intelligence operation of 'plumbers' whose job was to 'plug leaks' in cases like the Pentagon Papers affair, and to maintain surveillance over the ever-expanding list of those regarded as enemies of the presidency. Their activities involved burglaries and electronic surveillance, all carried out without a scintilla of legal authority.

The activities of the plumbers soon became entangled in electoral politics, and the forthcoming 1972 presidential election. Nixon faced several likely Democratic candidates, by far the most popular of whom was Edward M. Kennedy, whose prospects suffered a catastrophic setback in 1969 after a car which he had been driving crashed into a pond on Chappaquiddick Island, killing a young woman passenger. Concerned that his fortunes might revive, the Nixon team targeted him for special attention in 1972. The plumbers carried out sabotage operations to disrupt the campaigns of other likely Democratic candidates, so successfully that the party ultimately fielded George McGovern, its weakest possible standard bearer and the opponent Nixon was most likely to beat. One other likely Democratic candidate was George Wallace, who was shot and paralyzed during the campaign by one of the 'lone nuts' who had proliferated so conveniently the previous decade. In November 1972 Nixon defeated McGovern by a landslide majority of 18 million popular votes, and 520 votes in the electoral college compared with McGovern's trivial 17, one of the most devastating triumphs in American electoral history.

Nixon's triumph was short-lived. In June 1972 several of the plumbers were arrested while burgling the headquarters of the Democratic National Committee in Washington's Watergate Hotel. The affair was all the more embarrassing as the arrested burglars had ties both to the White House and to a bizarre underworld of CIA agents and anti-Castro Cuban activists. The Watergate affair was investigated by several newspapers, whose examination of the plumbers led them to uncover a vast illegal financing operation employed by the Nixon White House to fund covert operations. This money was critical because while Nixon probably had little direct knowledge of individual crimes, he would certainly have approved the large payments required to buy the silence of the arrested burglars. If proved, this would establish him as an accomplice after the fact, and destroy his presidency. Initially allegations about direct White House involvement in Watergate met widespread public skepticism, but evidence soon became overwhelming. By 1973 a Senate investigating committee was providing almost daily revelations about wrongdoing.

Watergate entered a critical new phase with the revelation that Nixon had been in the habit of taping conversations taking place in his office, leaving precise evidence of his involvement in illegal activities. Though the tapes contained long and unexplained gaps, what remained was ample to prove sufficient criminal involvement to justify impeachment. This procedure was voted for by the House Judiciary Committee in July 1974, and on 8 August, Nixon admitted the inevitable and resigned. He was succeeded by his vice president, Gerald R. Ford, the previous vice president having been forced to resign following charges of financial corruption unrelated to Watergate.

Just as the Watergate affair involved far more than one mere burglary, so the ensuing fallout went beyond the political destruction of Richard Nixon. The investigation and related activities resulted in the prosecution of many highly placed officials, including several White House aides, Attorney General John M. Mitchell and FBI director Patrick Gray. The need to prevent a recurrence of such behaviour also led to legislative changes, including a reform of campaign financing. In reality, these laws were largely counterproductive. Intended to curb the influence of big-money donors, the laws actually ensured that much power passed to PACs (political action committees), which coordinated the donations of a particular industry or interest group. A Freedom of Information law permitted citizens to gain access to information that federal agencies had collected about them.

The intelligence agencies suffered particularly heavy fallout. Between 1974 and 1976 several presidential and congressional committees undertook a searching exploration of the misdeeds of the intelligence community over previous decades, and the resulting exposés were devastating. The CIA was shown to have plotted the assassination of world leaders, and had almost certainly carried out such plans on occasion. These illegal schemes had proceeded hand in glove with the Mafia and foreign organized crime syndicates. The CIA and related agencies had also carried out illegal drug experiments, often on unsuspecting human guinea pigs, as part of ongoing attempts to control human behaviour, and possibly to create programmed assassins. Within the United States, the committees exposed COINTELPRO and the FBI's schemes to destroy leaders such as Martin Luther King. It was shown that Nixon's obsession with bugging and surveillance had for decades been part of the standard operating procedure of a lawless covert state. Public concern about these revelations was particularly excited by alleged official involvement in the notorious assassinations of the past two decades. These ideas were widely disseminated in popular culture, and pressure for a new investigation became overwhelming following two unsuccessful attempts on President Ford's life in September 1975. From 1976 to 1979 a controversial House Select Committee on Assassinations examined the murders of John F. Kennedy and Martin Luther King.

Though these accusations were sensational in themselves, they were part of a larger social trend in those years, a generalized suspicion of the federal government, of federal law enforcement and of large institutions in general, and an increased openness to conspiratorial interpretations of politics. Hostility to Washington and its tainted insiders played a powerful role in the 1976 presidential election, in which Gerald Ford was crippled by the full pardon he had issued to Nixon, while Democratic challenger Jimmy Carter represented himself as the ultimate outsider, a Southern Baptist from rural Georgia. Carter won convincingly.

THE FALL OF AMERICA?

The crippling of the executive branch had global repercussions, and began a traumatic period for US foreign policy. Vietnam offered an early example. Since 1969 Nixon's policy had been to withdraw US ground troops while bolstering the Vietnamese military and maintaining air support. The Americans renewed their intense bombing of Hanoi in December 1972, and the following month a ceasefire agreement ended the use of American ground troops. The idea was that South Vietnam could be supported by US air power, but over the next two years it became increasingly difficult for either Nixon or Ford to commit any forces whatever to support South Vietnam. In April 1975 both Vietnam and Cambodia fell to the communists, and television viewers worldwide saw the unforgettable spectacle of terrified refugees attempting to escape in the last American helicopters to leave Saigon.

Shortly afterwards the degree of public frustration with US involvement with the outside world was indicated by opinion polls showing that a large majority of those questioned would oppose military intervention to preserve any foreign country from foreign invasion or communist revolution, with the exception of Canada. Ferocious isolationism was reinforced by the effects of the assault on the intelligence community. The CIA was discredited, and in 1977 hundreds of agents were dismissed or retired, many of whom had been involved in illegal or improper activities. The new War Powers Act raised grave constitutional questions about the power of the presidency to intervene overseas without the full authority of Congress. With the United States crippled internationally, the Soviet Union succeeded in extending its influence to Third World countries it would not have dared to intervene in during earlier years, especially African countries such as Angola, Mozambique and Ethiopia. Ironically this overextension of Soviet power may well have contributed significantly to the collapse of that nation's economy in the 1980s, and thus to the ultimate US victory in the Cold War.

The perception of American powerlessness was aggravated by events in the Middle East, an area in which Americans had previously had little interest or knowledge beyond an emotional support for the Jewish state of Israel. In October 1973 the Arab–Israeli Yom Kippur War led to an Arab oil embargo against Western countries, and a general price increase with vast economic repercussions. In this case a foreign policy disaster had immediate consequences for American consumers, who found themselves standing in frustrating lines for supplies of increasingly expensive petrol. Together with another oil crisis in 1979, this event raised questions about the fundamental organization of American society, and the degree to which it had been structured around limitless supplies of cheap energy. The Middle East again provided shocks in 1979, when the Iranian revolution resulted in the seizure of power by a Muslim fundamentalist regime, which took hostage some fifty members of the US embassy staff. A rescue mission in April 1980 ended in disaster, and the hostages were not freed until after Ronald Reagan replaced Jimmy Carter as president in January 1981.

Public disaffection was enhanced by the perception that America's cities were collapsing. Though mass urban rioting declined sharply after 1968, the cities still found themselves in a grim fiscal situation and were forced to make cutbacks in services that caused a decline in the quality of life. By 1975 New York City was on the verge of bankruptcy, and public sector strikes in many cities even extended to the police. Soaring crime rates were a critical index of social decay. In 1961 violent crimes were recorded by the police at a rate of 145.9 for every 100 000 Americans, a figure that by 1981 had increased fourfold to 576.9; by the 1990s it was well over 700. Property crime rates rocketed, reaching one peak around 1981 and another a decade later. Though not ideal for statistical purposes, the homicide rate was also indicative. In 1965 around 10 000 Americans were murdered, giving a murder rate eight or ten times higher than that of most comparable Western societies. There were 20 000 murders a year by about 1980, approaching 25 000 in the early 1990s. In recent years there has been a dramatic rise in the proportion of murders involving young teenagers, both as victims and offenders.

LIBERALISM AND LIBERATION

Politically, American history in the 1960s and 1970s seems like a lengthy catalogue of disasters and disappointments, a picture that is quite at odds with the social experience of most ordinary people in those years. It was an era of enormous political and cultural liberalization and indeed liberation, a time of radical social change that would continue to influence behaviour for decades afterwards. Above all it was an age of prosperity, on a scale inconceivable in any previous time. In 1960 the US economy had a gross domestic product of $513 billion, a figure that grew dramatically, even allowing for the effects of inflation. GDP was one trillion dollars in 1970, over four trillion by 1985, 6.5 trillion in the mid 1990s. In terms of the average citizen, the long economic boom from the early 1950s to the early 1970s provided massive new opportunities, reflected in the move to the suburbs now made possible by universal car ownership, and the expansion of higher education. A lifestyle that would once have been confined to the rich now became available to a vast middle class.

Growing prosperity had a particular impact on the young people of this era, the 'baby boom' generation. At the start of the century the average birth rate was around 30 per 1000, a figure that declined to 20 or so in the 1930s. The 'boom' increased the average rate to around 25 from 1945–60, but thereafter it declined sharply. The birth rate remained around 15 throughout the 1970s and 1980s, reaching its lowest level for the years 1973–6. The sizable postwar cohort thus began its teenage years from the late 1950s, and entered maturity in the late 1960s and 1970s. Popular culture responded to the tastes of this wealthy market with the music of the Beatles and the British invasion, and later of the American rock and roll industry. In 1971 the baby boomers benefited from the 26th amendment to the constitution, which lowered the voting age to eighteen.

Social change was shaped by factors of gender as well as age. New forms of contraception served to separate sexuality from reproduction, especially the introduction of the contraceptive pill in 1961. Over the next two decades the 'sexual revolution' was marked by vastly greater experimentation and what a previous generation had described as promiscuity, a trend that was only stemmed by the discovery of the AIDS disease in the early 1980s. Sexual, social and political changes combined to transform the role of women in American society. Women of the 1960s and 1970s were much more likely to work outside the home, and to both achieve and expect an independent life that often could not be obtained within the framework of the traditional family. In 1970 about 43 per cent of women aged sixteen and over were in the labour force, a figure that had grown to 52 per cent by 1980 and approached 60 per cent in the early 1990s.

The new independence coincided with the aspirations of the feminist movement, and these factors contributed to the upsurge of divorce from the early 1970s. In 1958 there were roughly four marriages for every divorce in the United States. By 1970 the ratio was three to one; by 1976 it had reached about two to one, at which level it remained for the next two decades. The increased number of independent working women had a profound effect on the substance of politics, bringing to centre stage issues of gender and morality that would previously have been dismissed as trivial or even humorous. By the 1980s sexual harassment was defined as a social problem. In 1991 Senate hearings to confirm Judge Clarence Thomas to the US Supreme Court resulted in the airing of harassment charges that gave the issue the status of a national scandal.

The US Supreme Court became a symbol of a new social liberalism, ironically in view of that body's longstanding role as a reactionary bastion. The whole desegregation process was largely initiated by the 1954 Brown decision, described earlier, and both the high court and other federal courts made a strenuous effort to carry through the implications of that ruling. Criminal justice was revolutionized in these years, with race often a crucial but unspoken factor. When considering a case of police maltreatment of suspects, the court often explored the impact of a given law not on any given defendant in any court, but specifically on a black defendant before a racist southern court. The judiciary sought to eliminate 'badges of servitude', and the justice system was particularly rife with those symbols.

Between 1961 and 1966 the Supreme Court undertook a 'due process revolution' with a series of epoch-making decisions such as Miranda, which required that suspects be informed of their right to remain silent upon arrest, and Mapp, regulating procedures for search and seizure. Gideon confirmed the right to an attorney in criminal cases, and Escobedo threw out a prosecution where an accused person was denied access to legal advice. In all such cases the penalty for police misconduct or ignorance was sweeping, involving the loss of evidence or testimony improperly obtained. Prison conditions were examined so stringently that the penal systems of whole states were declared 'cruel and unusual punishment', and the states were ordered to make numerous detailed changes in their operating procedures. Though not actually abolished, capital punishment was effectively suspended in the United States after 1967, and the 1972 decision in the Furman case struck down all existing death penalty statutes. (Only after thorough revision were new statutes approved in 1976, to the surprise of many observers.) These reforms were less important for the specific changes introduced than for the general assumption that personal rights would continue to be expanded and enforced by courts, which would no longer turn a blind eye to flagrant police misconduct. Though these decisions were especially associated with the name of Earl Warren (Chief Justice 1953–69), the spirit of the 'Warren Court' survived until the end of the 1970s, and the effective implementation of the 'revolution' was often the work of lower court judges rather than the Supreme Court itself.

The activism of the Supreme Court also reached into issues of personal behaviour and morality, and free speech rights were vastly expanded by decisions such as Brandenburg (1969), which defended the advocacy of unorthodox and even violent opinions. The Court also faced the dilemmas raised by profound contemporary changes in sexual mores. In 1965 the case of Griswold and Connecticut not only overturned a state prohibition on contraception, but proposed a fundamental right to personal privacy. This case resurrected one of the most potentially powerful aspects of the constitution, the doctrine that the ninth amendment provides citizens with countless rights not specifically listed in the Bill of Rights, but which once discovered and recognized must be enforced with all the vigor hitherto reserved for freedom of speech or religion. In one of the most controversial decisions of the era, Roe v Wade (1973) found that women had a fundamental right to abortion as part of the right to privacy, ensuring that abortion would remain one of the most rancorous issues in

American politics well into the 1990s. Throughout the next two decades in the United States, an average of 1.5 million pregnancies a year would end in abortion.

Court decisions also revolutionized acceptable standards in film and literature. The 1957 the Roth decision provided an effective defence against obscenity charges, allowing the accused to argue that a work contained some degree of redeeming social importance, and also permitting contemporary community standards to be taken into account in judging the merits of a case. For better or worse, American books and films by the 1970s regularly included images and dialogue that a decade before would have marked a work as irredeemably pornographic.

The bleak political years of the 1960s and 1970s were also characterized by a flourishing of American culture, and especially literature, which was at its strongest during the years of sharpest political conflict. In fiction, writers at the peak of their creative energies included Norman Mailer, Jack Kerouac, William Burroughs, John Barth, Saul Bellow, E. L. Doctorow, Richard Brautigan, Robert Stone, John Updike, William Kennedy and Gore Vidal. Of the many distinguished novels of the period, particular critical attention focused on works such as Joseph Heller's *Catch 22* (1962), Kurt Vonnegut's *Slaughterhouse Five* (1969), Thomas Pynchon's *Gravity's Rainbow* (1973) and Robert Coover's *The Public Burning* (1977). In more sense than one, literary barriers were demolished in these years. Some of the most distinguished writing derived from genres that would once have been regarded as below the notice of serious literature, for example the science fiction and fantasy world that produced Vonnegut as well as Ursula K. LeGuin, Philip K. Dick and Harlan Ellison. While the notion of a canon of great works was severely challenged, any list of the most able writers of the era would now include a far larger contingent of women and minorities, including Alice Walker, Ishmael Reed, Ralph Ellison, Leslie Marmon Silko and Toni Morrison. In poetry, the beat generation found its leading exponent in Allen Ginsberg. In the visual arts, the most influential movements of the era trampled the boundaries between high and popular culture, notably with the Pop Art and related styles of Andy Warhol and Roy Lichtenstein.

REPEALING THE 1960s

Though the term is often a cliché, it is fair to describe the changes in American society between about 1965 and 1975 as constituting a social revolution, most marked in areas such as sexual conduct and family structure, with drug use a valuable indicator of respect for law. By the late 1970s the use of drugs (especially marijuana) was a common source of humour in the mass media, and a fad for cocaine use among middle-class white Americans reached its height about 1980. A social reaction soon set in, both against the excesses of the 1960s and against some of its most fundamental achievements. In racial matters, the civil rights revolution led to attempts to legislate fairness by means of affirmative action, and a quest for racial balance in school districts by means of court-mandated 'bussing': this involved the transportation of thousands of children of one race to distant areas of a school district populated by another race. Both policies were bitterly divisive, and bussing caused civil disorder in several northern cities in the mid 1970s, especially Boston.

Concern about the decline in moral values was reflected in a massive religious shift in those years, and the rise of conservative, fundamentalist and Pentecostal churches. Between the late 1960s and early 1980s liberal denominations such as Episcopalian, Methodist and Presbyterian suffered a cataclysmic drop in membership, sometimes losing 20 or 30 per cent of their faithful in two decades. Meanwhile conservative churches such as the Southern Baptist and Assemblies of God were recording increases of 50 or 100 per cent in the same era. Throughout the 1980s opinion polls regularly suggested that around a half of all Americans believed firmly in the account of creation described in the Book of Genesis, dismissing evolution as a secularist fad, and most wished this position taught in the public schools. The new evangelicalism achieved visibility through networks of Christian publications and bookstores, and the work of television evangelists such as Jerry Falwell and Pat Robertson. Politically, the new religious constituency was initially mobilized in support of the Baptist presidential candidate Jimmy Carter in 1976, but thereafter the evangelicals clung decisively to the secular far right.

From the late 1970s evangelical and political conservatives found common cause in the anti-abortion movement and the struggle to prevent states and cities from enacting 'gay rights' measures to extend civil rights protection to homosexuals. Also critical was the campaign against the proposed Equal Rights Amendment to the US constitution, ERA, which would prohibit gender discrimination. This amendment was passed by Congress with the necessary majority, but then needed ratification by the requisite number of states. This campaign galvanized the feminist movement: in 1978, 100 000 marched in Washington to support the measure, and NOW grew steadily. However opponents also mobilized, and ERA failed to gain the support of enough states. The Christian conservative movement found a structural base in the 'Moral Majority', founded in 1979. By the 1990s this had been replaced by the better organized Christian Coalition.

Concern about moral decline was bolstered by foreign policy issues, which galvanized the conservative right during the late 1970s. Apart from the Iranian hostage crisis and the petrol shortages, American weakness seemed evident from a proposed treaty that would allow control of the Panama Canal to revert to the nation of Panama. Meanwhile, Cold War fears were exacerbated by the Soviet invasion of Afghanistan in 1979–80. Even the relatively liberal President Carter responded by reintroducting of the selective service registration that was the necessary prerequisite for a renewed military draft. International tension seemed to confirm conservative claims about the imminence of global conflict and the necessity for rearmament, and justified tirades against ongoing arms limitation negotiations with the USSR. By 1980 the centre of American political debate had swung far to the right of where it had been three or four years previously. The Republican Party chose as its presidential candidate Ronald Reagan, who many had dismissed a decade previously as a right-wing extremist. Reagan's victory that November was assisted by the defection of millions of liberal voters away from Carter to the independent Anderson, but even so the Republicans won convincingly, taking control of the White House and the Senate, and initiating a decade of militantly rightist policies. From 1989 Reagan's policies were largely continued by his successor George Bush, the former vice-president .

Reagan's victories in 1980 and 1984 resembled those of Nixon in earlier years, in that both men benefited from shifts in electoral geography. As the Sunbelt states grew, they steadily acquired more electoral votes, while those of their northern counterparts contracted. Between 1952 and 1992 New York fell from 45 electoral votes to 33, Pennsylvania from 32 to 23, Ohio from 25 to 21, Illinois from 27 to 22. In the same years, Texas grew from 23 votes to 32, Florida from 10 to 25, California from 32 to 54. South-western states, which in 1950 had three or four electoral votes each, now generally had six or eight, with the likelihood of gaining more in the coming decades, making them a significant electoral force. It will not be too long before a candidate can win the presidency without a single electoral vote from the north-east or mid-west.

The rise of the Sunbelt and western states benefited the political causes and attitudes prevaling in those regions, such as greater hostility to government intervention and social welfare, more sympathy for the concerns of the religious right, and deeper commitment to the defence and aerospace industries, which are disproportionately located in those areas. The political rebirth of the south was also critical in that the civil rights struggles had first crippled and ultimately destroyed the century-long Democratic hegemony there. At first reluctantly, then enthusiastically, southern voters recognized their natural affinity for the conservative New Right, which found expression in the Reaganite Republican Party. Demographics laid a sound foundation for the new politics of God and country, flag and family.

THE REAGAN ERA

In its foreign policy the Reagan administration viewed most problems as stemming from the aggressive intentions of the Soviet 'evil empire', and its puppets worldwide. In this view the Third World War was not merely a possibility, it was already in progress through the systematic attacks on the West by covert communist forces, which was the label attributed to virtually any group struggling against an American ally. Terrorism was a Soviet tool to destabilize the West, which required an appropriate reaction in the form of the 'Reagan doctrine', the pledge to assist militant anticommunist forces in any red-dominated country. Throughout the Third World CIA clandestine forces were unleashed against weaker pro-Soviet governments: in Angola, Mozambique, Ethiopia, Cambodia, and above all Afghanistan, which was viewed as a potential Soviet Vietnam.

Covert warfare was accompanied by a massive build-up of American forces across the board, as well as a programme of modernization and revitalization that could only be justified against a background of imminent hostilities. The US Defense Department's budget rose from $136 billion in 1980 to $244 billion in 1985, and that figure takes no account of related expenditure concealed in the spending of other units such as the Department of Energy. The Reagan administration financed its defence build-up by means of deficit spending on a scale unprecedented in peacetime. Even at the height of the Vietnam War the US government had only rarely run up a deficit of some $25 billion in a single year, or 3 per cent of GNP, and in 1969 the US budget even ran a surplus. Under Reagan, however, previous restraints were abandoned, and annual deficits of $200 billion were common through the mid 1980s, around 5 or 6 per cent of GNP. Total public debt doubled between 1980 and 1985, and in 1987 the US finally recorded an expenditure in excess of one trillion dollars. The American deficit crisis was in large measure a direct product of the Reagan military spending spree.

Among much else, this money bought a new generation of nuclear missiles and weapons that were intended for fighting a nuclear war rather than merely deterring a potential enemy, weapons so accurate that the Soviets might well be forced to launch a nuclear strike in order to prevent the destruction of their command and control facilities. Most feared were the intermediate range Pershing and Cruise missiles, which were installed in Western Europe in 1983, giving rise to a massive antiwar movement in Britain, West Germany, Italy and other nations, which had no wish to serve as the 'European Theatre' in a potential cataclysm. Also around this time Reagan announced the beginnings of a programme of space-based missile defence vulgarly known as 'Star Wars', which, whatever its technical feasibility, increased the panic of the Soviet leadership about their nation's vulnerability. The crowning moment of the new Cold War came in 1983 when a frightened Soviet military shot down a Korean airliner that had penetrated its air space, apparently in the belief that this represented a test of radar defences prior to a US nuclear assault. By November 1983 the Soviets were close to mounting a preemptive nuclear attack, bringing global war closer than at any time since the Cuban missile crisis. No assessment of the Reagan administration can ignore the incredible risks American leaders ran, nor the degree to which the fate of the world depended on Soviet restraint in not reacting to provocations.

The new policy of confrontation was also evident in what conservative leaders repeatedly referred to as the nation's 'backyard', Central America and the Caribbean, which now replaced South-East Asia as the primary Cold War battlefield. Radical regimes established themselves in the 1970s in Nicaragua and Grenada, and by 1980 civil wars in El Salvador and Guatemala seemed likely to knock down more 'dominoes' in the Soviet cause. As elsewhere, these situations were seen entirely in terms of geopolitical conflict, with virtually no interest in the domestic rivalries and tensions that had produced the specific crises. The Reagan government reversed the Carter policy of restraint in Central America, pouring in aid to support the military establishments of the front-line states, even when the Salvadoran and Guatemalan wars were accompanied by massacres and death squad activities directed against anyone of a liberal, moderate or pro-labor bent, and especially against Indian populations.

A 1983 military coup in Grenada provided the excuse for a US military assault and occupation, leaving Nicaragua and Cuba as the only leftist havens in the hemisphere. Grenada enjoyed a symbolic significance far beyond its military importance, as a deliberate administration attempt to cure the 'Vietnam syndrome' and accustom the American people once more to the prospect of direct confrontation with communist forces, even if that meant US casualties. This attitude also shaped US counterterrorism policy, and the willingness to strike directly at alleged terrorist sponsor states, as occurred with the 1986 bombing of Libya. For some years Nicaragua seemed a likely candidate for invasion, but the government there was challenged and ultimately destroyed by the promotion of an anticommunist 'Contra' rebel force, created and armed by US advisers. Though the Contras could never defeat the Nicaraguan government, they caused enough bloodshed and economic dislocation to force the regime to the bargaining table, and the ruling Sandinista Party was defeated in elections in 1990. US-sponsored wars in Central America claimed hundreds of thousands of lives, mainly civilians, and regularly involved illegal conduct by US intelligence and military personnel.

Strangely, the Middle East was another area in which the new administration sought to challenge communism, which they saw as the motivating force behind the leftist and Muslim side in the Lebanese civil wars. In 1982 and 1983 US forces found themselves serving in Beirut, ostensibly against Soviet-inspired interests. In reality this intervention brought the United States into direct conflict with fundamentalist Islamic forces, mainly organized from Iran, and for several years US assets worldwide were targeted by Islamic terrorists. American and Western personnel in Lebanon were also taken hostage, and the ensuing diplomatic imbroglio came close to destroying the Reagan administration even more thoroughly than Watergate had wrecked the Nixon regime.

Briefly, the Reagan administration illegally sold weapons to Iran as part of a deal to win the release of the US hostages. About 1985 some of the profits from this deal were diverted to fund the Contras in Nicaragua, which the US Congress had refused to support in view of atrocities committed by them. The executive was thus in the position of setting up both a private alternative fiscal system and an intelligence network to carry on its policies, and illegality was piled upon illegality. The affair came to light in November 1986, and the 'Iran–Contra Affair' dominated the headlines for the next two years. Even the publicly available evidence gave ample grounds for impeaching the president and several of his closest advisers, and that took no account of the proliferating rumours of government involvement in drug trafficking and assassinations in support of the Contra cause. However the Congressional investigations in the case were restrained, anxious perhaps to prevent a recurrence of the intelligence disasters of the mid 1970s, and nervous about tackling a still popular president. Reagan thus succeeded in ending his term on schedule and without the political meltdown that had appeared inevitable in 1986–7.

It remains open to debate how far his foreign policies can be judged successful. American conservatives take full credit for the collapse of the Soviet Union and other communist

states from 1989 onwards, which they see as a direct response
to the failed attempt to match the US military build-up,
compounded by the Soviet disaster in Afghanistan. On the
other hand we can never know how events might have proceeded if the West had maintained a traditional policy of
containment, and had avoided the high-risk strategy that had
come close to incinerating both the 'free' and the communist
world in 1983.

The Reagan era did indeed succeed in reducing American
nervousness about overseas commitments, especially in Third
World conflicts. This was evident in policing actions such as
those carried out in Panama in 1989 and Haiti in 1994, and in
international intervention in Bosnia from 1995–6. Ironically
the vast quantities of hardware purchased during the 1980s
were employed not against the Soviet superstate but against
the far less imposing Iraqi leader Saddam Hussein, following
his occupation of Kuwait in 1990–1. This era also had its
share of conspicuous disasters, even when the enemies encountered were infinitely less technologically advanced than
the American forces. Losses in Beirut in 1983 and Somalia
from 1992–4 tended to reinforce the traumatic memories of
Vietnam.

THE NEW MORALITY

The military rearmament undertaken under Reagan was to
be accompanied by moral reconstruction, and the social
experiments of the 1960s were to be reversed as thoroughly
as the inheritance of Vietnam in foreign policy. The causes of
social problems were reevaluated, wrong-doing and deviancy
being seen as issues of personal sin and evil rather than social
or economic dysfunction. For conservatives of the Reagan
era, the central issue in questions of morality (as in econom-
ics) was a renewed emphasis on the responsibility of the
individual, and a denial of the effectiveness or validity of
solutions that emphasized the state or the social dimension.

Reaganite social policy involved heavy cutbacks in social spending and public welfare, while swelling the budgets of police and prisons. There was throughout a harsher and more punitive response to crime, replacing the social and therapeutic policies that had been advocated during President Johnson's 'Great Society' and afterwards. The new conservatism was aggressively expressed in the drug war declared in the middle of the decade, which reasserted the moral discipline that had been so widely questioned in recent years. Draconian penalties deterred most of the middle-class casual drug users of the 1970s, but at the cost of criminalizing millions of blacks and other minorities.

The practical consequences of these changes can be quantified by means of the nation's soaring prison population. The number of people incarcerated in federal, state and local prisons actually tripled between 1980 and 1995, even though the actual rate of violent crime was roughly the same in 1995 as it had been at the time of Reagan's inauguration. By the mid 1990s some 1.5 million Americans were incarcerated at any given time, the highest rate per capita on the planet, and between six and ten times the general European rate. Nearly four million more were in the hands of the state through the probation and parole systems. In the same years there was widespread restoration of the death penalty, the ultimate form of purely retributive punishment.

Conservative interpretations were also apparent in the stereotypes and moral panics that were so pervasive in the media and political debate during those years, the recurrent nightmares or waves of concern about various external forces that appeared to represent a grave threat to the American people. These included not only drug dealers and drug 'kingpins', but also terrorists, both foreign and domestic, and the serial killers, child molesters and pornographers believed to pose such a danger to American children. From 1983 the inept investigation of child abuse charges at a Californian pre-school promoted a decade of panic about Satanic ritual gangs said to be preying on children across the nation, a literal 'witch-hunt' that actually gave the accused fewer protections than his or her counterparts in seventeenth-century New England.

In the political context of those years, each of these apparently diverse threats served essentially similar functions, by personifying the immorality and outright evil that had arisen as a consequence of the moral and political decadence of recent administrations, the family breakdown and sexual hedonism of the previous fifteen years. 'Dangerous outsiders' were useful in justifying bureaucratic and legal changes to reverse the perceived decay. A series of panics about drugs, child abuse, serial murder and terrorism permitted the FBI and other police agencies to slough off the tight restrictions imposed in the 1970s after the exposés of COINTELPRO and other horrors.

By 1989, with the Soviet threat collapsing almost hourly, international drug cartels emerged as the new 'evil empire' to focus American policies, and to justify the maintenance of a largely obsolete national security establishment. That September, President Bush declared that 'All of us agree that the gravest domestic threat facing our nation today is drugs . . . our most serious problem today is cocaine and in particular crack . . . it is turning our cities into battle zones, and it is murdering our children. Let there be no mistake, this stuff is poison'.[2] In Panama shortly afterwards, the rhetoric of the drug menace was used to justify the invasion of an independent state.

THE ECONOMIC DIMENSION

Through most of his administration, Ronald Reagan presided over what initially appeared a substantial economic boom, fuelled by the defence build-up and the deregulation of financial markets, the decline of organized labour, and the evisceration of environmental restraints on business activity. The United States also moved irrevocably into the information age, with most of the key innovations in computing deriving from American firms such as IBM, Apple and Microsoft. The stock market boomed, though the expansion was patchy and there were signs of significant weakness. Manufacturing industries stagnated in the Rustbelt, while midwestern agriculture entered a period of severe crisis. In the middle of the decade, falling oil prices caused economic havoc in Texas and the 'oil patch'. And while employment figures appeared healthy during 'Reaganomics', there was concern that many of the jobs were relatively low-paid service positions, often lacking the permanence or the benefits associated with the manufacturing sector. Even taking account of such 'McJobs', the official unemployment rate rose from 6 per cent in 1978–9 to almost 10 per cent in 1982–3. The number of people officially classified as living below the poverty level rose by some 25 per cent between 1979 and 1983, to exceed 35 million individuals.

The international situation also showed worrying signs, with increasing competition from Japan and other nations of the Pacific rim. By 1993 the United States still claimed the world's three largest industrial corporations: General Motors, Ford and Exxon. However only eight other American names were found among the top forty firms, compared with ten Japanese and sixteen from Western Europe. In 1993 the United States was running a trade deficit of $60 billion with Japan, $22 billion with China and $10 billion with Taiwan.

Two of the most explosive growth areas in the early 1980s would ultimately produce long-term problems of a magnitude barely imaginable at the time. One was mergers and acquisitions, in which corporations acquired rivals in order to sell off the less profitable sections of the targeted firm. The whole process was heavily financed by debt, but it was felt to be socially advantageous in maintaining a kind of Darwinian evolution in which the less fit were driven from the marketplace. Also indicative of a radical free-market policy were changes in the financial sector, where the staid savings and loan institutions were deregulated and allowed to offer whatever interest rates they liked on deposits, and to fund these often very high rates through risky investments and speculations. Even the most outrageous investments were guaranteed by the federal government, which was legally required to bail out the rashest gambler. Huge fortunes were made, but the obvious problem was that money would inevitably flow to those institutions offering the highest rates, and thus having the shakiest economic foundations.

The crisis came in 1987–8. The stock market collapsed in October 1987, leaving the gurus of the mergers and acquisitions world to face a lengthy series of criminal trials for insider dealing and stock manipulation. Most savings and loans institutions evaporated between 1988 and 1991, leaving the federal government to pick up hundreds of billions of dollars in defaults. Southern and western states were especially hard hit, and the financial collapse had a domino effect on the real estate market. Subsequent investigations also revealed widespread political misconduct in the savings and loans disaster, the consequences of which were only mitigated by the refusal of either political party to pursue a matter in which their own people were also deeply embroiled. The economic disaster was compounded by the end of the Reagan boom in the Summer of 1990, which began a lengthy period of recession and worsening unemployment. This contributed to the social unrest that exploded in Los Angeles and other cities during the riots in the spring of 1992.

Against such a mixed economic and political background, it is perhaps remarkable that the Republicans maintained their position as well as they did, and this may well suggest the extent to which politics had shifted to the right since the mid 1970s. The Democrats contributed to their misfortunes by nominating in 1984 and 1988 two of the least charismatic figures possible – Walter Mondale and Michael Dukakis, who were chosen on the strength of their impeccable liberal credentials. As both elections showed, the left of centre views that won the support of the party's main pressure groups and ordinary faithful were guaranteed to destroy a presidential candidate. Dukakis acknowledged this when he ostentatiously rejected Reagan's accusation that he was 'a liberal'. Not until 1992 were the Democrats able to field in Bill Clinton a candidate who at least initially appealed to the religious and moderate values of the electorate, and who addressed the economic concerns and suffering the Bush administration was believed to be neglecting.

WHILE NOT THE PAST FORGETTING: WACO AND OKLAHOMA CITY

We are still too close in time to the Clinton administration for any realistic assessment to be made of its failings or achievements, except to say that much of what the president attempted to do made good sense from the perspective of other advanced nations. In the tradition of American liberalism, Clinton saw the state as a potential agent for good. He supported the expansion of state powers and obligations in areas such as the regulation of firearms, the removal of legal disabilities against homosexuals and the promotion of a national health-care system, the latter reform, however, suffering ruinous defeat in 1994. But while such ideas were quite reasonable from a British, French or Canadian standpoint, they encountered a degree of opposition that is incomprehensible unless understood as part of American traditions that are of very long standing, and indeed can be traced to the earliest English settlement.

The Clinton administration was viewed as not only sinister but almost diabolical by millions of Americans, who feared its internationalism was covertly promoting a one-world government, a 'New World Order' that would be one of the instruments of the Antichrist foretold in the Bible's Book of Revelation. This apocalyptic notion was as authentically

American as the liberal strand symbolized by Clinton, and had quite as powerful a resonance for large sections of the population, though their views were not so commonly represented in the mainstream media.

These two American strands came into fiery conflict in 1993 at Waco in Texas, when federal agents stormed a compound of the millenarian Branch Davidian sect in search of illegal automatic weapons. Several sect members and agents were killed in a firefight, and there began a siege that lasted until 19 April, when a final federal assault resulted in the death of some 80 Davidians. The incident is chiefly significant for the total incomprehension that separated the two sides, each of whom represented a wholly different thought-world and historical tradition.

The Davidians were scarcely unusual: there were hundreds of religious denominations in the United States with only a few hundred members, and many of those lived in some form of geographical seclusion. Millions also shared the apocalyptic expectations of the Davidians, and many shared the idea that Christians would in the last days have to take up literal rather than spiritual arms to resist the Babylonish forces of the Antichrist. There was nothing here that would have caused surprise among the early settlers of seventeenth-century Massachusetts or nineteenth-century Utah, the perfectionist colonies of Victorian America, the survivalist compounds of the modern Ozarks, or the successive fortresses that have been constructed in the American wilderness. The sexually promiscuous messiah was also a figure with a long history on this continent. What was new was that these ideas were now dismissed as insane and dangerous, and requiring intervention by a state mechanism that looked increasingly like national police forces elsewhere in the world, structured and armed on paramilitary lines. Even among those with little sympathy for the religious aims of the sectarians, there was little surprise at the relatively large arms hoards within the compound: why should every individual not possess and use an efficient modern rifle? On the other side, the federal forces failed to take seriously the apocalyptic warnings from inside the compound: 'Bible babble', they called it.

In turn the destruction of Waco mobilized these archaic trends still further, in the form of militias and paramilitary groups equally dedicated to resistance against the 'Beast' and One-Worldism. Not coincidentally, the second anniversary of the Waco fire storm was marked by a blow at the heart of the 'Beast', when over 160 people were killed in the bombing of a federal office building in Oklahoma City. The date was richly symbolic, commemorating not merely Waco and other government atrocities against survivalists, but also those classic tax protesters at Lexington in 1775. Though the media and politicians saw the action as mindless barbarism, it represented – albeit in a dark form – some American traditions that a government neglects at its peril: radical individualism, suspicion of government, apocalypticism and a willingness to strike back at perceived tyranny. While advanced Western nations appear to be moving ever closer towards a greater degree of social and cultural harmonization, incidents such as Waco and Oklahoma City indicate the often misleading nature of such resemblances, and the survival of distinctively American political and religious traditions.

Notes

1. These are quotes from the Weatherman communiqués, printed in Harold Jacobs (ed.), *Weatherman* (Berkeley, CA: Ramparts Press, 1971).
2. 'Text of President's Speech on Drug Control Strategy', *New York Times*, 6 September, 1989.

Appendix: The Declaration of Independence, 1776

When, in the course of human events, it becomes necessary to dissolve the political bands which have connected them with another, and to assume, among the powers of the earth, the separate and equal station to which the laws of nature and of nature's God entitle them, a decent respect to the opinions of mankind requires that they should declare the causes which impel them to the separation.

We hold these truths to be self-evident, that all men are created equal; that they are endowed by their Creator with certain inalienable rights; that among these are life, liberty, and the pursuit of happiness. That, to secure these rights, governments are instituted among men, deriving their just powers from the consent of the governed; that, whenever any form of government becomes destructive of these ends, it is the right of the people to alter or to abolish it, and to institute a new government, laying its foundation on such principles, and organizing its powers in such form, as to them shall seem most likely to effect their safety and happiness. Prudence, indeed, will dictate that governments long established, should not be changed for light and transient causes; and, accordingly, all experience hath shown, that mankind are more disposed to suffer, while evils are sufferable, than to right themselves by abolishing the forms to which they are accustomed. But, when a long train of abuses and usurpations, pursuing invariably the same object, evinces a design to reduce them under absolute despotism, it is their right, it is their duty, to throw off such government and to provide new guards for their future security. Such has been the patient sufferance of these colonies, and such is now the necessity which constrains them to alter their former systems of government.

The history of the present King of Great Britain is a history of repeated injuries and usurpations, all having, in direct object, the establishment of an absolute tyranny over these States. To prove this, let facts be submitted to a candid world:

He has refused his assent to laws the most wholesome and necessary for the public good.

He has forbidden his governors to pass laws of immediate and pressing importance, unless suspended in their operation till his assent should be obtained; and, when so suspended, he has utterly neglected to attend to them.

He has refused to pass other laws for the accommodation of large districts of people, unless those people would relinquish the right of representation in the legislature: a right inestimable to them, and formidable to tyrants only.

He has called together legislative bodies at places unusual, uncomfortable, and distant from the depository of their public records, for the sole purpose of fatiguing them into compliance with his measures.

He has dissolved representative houses repeatedly for opposing, with manly firmness, his invasions on the rights of the people.

He has refused, for a long time after such dissolutions, to cause others to be elected; whereby the legislative powers, incapable of annihilation, have returned to the people at large for their exercise; the state remaining, in the meantime, exposed to all the danger of invasion from without, and convulsions within.

He has endeavored to prevent the population of these States; for that purpose, obstructing the laws for naturalization of foreigners, refusing to pass others to encourage their migration hither, and raising the conditions of new appropriations of lands

He has obstructed the administration of justice, by refusing his assent to laws for establishing judiciary powers.

He has made judges dependent on his will alone, for the tenure of their offices, and the amount and payment of their salaries.

He has erected a multitude of new offices, and sent hither swarms of officers, to harass our people, and eat out their substance.

He has kept among us, in time of peace, standing armies, without the consent of our legislatures.

He has affected to render the military independent of, and superior to, the civil power.

He has combined, with others, to subject us to a jurisdiction foreign to our Constitution, and unacknowledged by our laws; giving his assent to their acts of pretended legislation;

For quartering large bodies of armed troops among us:

For protecting them by a mock trial, from punishment, for any murders which they should commit on the inhabitants of these States:

For cutting off our trade with all parts of the world:

For imposing taxes on us without our consent:

For depriving us, in many cases, of the benefit of trial by jury:

For transporting us beyond seas to be tried for pretended offenses:

For abolishing the free system of English laws in a neighboring province, establishing therein an arbitrary government, and enlarging its boundaries, so as to render it at once an example and fit instrument for introducing the same absolute rule into these colonies:

For taking away our charters, abolishing our most valuable laws, and altering, fundamentally, the powers of our governments:

For suspending our own legislatures, and declaring themselves invested with power to legislate for us in all cases whatsoever.

He has abdicated government here, by declaring us out of his protection, and waging war against us.

He has plundered our seas, ravaged our coasts, burnt our towns, and destroyed the lives of our people.

He is, at this time, transporting large armies of foreign mercenaries to complete the works of death, desolation, and tyranny, already begun, with circumstances of cruelty and perfidy scarcely paralleled in the most barbarous ages, and totally unworthy the head of a civilized nation.

He has constrained our fellow citizens, taken captive on the high seas, to bear arms against their country, to become the executioners of their friends, and brethren, or to fall themselves by their hands.

He has excited domestic insurrections amongst us, and has endeavored to bring on the inhabitants of our frontiers, the merciless Indian savages, whose known rule of warfare is an undistinguished destruction of all ages, sexes, and conditions.

In every stage of these oppressions, we have petitioned for redress, in the most humble terms; our repeated petitions have been answered only by repeated injury. A prince, whose character is thus marked by every act which may define a tyrant, is unfit to be the ruler of a free people.

Nor have we been wanting in attention to our British brethren. We have warned them, from time to time, of attempts made by their legislature to extend an unwarrantable jurisdiction over us. We have reminded them of the circumstances of our emigration and settlement here. We have appealed to their native justice and magnanimity, and we have conjured them, by the ties of our common kindred, to disavow these usurpations, which would inevitably interrupt our connections and correspondence. They, too, have been deaf to the voice of justice and consanguinity. We must, therefore, acquiesce in the necessity which denounces our separation, and hold them, as we hold the rest of mankind, enemies in war, in peace, friends.

We, therefore, the representatives of the United States of America, in general Congress assembled, appealing to the Supreme Judge of the world for the rectitude of our intentions, do, in the name, and by the authority of the good people of these colonies, solemnly publish and declare, that these united colonies are, and of right ought to be, free and independent states: that they are absolved from all allegiance to the British Crown, and that all political connection between them and the state of Great Britain is, and ought to be, totally dissolved; and that, as free and independent states, they have full power to levy war, conclude peace, contract alliances, establish commerce, and to do all other acts and things which independent states may of right do. And, for the support of this declaration, with a firm reliance on the protection of Divine Providence, we mutually pledge to each other our lives, our fortunes, and our sacred honour.

Further Reading

Though a bibliographical essay on American history could quite easily exceed the total length of this present book, it might be useful to offer some brief suggestions for further reading. The following discussion is chiefly aimed at suggesting authors whose work are most valuable on particular themes and eras: most of these scholars are highly prolific, and while only one or two specific titles are mentioned in each case, their other works should also be pursued. Given the constrains of length, this account is, necessarily, highly subjective.

GENERAL THEMES

A number of major works examine themes spanning the course of American history, and draw examples from that history. Some excellent starting points for this general overview would include works of Richard Hofstadter such as *The American Political Tradition* (first published New York: A.A. Knopf 1948, and often reprinted) or *The Paranoid Style in American Politics* (New York: Knopf 1965). The 'paranoid style' is also the subject of David H. Bennett's *The Party of Fear* (second edition New York: Vintage 1995), a fine study of racist, nativist and xenophobic strands in American history.

Hofstadter's model of using biographical studies to illustrate the development of a theme has been imitated in books such as G. Edward White's *The American Judicial Tradition* (New York: Oxford University Press. Revised edn 1988). The development of American law is also well covered by Lawrence M. Friedman in *A History of American Law* (New York: Simon & Schuster second edition ca 1985), and his *Crime and Punishment in American History* (New York: Basic 1993). The classic writings of Merle Curti provide an overview of American intellectual history, while Sydney Ahlstrom's *A Religious History of the American People* (Yale University Press 1972) offers a fine introduction to the American religious tradition. So does Garry Wills' *Under God: Religion and American Politics* (New York: Simon & Schuster 1990).

Richard Slotkin's series of volumes on the frontier tradition and violence themes in American history are a rich mine for social and cultural history. See for example his *Regeneration through Violence: the Mythology of the American Frontier, 1600–1860* (Middletown, CT: Wesleyan University Press 1973), *The Fatal Environment: the Myth of the Frontier in the Age of Industrialization, 1800–1890* (New York: Atheneum 1985), and *Gunfighter Nation: the Myth of the Frontier in Twentieth-Century America* (New York: Atheneum 1992). Another general history that is quite invaluable for social topics is *Intimate Matters: a History of Sexuality in America* by John D'Emilio and Estelle Freedman (New York: Harper & Row 1988).

THE COLONIAL AND REVOLUTIONARY PERIODS

Many older works are still major sources for the study of the colonial era, especially the work of Perry Miller from the 1950s. His works include *The New England Mind: from Colony to Province* (Harvard University Press ca 1953) and *Jonathan Edwards* (Cleveland: World, 1965), as well as collections of documents such as *The Puritans* (revised edition, New York: Harper & Row 1963). Miller also published important work on the transcendentalists. Other important work on the colonial era is found in the writings of Bernard Bailyn and Edmund S. Morgan. Bailyn's work on political thought and ideology is especially significant: see for example his *The Ideological Origins of the American Revolution* (Cambridge, MA: Belknap, enlarged edition, 1992). His concern to place American developments firmly in their international context is evident from studies such as *The Peopling of British North America* (New York: Knopf 1986) and *Strangers within the Realm: Cultural Margins of the First British Empire* (Chapel Hill, NC: University of North Carolina Press 1991). Morgan's work on the revolutionary era is well represented in his *The Birth of the Republic, 1763–89* (University of Chicago Press third edition 1992) and *American Slavery, American Freedom: the Ordeal of Colonial Virginia* (New York: Norton 1975). Hofstadter's *America at 1750: a Social Portrait* (New York: Knopf 1971) is also a model survey. Gary B. Nash is another prolific scholar on this era, the author of books such as

Red, White and Black: the Peoples of Early America (Englewood Cliffs, NJ: Prentice-Hall 1974) and *The Urban Crucible: Social Change, Political Consciousness, and the Origins of the American Revolution* (Harvard University Press 1979). The much debated witchcraft cases are discussed by John P. Demos, *Entertaining Satan: Witchcraft and the Culture of Early New England* (Oxford University Press 1982) and Carol F. Karlsen *The Devil in the Shape of a Woman: Witchcraft in Colonial New England* (New York: Norton 1987). Other active scholars include Stephen Saunders Webb, whose book *1676: the End of American Independence* (New York: Knopf 1984) emphasizes the imperial dimensions of colonial history; while David Hackett Fischer's controversial thesis presents colonial social patterns as reflecting the British home areas from which migrants stemmed (in *Albion's Seed: Four British Folkways in America* (New York: Oxford University Press 1989).

Though older scholarship focused on the affairs of New England and Pennsylvania, much recent work concerns the Chesapeake region. Particularly noteworthy here is Allan Kulikoff's *Tobacco and Slaves: the Development of Southern Cultures in the Chesapeake, 1680–1800* (Univ. of North Carolina Press 1986). Russell R. Menard is the author of *Economy and Society in Early Colonial Maryland* (New York: Garland 1985) and *The Economy of British America, 1607–1789* (University of North Carolina Press 1985, with John J. McCusker). William Cronon's *Changes in the Land: Indians, Colonists, and the Ecology of New England* (New York: Hill & Wang 1983) is a magnificent example of a new environmental approach to colonial history.

From much distinguished scholarship on Native American affairs, see especially the work of Francis Jennings, in books like *The Ambiguous Iroquois Empire* (New York: Norton 1984) *Empire of Fortune: Crowns, Colonies, and Tribes in the Seven Years War in America* (New York: Norton 1988) and *The Founders of America* (New York: Norton 1993).

THE NINETEENTH CENTURY

On the post-revolutionary and early national era, see Stanley Elkins and Eric McKittrick, *The Age of Federalism: The Early American Republic 1788–1800* (New York: Oxford University Press,

1993). Still useful is Hofstadter's *The Idea of a Party System: the Rise of Legitimate Opposition in the United States, 1780–1840* (University of California Press 1969), while the national politics of the early nineteenth century are discussed by Merrill D. Peterson in *The Great Triumvirate: Webster, Clay, and Calhoun* (New York: Oxford University Press 1987)

Issues of race, slavery, reconstruction and segregation have attracted a vast literature, in which some of the most important writers include Herbert Gutman, Leon Litwack, Eugene Genovese, Elizabeth Fox-Genovese, Eric Foner and Kenneth Stampp. Among numerous books, some of the most significant include Gutman's *The Black Family in Slavery and Freedom, 1750–1925* (New York: Pantheon 1976), Genovese's *Roll, Jordan, Roll: the World the Slaves Made* (New York: Pantheon 1974), Litwack's *Been in the Storm so Long: the Aftermath of Slavery* (New York: Knopf 1979), Stampp's *The Peculiar Institution: Slavery in the Antebellum South* (New York: Vintage, new edition 1989), Foner's *Reconstruction: America's Unfinished Revolution, 1863–1877* (New York: Harper & Row 1988) and Fox-Genovese's *Within the Plantation Household: Black and White Women of the Old South* (University of North Carolina Press 1988).

A very strong radical tradition in American historiography focuses on the lives of working people of all races, and the interplay of elite and plebeian interests in party politics at local and national level. Some major authors here would include Herbert Gutman, Eric Foner and Eugene Genovese, as well as David Montgomery. All are very prolific. See for example Gutman's *Work, Culture, and Society in Industrializing America: Essays in American Working-Class and Social History* (New York: Knopf 1976) and Foner's *Free Soil, Free Labor, Free Men: the Ideology of the Republican Party before the Civil War* (New York: Oxford University Press 1970). Montgomery's books include *The Fall of the House of Labor: the Workplace, the State, and American Labor Activism, 1865–1925* (Cambridge University Press 1987) and *Citizen Worker: the Experience of Workers in the United States with Democracy and the Free Market during the Nineteenth Century* (Cambridge University Press 1993). Though the history of the 'lower orders' was certainly not an uninterrupted series of conflicts and disturbances, nineteenth-century America did have a strand of public and private violence, which is studied for example in Michael Feldberg's *The*

Turbulent Era: Riot and Disorder in Jacksonian America (New York: Oxford University Press 1980). William Cronon's book *Nature's Metropolis: Chicago and the Great West* (New York: Norton 1991) is impressive on the interaction between urban growth and western expansion, and the role of technological change in both.

The literature on the Civil War is so vast as to constitute a historical genre in its own right, and there are numerous case studies of all the major political and military figures, as well as the battles and campaigns. Good entry points to this literature include Shelby Foote's *The Civil War: a Narrative* (New York: Random House, three volumes, 1958–74), while much of value can still be found in older popular histories of the war, for example Bruce Catton's series dating from the 1950s. The political history of the era is the subject of important work by David H. Donald.

Popular movements at the end of the nineteenth century are also the subject of a rich literature, whether we are dealing with populists and progressives, or the racist and nativist movements that achieved such influence in these years. One great name in southern history is C. vann Woodward, author of *The Strange Career of Jim Crow* (New York: Oxford Univ. Press revised edition 1974). The changing ethnic basis of American society is discussed in John Higham's *Strangers in the Land: Patterns of American Nativism, 1860–1925* (New Brunswick, NJ: Rutgers University Press 1988).

THE TWENTIETH CENTURY

The historical literature on twentieth-century America is huge, and can only be approached here by emphasizing certain themes.

The critical years of the Depression and the New Deal have served as foci of research. Major writers include Alan Brinkley, author of *Voices of Protest: Huey Long, Father Coughlin, and the Great Depression* (New York: Knopf 1982); and Robert S. McElvaine, whose books include *The Great Depression: America, 1929–1941* (New York: Times Books 1984). The copious publications of Kenneth S. Davis include an impressive multivolume biography of Franklin D. Roosevelt.

As in earlier epochs, racial matters have long fascinated historians, and the civil rights movement is the subject of much fine scholarship. Particularly outstanding is the work of David Garrow, in books such as *Bearing the Cross: Martin Luther King, Jr., and the Southern Christian Leadership Conference* (New York: W. Morrow 1986) and *We Shall Overcome: the Civil Rights Movement in the United States in the 1950s and 1960s* (Brooklyn, NY: Carlson 1989).

Each of America's wars has exercised a like attraction. One model study is David M. Kennedy's *Over Here: The First World War and American Society* (New York: Oxford University Press 1980), which integrates military and civilian aspects of the struggle. From countless books on the Second World War and Korea, some of the most important writing is found in the many books of Stephen E. Ambrose, the biographer of Eisenhower. Ambrose is also the author of *Rise to Globalism: American Foreign Policy since 1938*, which is now in its seventh (1993) edition (New York: Penguin). Russell F. Weigley is another very distinguished author on the American politico-military tradition. The impact of military and national security considerations on virtually every aspect of American life is the theme of Michael S. Sherry, *In the Shadow of War: The United States since the 1930s* (New Haven, Conn.: Yale University Press, 1995). This influence was particularly evident in the years after the second world war, which is the subject of James T. Patterson's *Grand Expectations: the United States 1945–74*, a recent volume in the impressive *Oxford History of the United States* (New York: Oxford University Press 1996).

The crisis of the anticommunist purge is the subject of many books that deal both with Senator McCarthy himself and the impact of the panic on American culture and society. Important books here include David M. Oshinsky's *A Conspiracy so Immense: the World of Joe McCarthy* (New York: Free Press 1983), while Michael Kazin's *The Populist Persuasion: An American History* (New York: Basic Books 1995) traces the populist theme through this era.

Many important historical works address the politics and culture of recent decades, including Todd Gitlin's *The Sixties: Years of Hope, Days of Rage* (New York: Bantam 1987) and Garry Wills' *Reagan's America: innocents at home* (Garden City, NY: Doubleday 1987). However the closer we come to the present day, the more matters of social and political history can properly be explored through the literature of sociology and political science, as well as through biography and autobiography, and of course journalism.

Index

3/98   3   2/98
1/03   21   11/02